EFFECTIVE
Public Speaking

EFFECTIVE
Public Speaking
FOURTH EDITION

Joe Ayres
Washington State University

Janice Miller
Washington State University

WCB Brown & Benchmark
PUBLISHERS

Madison, Wisconsin • Dubuque, Iowa • Indianapolis, Indiana
Melbourne, Australia • Oxford, England

Book Team

Executive Editor *Stan Stoga*
Developmental Editor *Kassi Radomski*
Production Editor *Peggy Selle*
Photo Editor *Robin Storm*
Permission Coordinator *LouAnn Wilson*
Visuals/Design Developmental Consultant *Marilyn A. Phelps*
Visuals/Design Freelance Specialist *Mary L. Christianson*
Publishing Services Specialist *Sherry Padden*
Marketing Manager *Carla J. Aspelmeier*
Advertising Manager *Jodi Rymer*

Brown &
Benchmark
A Division of Wm. C. Brown Communications, Inc.

Executive Vice President/General Manager *Thomas E. Doran*
Vice President/Editor in Chief *Edgar J. Laube*
Vice President/Sales and Marketing *Eric Ziegler*
Director of Production *Vickie Putman Caughron*
Director of Custom and Electronic Publishing *Chris Rogers*

Wm. C. Brown Communications, Inc.

President and Chief Executive Officer *G. Franklin Lewis*
Corporate Senior Vice President and Chief Financial Officer *Robert Chesterman*
Corporate Senior Vice President and President of Manufacturing *Roger Meyer*

Cover design and illustration by Ellen Pettengell Design

The credits section for this book begins on page 341 and is
considered an extension of the copyright page.

A Times Mirror Company

Library of Congress Catalog Card Number: 92–82988

ISBN 0–697–12911–X

Printed in the United States of America by Wm. C. Brown Communications, Inc.,
2460 Kerper Boulevard, Dubuque, IA 52001

10 9 8 7 6 5 4 3 2 1

Contents

4

Selecting the Topic and Stating the Specific Purpose *61*

5

Gathering Materials *75*

6

Organizing the Speech *97*

7

The Body of the Speech: Developing Your Ideas *115*

Contents

16

Speaking for Special Occasions *309*

Preface

The fourth edition of *Effective Public Speaking* continues to present, clearly and concisely, what the student needs to know to speak effectively in a variety of public settings. However, we have made strategic changes in every chapter that strengthen the text throughout. For instance, in chapter 1 (An Overview), we highlight the importance of public speaking by pointing out its impact on professional and everyday life. A model of the public speaking process also has been added to help students visualize the dynamics of the speaking situation. Chapter 2 (Speech Anxiety) has been revised to include performance visualization—a procedure that has been demonstrated to enhance performance as well as reduce speech anxiety. In chapter 3 (Listeners and Listening), we have sharpened the discussion of audience analysis and ways to improve listening. As is evident from the title, "Selecting the Topic and Stating the Specific Purpose," chapter 4 now includes specific purpose construction as well as topic selection. This was done to take advantage of the natural affinity between selecting what you are going to talk about and your purpose for speaking.

In chapter 5 (Gathering Materials), we have condensed the treatment of interviewing and expanded the treatment of electronic information services. These changes were made to more closely approximate the information gathering activities that accompany speech preparation. In chapter 6 (Organizing the Speech), you will find an expanded speech preparation checklist. Chapter 7 (The Body of the Speech) extends the treatment of some aspects of development. For instance, more precise guidelines are offered with regard to the use of restatement and repetition to help students master this effective but underutilized tactic. In chapter 8 (Introductions, Conclusions, and Transitions), you will find an extended treatment of the use of humor in the introduction of a speech. This change should help students make better use of this important attention-gaining device.

Chapter 9 (Visual Aids) includes additional examples on the value of relevant visual aids. Chapter 10 (Language Use) now includes a discussion of sexist and racist language to develop a sensitivity to this important aspect of speaking. In chapter 11 (Delivery), we have added information about how to cope with nervousness and miscues. This material should be of considerable pragmatic value to students. In chapter 12 (The Speech to Inform), as in every chapter that includes sample speeches and commentary, the commentary now appears in a separate column beside the material being commented upon. This change makes the material more visually appealing and easier to read.

Chapter 13 (Bases of Persuasion) presents the "Psychological Bases of Persuasion" in a much more direct, understandable fashion. In chapter 14 (Constructing the Persuasive Speech), we include an outline for Jan Moreland's speech. In the past, we had presented an outline of a different speech. We think presenting the outline for Moreland's speech will help students better appreciate the relationship between outlining and speech-making. Chapter 15 (The Speech to Entertain), includes more examples to help students master this difficult form of speaking. In chapter 16 (Speaking for Special Occasions), we have also added additional examples. In particular, we now include a complete speech of introduction, which should help students organize and develop their own speeches of introduction. The Appendix (Performance of Literature) now includes a complete illustration of how to analyze material.

Despite these and other changes, the book remains about the same length. We have retained the organizational structure that has proven effective in earlier editions. Chapters 1–11 discuss basic principles, while chapters 12–16 deal with various speech forms.

We are indebted to a number of people for assistance in this project. Our children and our spouses, Frances and Bob, have been most understanding and helpful throughout. Frances Ayres provided valuable typing assistance. We have been grateful for our colleagues' support through the years. Special thanks for their help with specific sections goes to Mary and Robert Nofsinger, Robert and Nancy Ivie, Glenn Johnson, Tim Hopf, David B. Strother, and Gail Miller. Alexis Tan, the Director of our School of Communication, has been most generous in providing needed support.

Further, we wish to thank the following reviewers for their numerous and valuable insights: Renie Braswell, Mayland Community College; Craig Grossman, Irvine Valley College; James Mooney, Immaculata College; and Julia Overton, University of Pittsburgh–Bradford. We are also grateful to the staff at Brown & Benchmark for their patience, understanding attitude, and expertise.

Joe Ayres
Janice Miller

EFFECTIVE
Public Speaking

1 An Overview

Chapter Outline

And it is so plain to me that eloquence, like swimming, is an art which all men might learn, though so few do.

Ralph Waldo Emerson

The Importance of Public Speaking

A variety of research can be cited to verify the importance of oral communication. In one study, for instance, top managers in business identified "effective speaking, working efficiently with individuals and groups, effective communication in the organization, and listening skills" as critical to their success.[1] Business school graduates have stated that speaking is more important than writing to their success.[2] For those who doubt the importance of communication, we have listed a number of references at the end of this chapter that attest to the importance of good communication.[3] This research demonstrates something we all know intuitively: The more effective you are in communicating, the more likely you are to obtain a better job, receive higher pay and earlier promotions, and be given more responsibility.[4] The value of effective communication extends into the political arena, as well as our private lives. The message is clear—the better communicator you are, the better your chances for a rich, satisfying life.[5]

Public speaking is one form of communication that can make a vast difference in your ability to influence decisions in the public and private sectors.[6] In a public speech, you have the opportunity to deliver an uninterrupted message to a few individuals or a few million individuals. Few other modes of communication afford opportunities of this magnitude, so when these opportunities come your way, you want to be able to take advantage of them.

Rozanne Weissman, vice president for the Corporation for Public Broadcasting, says her corporation benefits when she sees each speech as "an opportunity to advance the interests of public broadcasting." And Weissman benefits as well because, as she points out, "putting together a presentation improves my speaking skills and thought processes—it makes me organize things in ways I may have not thought of before." Ray Heibert, a journalism professor, points out another benefit of public speaking: "I always learn something new from the people I address, because making a presentation requires me to get up to date on their issues by researching my audience and topic."[7]

Understanding the principles of effective public speaking is vital to receiving these and other benefits. This book is designed to present those principles in a direct, understandable fashion.

Public speaking shares much with other types of communication. It is also different in a number of respects. In this book, we will point out some of these similarities and differences. The remainder of this chapter discusses the basic aspects of the model of public speaking presented in figure 1.1.

Figure 1.1 Model of Public Speaking.

Basic Components of the Speech Act

As shown in figure 1.1, the basic components of public speaking include: (1) the speaker or source—the encoder of the message; (2) the message; (3) the audience—decoders of the message; (4) the channel through which the message is transmitted; (5) feedback; (6) noise, which interferes with the speech transaction which is taking place; (7) the setting; (8) the interrelatedness of all these components. In the remainder of this chapter, we will discuss these eight basic elements of communication as they relate to public speaking.

Speaker

One of the major components of the act of speaking is the speaker, who is the source of the message. These three factors need to be considered about any speaker: his or her motivation, credibility, and delivery.

Speaker Motivation

Psychologists have long wondered why people behave as they do. This is what we have in mind when we consider a speaker's *motivation*. In a public speaking class, you may often give a speech because it is required in order to get a grade; but, beyond this surface motivation, most people desire to

> True confidence abides in him alone who in the silent moment of his inward thought, can still suspect, yet still revere, himself.
>
> *William Wordsworth*

appear knowledgeable and interesting to others and are genuinely interested in self-improvement. You may talk to others to give information, to get help in solving a problem, or to convince them of your point of view.

One way to look at *motivation* is to consider what the *speaker* is getting out of speaking, or what the rewards are. Rewards come in many shapes. Some dedicated people get rewards from sacrificing personal gains in order to help others. Mahatma Gandhi, for instance, fasted often in order to focus attention on the deplorable conditions of poor people in India, and Martin Luther King, Jr. faced ridicule and physical danger as he fought for the civil rights of his fellow black Americans. Some people give up immediate rewards to achieve rewards at a later time. Students, for example, spend years in school at the sacrifice of immediate income, in hopes of eventually making more money and leading more fulfilling lives than they would if they had not gone to college.

A *speaker's motivation* can be examined in two ways: first, whether direct personal rewards (e.g., making money from a sale) or indirect rewards (e.g., feeling good about helping others) are involved; and second, whether immediate rewards (e.g., having money today) or delayed rewards (e.g., getting a degree after four years in college) play a part. A speaker could be motivated by one or more of these factors. Thus, a salesperson may be interested in helping a customer buy a reliable car as well as by a desire to make a profit. That short-term "making a living" is important, but so is the need to feel that the work performed is of some long-term benefit and significance.

Motives can be unethical as well as ethical. *Ethics* is a very complex subject because human beings genuinely differ on whether certain acts are "ethical" or "unethical." At a very basic and oversimplified level, it can be said that if you are presenting your motives forthrightly, you are being ethical. If you have one motive and act as though you have another, you are being unethical. By this definition, a student who appears at a professor's office to ask a question and who genuinely wants to know the answer is being ethical. Conversely, the student who asks the professor a question and really doesn't care about the answer, but wants the professor to think he or she does, is acting unethically.

Before speaking you should consider what your motives are. Let's say you urge the City Council to approve placing the new post office at a certain location, and you happen to *own* that piece of property. No matter how genuine your reasons for considering that site to be the best location for the post office, if you fail to acknowledge the possible conflict of interest, you risk being labeled unethical. Your private and public motives seem to clash.

If you analyze your motives, clearly understand them, and present speeches that represent the full range of your goals, you can avoid this problem.

Speaker Credibility

Speaker credibility rests on a speaker's trustworthiness, competence, and good will. The speaker who is consistently honest and fair in his or her presentation will be seen as trustworthy, and the speaker who appears to be well-informed and well-organized will be considered competent. Good will is established when the speaker seems to have the best interests of the audience in mind.

In large measure, a speaker's ideas are accepted as believable only to the degree that the speaker is perceived to be credible. The famous writer/philosopher Ralph Waldo Emerson put it this way: "Don't *say* things. What you are stands over you the while, and thunders so that I cannot hear what you say to the contrary." This tendency to identify the speaker with the content of the message is not new. In fact, the ancient Greeks carried this inseparability of the speaker and the message to the extreme; the messenger who brought bad news was killed on the spot!

The speaker who is attractive and dynamic will be seen as more credible than one who is not. In the 1960 Nixon-Kennedy television debates, Nixon appeared to be unshaven and ill at ease (even his mother called to ask if he was feeling well). This projected an unattractive and unreliable image, while Kennedy looked vital and confident and thus inspired trust in his listeners and viewers.

The most fundamental part of a speaker's image is the attitude the speaker has toward himself or herself. The person who is not sure that the speech is interesting or worthwhile, or is not well-prepared will telegraph that attitude to the audience. An unprepared speaker may look out the window or at the floor, use a disorganized thought pattern, or speak in a weak, unsteady voice. The speaker's lack of confidence often leads the audience to agree with the speaker's low self-assessment.

> The limits of my language are the limits of my world.
>
> *Wittgenstein*

There are, however, several specific ways a speaker can influence the audience to see her or him as credible:

1. Highlighting personal experiences, as long as it is not boastful, tends to increase perceived trustworthiness and dynamism.
2. Citing highly credible authorities who agree with the speaker increases perceived competence.
3. Demonstrating shared common beliefs, attitudes, and values with the audience increases perceived trustworthiness.
4. Well-organized speeches enhance perceived competence.
5. Sincerity also enhances perceived trustworthiness.

Speaker Delivery

Delivery, using voice and body to communicate the feelings that comprise the speech, should complement the speech objective. These delivery techniques will be discussed in more detail in chapter 11.

Message

Messages are what the speaker says; sometimes the term *message* refers to everything a speaker does or says. The verbal component may be analyzed in terms of its content, style, and structure.

Content

Whether your chosen topic concerns politics, sex, football, or some other subject, content refers to what you have to say about your chosen topic. The first step in getting ready to speak is to pick a subject and research it thoroughly. Once that is done, you will need to decide how much to say about each aspect of your subject. An effective speaker is one who says enough about each aspect of the topic to accomplish the goal of the speech. You have to take the audience's needs, time limits, and other items into consideration as you prepare and present the content of the speech.

Style

Style concerns the manner in which you present the content of your speech. Speaking styles range from the very informal to the very formal; informal styles tend to be conversational, perhaps using popular expressions of the day, while a formal style takes great care to use proper English and avoid slang. Most presentations fall between these extremes, and in every case style should be determined by what is appropriate to the speaker, the topic, the audience, the occasion, and the setting.

Structure

The structure of a message is its organization. A well-organized speech must have all of its elements placed in logical relationship to each other. We will talk about organizational variations, but in each of these variations the

structure will include an introduction, a body, and a conclusion. Within these major divisions, major points should stand out as main points; minor points should appear as subpoints to the main points; and everything should contribute to the speaker's purpose. The desire for form and order is an innate human characteristic, and lack of order makes both speaker and audience feel uncomfortable. When speeches are poorly organized, the impact of the message is reduced and the audience is less likely to accept the speaker or the speaker's ideas.

Audience

You must analyze your listeners to decide how to present your ideas. An analysis of the audience should include attempts to learn as much as possible about audience characteristics, including age, sex, race, social background, income, occupation, religion, geographic location, and group memberships. By using such information, you can make educated guesses regarding what the audience already knows about the topic you have chosen, the extent of the audience members' interest in the topic, and how strongly sympathetic or hostile they are toward you and toward your point of view on the planned topic. For example, if you intend to discuss the subject "Future Careers," knowing the age of your audience members would be vital. An audience of young people would have different needs and expectations than would retired people who were looking forward to starting a second career.

In this way, you will develop your rhetorical sensitivity, an awareness of the need to respond to listener needs and the demands of the speaking situation while retaining your integrity as a speaker who stands behind his or her ideas.[8]

Channel

Channel refers to the means you use to convey your message. When you speak directly to an audience, you employ a variety of means to convey your message, including (1) visual—gestures, facial expressions, bodily movement, and posture; (2) pictorial—diagrams, charts, graphs, pictures, and objects; (3) aural or paralinguistic—tones of voice, variations in pitch and loudness, and other vocal modulations produced in a speaker's stream of sounds; mostly you will use (4) verbal means to communicate—words.

Communication may occur through other sensory channels as well, such as smell or touch, but most messages are sent via light waves and sound waves and are received by the eyes and the ears.

Listing these items separately does not mean that they are separate in practice. Just as the bowler must learn to master hand, foot, and eye coordination, all together, in order to throw a strike, so must the speaker attend to transmitting his or her message through these several channels simultaneously. The more sensory channels a speaker employs at the same time, the more effective the presentation will be. This complexity is not a reason for discouragement. People do learn to bowl, to ski, to golf, and many other activities. You have been practicing your speech skills for many years already, so you should have a solid base on which to build in becoming an effective speaker.

Feedback

Feedback is the process whereby the speaker learns how his or her message has been received and, in turn, responds to those cues. The feedback process is not complete until the speaker has responded to the listener. The process includes the listener's reaction to the speaker's response, and so forth. This phenomenon in human communication can be likened to the operation of a thermostat, which turns heat on or off in response to a change in temperature.

In a public speaking situation, you can often ask your listeners if they understand a point you have just made. You can also watch the audience's reaction to your presentation.

It is very important to be aware of how others are reacting to your presentation. Often you will discover that others do not react in the way you expect. One student we had in class thought that sitting on the edge of the table in front of the audience would convey a friendly, relaxed attitude, and he often used that tactic. This style of delivery was quite effective when he talked about repairing bicycles, but the strategy backfired when he talked about finding a cure for cancer. A number of audience members felt that his posture indicated that he really didn't care about cancer research, that he was instead just fulfilling a class assignment.

Chapter 1

Years ago I started with the question: How do body motions flesh out words? . . . These days I put it another way: man is a multisensorial being. Occasionally he verbalizes.

Ray Birdwhistell

Even if you have made a diligent effort to analyze the makeup and attitudes of your audience before you speak, you must be alert and responsive to reactions throughout your speech. Those audience attitudes may change, in interaction with one or more of the other factors in the communication situation, as you are speaking. Audience cues are usually subtle and ambiguous, and it is possible to misread them. A frown may mean disagreement or it may mean that the listener is concentrating. You can only do your best to interpret these nonverbal responses correctly and to continue to develop your sensitivity to their meanings.

Noise

"I know you believe you understand what you think I said, but I am not sure you realize that what you hear is not what I meant to say."

This familiar maxim illustrates the point that interference may occur in the communication process and result in a distorted message. *Noise* can originate externally and be physical in nature or it can originate in the speaker and/or the listener.

External Noise

Interference that originates externally may be in the form of sound: people talking, coughing, or shifting position; the seating of latecomers; the noise of equipment such as air conditioners or radiators; a lecturer in the room next door; or traffic noises from outside. Poor acoustics might also cause the speaker's words to be inaudible to some or all of the listeners. Visual interference can result from poor lighting, from something interesting being visible through the window, or from the listener's inability to see the speaker. Physical discomfort, being too hot or too cold, or poor ventilation can interfere with the smooth flow of communication response between speaker and listeners.

Most of these external sources of noise are outside the listener's control and are only somewhat subject to the prior control of the speaker. Thus it is the speaker's responsibility to adjust and adapt as well as possible under the circumstances.

Internal Noise

Interference may occur at the source of the message if the speaker is confused or unclear about what he or she wants to express. Internal noise can also arise if the speaker does not know or misanalyzes the field of experience, knowledge of the subject, vocabulary level, or attitudes of the audience. Communication does not take place in a vacuum; the role of the

Be alert to cues from your audience that tell you how they are responding as you speak.

audience is of central concern to the speaker. The audience and the speaker are simultaneously communicating with each other. It is this *transactional nature* of speech that makes feedback and the attempt to eliminate noise so important. Speaker and listener are interdependent, so successful communication requires that both participate actively.

Sometimes internal noise occurs because the speaker and/or listeners lack the words and word skills needed to construct the message. On most of the topics that you normally speak about, you use a vocabulary of 500 to 800 words. The average high school freshman has a general working vocabulary of 8,000 words, while the average adult has a vocabulary around 80,000 words. If you have a large working vocabulary, your chances of having the right word at the right time are increased.

Another source of noise surfaces when speakers and/or listeners let personal biases cloud an objective analysis of the situation. Of these sources of internal noise, the most difficult to recognize and control are our own personal biases. Presumably, though, as we gain experience and knowledge, we come to recognize and discard some of these preconceptions. Most of us have experienced at some time a feeling of prejudice against students at a rival school, but have since come to see that as a rather foolish bias. Such

Audience reaction affects the speech.

issues as racism and religious discrimination are much more serious and difficult to overcome. We should all examine our own beliefs and begin to let go of those that create "internal noise."

Counteracting Noise

Perhaps the most specific means the speaker can use to increase message *fidelity* (i.e., the degree to which the message you intend to send is the one the listener actually receives) and to *combat noise* are (1) to use more than one channel at the same time (especially verbal and nonverbal) and (2) to use repetition and restatement.

Listeners cannot "go back and reread that paragraph." Using multiple channels, repetition, and restatement can help listeners counteract noise.

Setting

Setting includes the *place* and the *occasion* of a speech.

Place

The place in which you deliver your speech may be one that enhances or that interferes with the effectiveness of the presentation. Most presentations to a speech class will be in a classroom. This setting generally lends itself well to a speaker/audience relationship, but the student speaker may want to make some changes in the "non-permanent" aspects of the setting (e.g., rearranging the chairs), if that will help the success of the presentation.

If possible, whenever you speak try to determine ahead of time what the room and furniture will be like. Sometimes presentations are ruined because the speaker did not anticipate problems within the physical setting. In preparing a speech on posture, you might be planning to use your own body movements to illustrate your points, only to find that the seats are arranged in such a way that you have very little room to move. If you learn this ahead of time, you could change your plan of delivery or make adjustments in the setting.

Occasion

Occasion refers to the purpose that brings the group together. Is the occasion a high school graduation, or a ceremony at which awards will be presented? Is the group interested in obtaining technical information or does the occasion call for a speech on a topic of general interest? A presentation prepared for the regular meeting of a group will not use the same materials or style of presentation as one for the annual banquet meeting.

Interrelatedness

The use of machine-oriented terms such as *channel, feedback,* and *noise* to describe human communication suggests a mechanistic view of the speech process. People are not machines, and "breakdowns in communication" are only slightly similar to mechanical breakdowns. Using symbols to communicate meanings—a subtle and complex activity—is uniquely human. We should not be deceived by the directness of these mechanical terms and expect simple solutions to our problems in communicating.

The speaker, the message, the audience, the channel, feedback, noise, and the setting have been discussed individually, but in reality all of these items are part of one process. Throughout our discussion, we have used terms such as *transaction* and *simultaneous* to indicate that a message is always presented by a speaker, in a setting, to an audience, using some channel, using varying degrees of feedback, and that noise or interference could occur at any one of these points. The effective public speaker needs to attend to all of these items at once.

If your topic is the Supreme Court's decision that Medicaid can not be used (with limited exceptions) to finance abortions for women receiving public assistance, you will have to make choices based on why you selected the subject, what the audience already knows and thinks about the subject, whether the audience would be more receptive to a formal or an informal style, and many other matters. As we proceed, you will learn more of the theory behind these decisions and gain practice putting those theories to work.

Summary

The ability to communicate effectively is essential both to individuals and to society. A course in public speaking can help you learn necessary skills and gain insights into the nature of human communication.

The seven basic components in the speaking process are: speaker, message, audience, channel, feedback, noise, and setting, which are all interrelated. The speaker needs to take into account his or her motivation for speaking, assess his or her credibility with the audience, and assume responsibility for the organization and delivery of the message. Messages are what a speaker says to an audience; three basic elements of a message are content, structure, and style. Channels are the means used to convey the message, which may be visual, nonverbal, and oral. A speaker needs to consider the composition of the audience (e.g., age, sex, knowledge level, etc.) as the speech is prepared and delivered. Feedback is the information a speaker receives from an audience about the presentation and the speaker's response to that audience reaction. The speaker must be alert to both external and internal noise and move to counteract their effects. The setting is the place in which a speech is given and the occasion is the reason the audience has gathered. These basic ingredients in the speaking process are highly interrelated, with each affecting and being affected by all the others.

Exercises

1. In order to learn about the other people in your class—those who will be listeners when you speak—we suggest that you pair off with another class member to interview one another. If there is an odd number of students in class, form a triad, having person 1 introduce person 2, person 2 introduce person 3, and person 3 introduce person 1. Each of you should learn the other's age, interests, occupational background, and occupational goals, where he or she has lived, and any unusual experiences that person might have had. You should ask what your partner thinks about current issues and which ones she or he feels strongly about. You will then introduce each other to the class. Try to include an introduction, a body, and a conclusion in your presentation.

2. Another means of getting acquainted with other students and becoming aware of each other as members of the audience is the Brown Bag Speech. Each student should bring to class a brown grocery bag containing three objects or symbolic representations of those three objects. The three objects are to be the things you would want to have if you were marooned on an island in the ocean. Assume that while on the island your basic needs for survival (food, water, and shelter) will be met; none of your three objects need be anything required to survive. However, a luxury item (ice cream, steak, coffee) might be included, if that item is important to you. In three to four minutes (or in the time allotted by your instructor),

show the objects or the symbols to the class, explaining why you would choose to take them along. Try to present the objects in some logical order and have an introduction and a conclusion.

3. The part played by the channel used to communicate can be shown by a "serial transmission of information" exercise. Select a group of six students. Five of them should leave the room. The person remaining will be the message source. This person is given a written message to read and the other class members in the room are also given copies of the message. One of the five students is then called back into the room and told she or he will be read a message to remember and pass on accurately to the next person to be called in. Then student Number two will relay the message to student Number three. This process should be repeated until all five persons have been called in, with each person relaying the message to the person following. Class members may discuss what happened to the message as it was passed from person to person and suggest ways to avoid message distortion.

4. To illustrate the importance of feedback, place one person aside from the group. Present the person with a drawing of a geometric figure. His or her task is to describe the figure so that the other class members can draw it accurately. No one else may comment or ask questions of the speaker. Discuss these results, then assign another person to direct the class in drawing another figure, this time allowing the class to comment and ask questions.

Assignments

1. Listen to an out-of-class speech, paying particular attention to the items discussed in this chapter: speaker, message, audience, channel, feedback, noise, and setting.
2. Write a brief paper describing the physical location, noise factors in the situation, and feedback available in the speech you listened to outside of class.

Suggested Reading

Aristotle. *The Rhetoric of Aristotle*. Translated and edited by Lane Cooper. New York: Appleton-Century-Crofts, 1932.

Becker, Samuel L. and Ekdom, Leah R. V. "That Forgotten Basic Skill: Oral Communication," *Association for Communication Administration Bulletin* # 33 (August, 1980).

Bormann, Ernest G. *Communication Theory*. New York: Holt, Rinehart & Winston, 1980.

Burgoon, Michael and Ruffner, Michael. *Human Communication: Studies and Applications*. New York: Holt, Rinehart & Winston, 1978. Chapter 1.

Cicero. *De Oratore*. Translated by E. W. Sutton and H. Rackham. 2 vols. Cambridge, Mass.: Harvard University Press, 1953.

Hickson, Mark L., III and Stacks, Don W. *Nonverbal Communication: Studies and Applications*. Dubuque, Ia.: Wm. C. Brown Co. Publishers, 1985.

Notes

1. Speech Communication Association, "Speech Communication and Careers" (Falls Church, Va.: 1977).
2. *Bulletin of the Association for Business Communication,* December, 1987.
3. National Council on Education, *Higher Education and National Affairs,* June 10, 1977; Denise R. Mier, "Learning the Art of Management Through the Art of Oral Reading," *Communication Education* 32 (July 1983): 298; Andrew D. Wolvin, "Meeting the Communication Needs of the Adult Learner," *Communication Education* 33 (July 1984); U.S. Office of Personnel Management, "Employee Training in the Federal Service Fiscal Year 1980" (Washington, D.C.: OPM, 1981): 2, 3, 6; Herbert W. Hildebrandt, "International/Intercultural Communication: A Comparative Study of Asian and U.S. Managers," *World Communication,* Vol. 17, No. 1 (1988): 49–68; Ann S. Bisconti and Lewis C. Solmon, *College Education on the Job . . . The Graduate's Viewpoint* (College Placement Council Foundation: 1976); John Muchmore and Kathleen Galvin, "A Report of the Task Force on Career Competencies in Oral Communication Skills for Community College Students Seeking Immediate Entry into the Work Force," *Communication Education* 32 (April 1983): 207–20; Kathleen Edgerton Kendall, "Do Real People Ever Give Speeches?" *Central States Speech Journal* (Fall 1974): 233–35; Robert T. Oliver, Pennsylvania State University, Annual Convention of Toastmasters International, New York, 1965; "Communication Careers" (brochure), Association for Communication Administration (Falls Church, Va.: 1981).
4. Virginia P. Richmond and James C. McCroskey, *Communication Apprehension, Avoidance, and Effectiveness* (Scottsdale, Az.: Gorsuch Scarisbrick Publishers, 1985): 63–64.
5. Lynne Kelly and Arden K. Watson, *Speaking with Confidence and Skill* (New York: Harper & Row, 1986): 11–12.
6. Ruth E. Thaler-Carter, "And Now a Few Words From Myself," *Communication World* (October 1990): 16–191.
7. Ruth E. Thaler-Carter, "And Now a Few Words From Myself," *Communication World* (October 1990): 17.
8. Roderick P. Hart and Don M. Burks, "Rhetorical Sensitivity and Social Interaction," *Speech (Communication) Monographs* 39 (1972): 75–91; and Roderick P. Hart, Robert E. Carlson, and William F. Eadie, "Attitudes Toward Communication and the Assessment of Rhetorical Sensitivity," *Communication Monographs* 47 (1980): 1–22.

2 Speech Anxiety

Chapter Outline

Introduction

Lynne: Boy, am I glad that's over.
Dawn: I thought it was a great speech.
Lynne: You did?
Dawn: Sure.
Lynne: But I was so nervous I thought everybody would notice.
Dawn: You didn't seem to be very nervous.

Conversations like this one frequently occur as students leave the classroom. Speech anxiety, the fear associated with delivering a speech, is an important issue for many people.[1] We have found that 14 percent of the people enrolled in the basic public speaking course at our school suffer from extreme speech anxiety, a great many other students report speech anxiety to be an important problem, and almost all of our students report having experienced speech anxiety at one time or another.[2] Of course, speech anxiety is not restricted to students in public speaking courses. A 1973 survey of American adults revealed that 41 percent of the respondents listed public speaking as their number one fear, while only 19 percent of the respondents listed dying as number one.[3] Even prominent entertainers, reporters, and politicians like Johnny Carson, Joan Sutherland, Carol Burnett, Barbara Walters, Margaret Thatcher, and John Fitzgerald Kennedy occasionally experienced speech anxiety. Speech anxiety was a major problem for Gloria Steinem, the prominent women's rights advocate. She was so compelled to speak out on issues affecting women that she confronted her fear of public speaking because she knew it "wouldn't kill her."[4] Therefore, if you feel your fear of public speaking is abnormal, think again, because some degree of speech anxiety is often the rule, rather than the exception. Of course, knowing that others suffer from speech anxiety may not help you cope with your anxiety. It only lets you know that others may have more sympathy for your problem than you realize. Thus, we turn our attention to developing an understanding of why speech anxiety occurs and how we can cope with it.

Anyone who has experienced speech anxiety knows how it feels, so we do not have to describe the symptoms in detail here. For those who are interested, a description of the physiological changes one undergoes when experiencing speech anxiety can be found in Rollo May's book *The Meaning of Anxiety*.[5] When we experience speech anxiety our bodies are in a state of extreme alertness—ready to fight or flee. One fascinating line of research provides evidence that these changes are similar to the changes non-nervous people experience when confronting a speech situation, but these speakers report being excited, not nervous, about delivering the impending speech.[6] Another line of research, though, suggests that physiological changes differ when people are excited or nervous.[7] One thing is clear, people who report

> I saw that all the things I feared and which feared me had nothing good or bad in them save in so far as the mind was affected by them.
>
> *Spinoza*

Even accomplished speakers occasionally experience speech anxiety.

being excited exalt in their ability to think more clearly, to react more quickly, etc. Those who feel anxious focus on their nervous reactions and take them as evidence that the situation is terrible.

Of considerable interest is the question of why some people experience the speaking situation as anxiety provoking, while others find it exhilarating. Although there is certainly evidence that these tendencies could be inherited, we think that such anxiety is best understood as a learned response.[8]

Speech Anxiety as a Learned Response

Knowing that the physiological reactions of excitement or fear are similar does not tell us why one person feels fearful and another excited in the same situation (though it may explain why audiences are not very accurate in identifying which speakers are nervous and which are not).[9] A number of explanations have been advanced to account for this phenomenon, but we will only consider those that have received empirical support.[10] Reinforcement theory suggests that we have learned to fear public speaking by associating aversive (negative) consequences with speaking behavior.[11] Perhaps when we have spoken at family gatherings, in classes, or at work, the reactions of others seemed negative, thus we came to associate public speaking with negative consequences. If negative consequences are encountered in every speaking situation, we will most likely develop a general trait of speech anxiety. However, if we associate negative consequences with only one setting, for example, when speaking in class, our anxiety may be restricted to that setting.[12] We can also learn to fear public speaking by modeling, or watching the reactions of others.[13] When others we admire act fearful about speaking, we learn that speaking is something to be avoided. A pattern of uncertain or negative reinforcement and exposure to nervous role models seems sufficient to produce speakers who feel their ability to present speeches is minimal.[14]

Aspects of Speech Anxiety

Three aspects of a situation contribute to the degree of speech anxiety a person feels: novelty, conspicuousness, and audience characteristics.[15]

Novelty

Novelty concerns doing things that are new and unfamiliar. For many people, giving a speech is a rare event. But even experienced speakers can encounter novel circumstances. For instance, teachers who are comfortable talking to students encounter a novel situation when asked to address their peers or to deliver a course to a television camera for the first time. Fear of doing new things is probably tied to failure in such situations in the past.

Conspicuousness

Conspicuousness means that you stand out from the audience. For instance, you probably feel conspicuous when, after quietly sitting in a large audience, you stand to make a remark. You are suddenly the center of attention. Standing apart from the audience, as is the case in delivering a speech, provides a degree of conspicuousness that can intensify feelings of speech anxiety.

Audience Characteristics

Audience characteristics can greatly affect speech anxiety. These include size, status, familiarity, similarity, and behavior. Most people feel more fear with larger audiences.[16] We usually experience more fear facing higher status audiences, because individuals with higher status are in positions to reward or punish us. In essence, the risk potential is higher with such an audience than with one of lower status. Unfamiliar audiences produce higher

anxiety because we are less able to predict their responses. Lastly, the audience's behavior can influence our feelings of speech anxiety. If the audience is visibly angry, bored or inattentive, such behavior may heighten our anxiety.

All of these sources of anxiety can interact to influence anxiety levels. Being quite conspicuous; in a novel situation; in front of a large, hostile, unfamiliar audience of higher status; and having failed in previous speech situations would be enough to produce speech anxiety for almost anyone. What, then, can a person do to cope with these sources of anxiety? The advice offered here is divided into two sections. The first includes advice about dealing with speech anxiety in any situation. The second provides information on how to cope with anxiety in a specific speech. Of course, such a division is somewhat artificial, in that information about how to cope with anxiety in a specific speech will find some value in more general situations and vice versa.

Learning to Cope with General Speech Anxiety
Take a Public Speaking Course

That which we have learned can be unlearned. Public speaking courses are designed to help people learn to deliver effective public speeches. Numerous studies attest to the fact that students report much lower levels of speech anxiety toward the end of a public speaking course than they do at the beginning of the course.[17] However, some public speaking courses increase students' fear of speaking.[18] If your anxiety seems extreme, you ought to consider taking some of the steps outlined below concurrently with or prior to your enrollment in a public speaking course.

Enroll in a Special Program

Gerald Phillips at Pennsylvania State University has constructed a very successful treatment program for speech anxiety based on the assumption that people avoid communication because they lack the skills necessary to communicate effectively.[19] To develop such skills, students in his program learn to identify goals they might reasonably achieve with a specific audience, general strategies for achieving these goals, and specific things to say in order to accomplish their goals. Special courses based on this principle and others are available at some colleges and universities.[20]

Seek Professional Help

Psychologists have developed several techniques for helping people learn to feel confident about speaking. A widely used procedure, systematic desensitization, is based on the notion that a person can not be tense (frightened) and relaxed at the same time.[21] Consequently, people are taught how to relax by using a set of muscle relaxation exercises. After relaxation is thoroughly mastered, the speaker, with the assistance of a clinician, works through a variety of fear provoking speaking situations ranging from not very frightening encounters (i.e., saying grace before a meal with one's family) to encounters that are personally frightening (i.e., convincing an audience of strangers that you did not engage in unethical conduct). The basic idea is to learn to associate speaking situations with pleasant, relaxing sensations rather than with tense, fearful ones.

Another clinical procedure demonstrably helpful in coping with speech anxiety is rational emotive therapy (RET).[22] Developed by Albert Ellis, RET presumes that people may have emotional reactions, that stem from irrational thinking, to speaking situations. Such reactions are grounded in the speaker's belief that everyone has to like his or her speech, that everyone will think he or she is stupid, that everything must go according to plan, etc. Ellis believes that, if people will adopt less extreme expectations, they should experience lower levels of speech anxiety. Using this principle, clinicians help people to identify irrational beliefs, to challenge those irrational beliefs, and to restate those irrational thoughts into rational ones. For instance, let us assume that I believe everyone must like my speech. According to Ellis, that is an irrational expectation since there are very few things everyone likes, including speeches. If this is pointed out to me, I can learn to restate my expectation into a more reasonable form—i.e., wanting the majority of the audience to respond favorably. Of course, the appropriate counter-statement depends on the situation. If I were presenting a pro-life speech to a pro-choice audience, it would be unreasonable to expect the majority to like my speech. Just getting them to listen might be a reasonable expectation.

If you feel your anxiety is extreme, you should contact your instructor or a counselor to see about receiving special help. A professional clinician has resources and time that are not usually available to the classroom teacher.

Be Prepared

One source of fear is lack of preparation. Preparation includes all aspects of getting ready for the speech: topic selection, audience analysis, research, speech construction, and rehearsal. All of these factors can help in coping with speech anxiety. Fear is often associated with a concern of how the audience will react to you. In most situations, the audience will be interested in what you have to say about a particular issue and will not be especially concerned with you. If you choose a topic that fascinates you, it will be easier not to worry about what the audience will think of you and to focus on the topic.

How the audience will react to your topic does need to be carefully considered. While we discuss audience analysis in more detail in chapter 3, the essence of that discussion will be to find out enough information about your audience to relate your topic to the audience's concerns. I once had a student deliver a speech on the proper way to cultivate coffee trees. She discovered that most of the people in that class were not very interested in the specifics of cultivating such trees. With a little thought she might have anticipated that growing coffee trees does not command attention for the typical college freshman. Even though she had chosen a subject of great interest to her—she was from Colombia, had grown up on a coffee plantation, and was studying agronomy—she still experienced considerable anxiety during this speech. The audience, though polite, was obviously bored. This speaker needed to consider how to make her topic interesting for her audience, perhaps by pointing out how coffee growing practices were related to some of the audience's concerns (e.g., the quality and cost of coffee). Since anxiety can arise due to audience reactions to your subject, you need to locate a subject of mutual interest to you and your audience.

Do the necessary research on your topic. In a speech advocating additional government assistance for housing programs, for example, you should be aware of existing and past programs, as well as counter-arguments. Such an awareness will help you develop a sense of confidence that can only be gained from thorough research.

When you construct your speech, prepare a clear outline. Once the outline is developed, try to anticipate the audience's reaction to your speech. The speech construction process not only requires getting the speech together, it also means thinking about the speech in relation to the audience. By carefully considering all aspects of the speech you will be able to pinpoint possible sources of speech anxiety. If you are aware that you get nervous when audience members react in a hostile manner, yet are intending to do something to provoke anger, anticipate your reaction and take steps to deal with it. Several tactics used to cope with anxiety in situations like this are discussed later in this chapter.

After you analyze the audience, complete the research, and construct the speech, be sure to allow sufficient time for rehearsal. As a general rule, the more familiar you are with your material, the less anxious you will be. A good idea is to practice delivering the speech to a friend. In that way you can get some useful feedback. Don't hesitate to ask your friend about any aspect of the speech that concerns you.

Plan to Use Movement

You will recall that anxious and excited speakers experience similar physical reactions when they anticipate presenting a speech. This reaction is often brought on by feeling conspicuous, being in a novel situation, and/or the composition of an audience. Good speakers use their arousal to energize the speech. These speakers use vocal variety, gestures, and movement to communicate their involvement and interest in the topic. Movement and gestures are especially good methods for reducing feelings of anxiety. Your body is ready for physical exertion, and moving and gesturing helps release some of this pent-up energy. You don't want to pace or wander aimlessly, so walk toward a visual aid or move on a point to emphasize it. In addition to helping relieve anxiety, purposeful movement helps to gain and maintain attention.

Flexibility

Anxious speakers are often apprehensive about the opinions of others. Such speakers tend to search for rules that will enable them to receive good evaluations. These speakers take suggestions for speech-making to be ironclad laws that must be followed. As a consequence, if they "break one law," they can become very anxious. Suggestions such as "Don't pace back and forth" should not be taken to mean that pacing should never be done; you may want to pace, to appear to be very "worked up" about an issue. Even if one paces, in a nonpurposeful fashion, it is not the end of your speaking career. The pacing distracts from the overall impact of the speech, but it seldom ruins the entire speech.

A flexible approach will also be helpful if your speech does not go exactly as planned. Anxious speakers tend to get rattled when their speeches differ from the way they have practiced them. Such deviations are routine and usually invigorate the speech. Besides, you are the only person who knows that something did not go as planned. You might have had the experience of telling the same story to several different people, perhaps somewhat differently each time, but still with good effect. Speeches are much like that. They can be presented in a number of different ways. It is a worthy goal to try to present the speech to attain the optimum effect, but it is hardly a disaster when you don't achieve the optimum effect. Expecting such perfection is a little like a football team expecting to score a touchdown on every play, then quitting when the first play gains only thirty yards!

Learning to Cope with Specific Speech Anxiety
Performance Visualization

By imagining a negative speech outcome, you can help create a poor performance.[23] Negative thinking has been linked with a variety of presentation difficulties. For instance, students who engage in negative thinking also have been found to be more agitated (e.g., to pace) and more disfluent (e.g., stutter and the like[24]). We have developed a procedure called performance visualization to help people eliminate these behavioral manifestations of speech anxiety, as well as reduce negative thinking.[25] This procedure begins by helping people understand that positive thinking facilitates good performances while negative thinking does not, as any athlete will tell you. The next step is to have students visualize giving a speech. Research has demonstrated that speech-anxious, as well as non-speech-anxious, people who were given detailed instructions in visualization felt more confident about speaking than people who were not provided with instruction in visualization.[26] The following script is for an informative speech, but it can

The best speakers know enough to be scared. Stage fright is the sweat of perfection. The only difference between the pros and the novices is that the pros have trained the butterflies to fly in formation.

Edward R. Murrow

PEANUTS reprinted by permission of UFS, Inc.

easily be adapted to other speech purposes. A good way to use this script is to have someone read it to you, while you imagine yourself presenting a specific speech to a specific audience.

Visualization Script for an Informative Speech

Close your eyes and allow your body to get comfortable in the chair in which you are sitting. Move around until you feel that you are in a position that will continue to be relaxing for you for the next ten to fifteen minutes. Take a deep, comfortable breath and hold it . . . now slowly release it through your nose (if possible). That is right . . . now take another deep breath and make certain that you are breathing from the diaphragm (from your belly) . . . hold it . . . now slowly release it and note how you feel while doing this . . . feel the relaxation fluidly flow throughout your body. And now, one more *really* deep breath . . . hold it . . . and now release it slowly . . . and begin your normal breathing pattern. Shift around, if you need to get comfortable again.

Now begin to visualize the beginning of a day in which you are going to give an informative speech. See yourself getting up in the morning, full of energy, full of confidence, looking forward to the day's challenges. You are putting on just the right clothes for the task at hand that day. Dressing well makes you look and feel good about yourself, so you have on *just* what you want to wear, which clearly expresses your sense of inner well-being. As you are driving, riding, or walking to the speech setting, note how clear and confident you feel, and how others around you—as you arrive—comment positively regarding your fine appearance and general demeanor. You feel thoroughly prepared for the task at hand. Your preparation has been exceptionally thorough, and you have really researched the issue you will present today. Now you see yourself standing or sitting in the room where you will present your speech, talking very comfortably and confidentially with others in the room. The people to whom you will be presenting your speech appear to be quite friendly, and are very cordial in their greetings and conversations prior to the presentation. You feel *absolutely* sure of your material and of your ability to present the information in a forceful, convincing, positive manner. Now you see yourself approaching the area from which you will speak. You are feeling very good about this presentation and see yourself move eagerly forward. All of your audio-visual materials are well-organized, well-planned, and clearly aid your presentation.

Now you see yourself presenting your talk. You are really quite brilliant and have all the finesse of a polished, professional speaker. You are also aware that your audience is giving head nods, smiles, and other positive responses, conveying the message that you are truly "on target." The introduction of the speech goes the way you have planned. In fact, it works better than you had expected. The transition from the introductory material to the body of the speech is extremely smooth. As you approach the body of the speech, you are aware of the first major point. It emerges as you expected. The evidence supporting the point is relevant and evokes an understanding response from the audience. In fact, all the main points flow in this fashion. As you wrap up your main points, your concluding remarks seem to be a natural outgrowth of everything you have done. All concluding remarks are on target. When your final utterance is concluded, you have the feeling that it could not have gone better. The introduction worked, the main points were to the point, your evidence was supportive, and your conclusion formed a fitting capstone. In addition, your vocal variety added interest value. Your pauses punctuated important ideas, and your gestures and body movements were purposeful. You now see yourself fielding audience questions with brilliance, confidence, and energy equal to what you exhibited in the presentation itself. You see yourself receiving the congratulations of your classmates. You see yourself as relaxed, pleased with your talk, and ready for the next task to be accomplished that day. You are filled with energy, purpose, and a sense of general well-being. Congratulate yourself on a job well done!

Now I want you to begin to return to this time and place in which we are working today. Take a deep breath . . . hold it . . . and let it go. Do this several times and move slowly back into the room. Take as much time as you need to make the transition back.

The most important ingredient of this visualization script is its emphasis on positive thinking. *Do not allow negative thoughts to creep in.* When the script suggests thinking about some aspect of a speech, you should be thinking about a specific presentation.

The next step involves having people model their presentations after the presentation of a really good speaker. This step is based on procedures athletes use to improve their performance. Let us say you are having trouble with your backhand in tennis. Performance visualization involves very carefully watching someone who has an excellent backhand. You watch that person so intently that you make a mental movie of that person hitting a backhand shot. The mental movie is so crisp you can see the person's backhand stroke when you close your eyes just as clearly as if you are actually seeing the person. The next step is to see yourself as the person in the movie. Finally, you actually practice the stroke. Performance visualization for speaking follows these same steps except the focus is on a speaker. The speech we have used most often for this purpose is Barbara Jordan's keynote speech at the 1968 Democratic National Convention. We tell students to ignore the content and focus on Jordan's delivery style, which is conversational in nature. We have used good student speeches for this purpose with excellent results as well.

Using a visual aid is one way to relieve anxiety.

In effect, we play a videotape of Jordan's speech over and over until the student has made a mental movie of it, then the student "plays" the movie over and over in his or her mind with himself or herself as the "star," and, eventually, the student practices delivering the speech.

Performance visualization, systematic densensitization, and other procedures for helping people cope with speech anxiety have been detailed in a recent book.[27] Another promising procedure that has been demonstrated to reduce speech anxiety is available on videotape. It helps people deal with cognitive, affective, and behavioral aspects of speech anxiety.[28] Any and all of these procedures can be of value as you prepare for a specific speech.

**Coping Tactics:
Immediately Prior
to the Speech[29]**

Generally, audience members will be in attendance to listen to what you have to say; they will not be there hoping you will fail. Stress positive thoughts about the audience and its attitude toward you, mentally rehearse the introduction to your speech and go over the main points and specific purpose of the speech. If there is one particular part that seems more difficult than another, review that part as many times as you can.

Be sure your notes are in the proper order and that all of your audiovisual materials are on hand. Try to keep your mind focused on the content of your speech.

**Coping Tactics:
During the Introduction**

If you are particularly anxious during the introduction of a speech, start with a useful, relevant visual aid to focus attention on the aid rather than on you. Combine the use of a visual aid with other introductory techniques detailed in chapter 8, i.e., relating a personal story, talking about the occasion, or asking rhetorical questions. If you do stumble when you deliver the introduction, forge ahead. More than likely, any problem in the introduction will seem more important to you than it does to the audience. Considerable evidence indicates that anxiety is highest just prior to and in the very beginning of the speech. Anxiety then drops rapidly, as the speaker gets into the body of the speech.[30] By plowing ahead, you should experience relief as you adjust to the novelty and conspicuousness of the speaking situation.

A good way to reduce nervous energy during the introduction of the speech is to move and to gesture. Locking yourself in one place tends to build up tension. Moving and gesturing will help relax some of that tension. Of course, these movements and gestures should be purposeful.

Coping Tactics: During the Body

One way to cope with the anxiety that arises during the body of a speech is to prepare detailed notes. A former colleague of ours, Robert L. Ivie, developed a note form (called the split form outline—see chapter 6 for an example of this note form) that is particularly useful in dealing with anxiety. To construct a split form outline, put your speaking notes in one column and the text of your speech in the other column. If you are not having trouble delivering the speech, just flow through the speaking notes on the left, but if you encounter difficulty, shift over to the detailed speech on the right.

A visual aid in this portion of the speech can also be helpful. If the aid contains vital information, it can serve as a form of speaking notes.

Coping Tactics: During the Conclusion

Few people report problems with nervousness when wrapping up their speech, but if you do, follow the advice provided for introductions. Use commonly accepted procedures for concluding your speech, such as a summary in connection with a story or with a relevant quotation. Frequently, you will be able to reuse the visual aid used in the beginning.

Coping Tactics: Question and Answer Period

Speakers are not usually anxious after the speech has been completed, but an unexpected question can unnerve you. If you have tried to anticipate possible questions and answers, such surprises should occur infrequently. When a topic you have not anticipated does arise, don't bluff. Bluffing serves to increase anxiety, because you risk discovery and loss of face. After all your hard work in preparing the speech, why put yourself in this situation? If a question you are not prepared to deal with comes up, don't fake an answer. You might consider explaining why you are unsure of the answer and offer to do additional work to locate the information.

Summary

In this chapter, speech anxiety is defined as fear associated with delivering a public speech. Speech anxiety is often a learned response, and situational factors including novelty, conspicuousness, and audience characteristics can affect anxiety levels. General methods for coping with anxiety include: taking a course, getting professional help, being thoroughly prepared, using purposeful movements, and being flexible. Performance visualization, a procedure designed to develop positive thinking and improve delivery, is a means of reducing anxiety associated with a specific speech. Positive thinking and focusing on the content of the speech are ways to cope with anxiety just prior to delivering a speech. Using visual aids and purposeful movements are useful tactics for coping with nervousness in the introductory portion of the speech. Using detailed notes and visual aids are useful coping tactics during the body of the speech. To deal with nervousness during the conclusion of the speech, use proven techniques for ending the speech. Being prepared and being forthright are ways to cope with anxiety during the question and answer period following a speech.

Exercises

1. Discuss the factors that converge to create a peak of anxiety at the beginning of a speech.
2. Most speakers would not want to get rid of all anxiety. Why not?
3. Most people report much higher levels of anxiety about delivering a speech than they do about conversing with one other person. What factors do you suppose produce higher levels of anxiety in the public speech setting than in the interpersonal setting?
4. Write an autobiography of your speech anxiety/confidence. What experiences increased/decreased your anxiety/confidence? If you could change any of those experiences, what, if anything, would you change? Why?

Assignments

1. List a variety of speaking situations you might confront. Rank these situations in order, starting with the one that is the most fear provoking. Analyze these situations to figure out why they are fear provoking. Identify steps you could take to cope with your fear in each situation.
2. Locate a person who admits to experiencing speech anxiety. Ask that person to describe his or her experience. After you have finished talking to that person, analyze the conversation to see if you can point out what aspects of the speaking situation produced the person's feelings of anxiety.

Suggested Reading

Ayres, J. "Perceptions of Speaking Ability: An Explanation for Stage Fright." *Communication Education* 35 (1986): 275–87.

Daly, J. A., and Buss, A. H. "The Transitory Causes of Audience Anxiety." In J. A. Daly & J. C. McCroskey (eds.). *Avoiding Communication.* Beverly Hills: Sage, 1984: 67–78.

Kelly, L., and Watson, A. K. *Speaking with Confidence and Skill.* New York: Harper and Row, 1986.

Richmond, V. P., and McCroskey, J. C. *Communication: Apprehension, Avoidance, and Effectiveness.* Scottsdale, Az.: Gorsuch Scarisbrick, publishers, 1989.

Notes

1. James C. McCroskey, "The Implementation of a Large-scale Program of Systematic Desensitization for Communication Apprehension," *Speech Teacher,* 21 (1972): 255–64.
2. Joe Ayres and Theodore S. Hopf, "Visualization: A Means of Reducing Speech Anxiety," *Communication Education* 34 (1985): 318–23.
3. David Wallechinsky, Irving Wallace, and Amy Wallace, *The Book of Lists* (New York: Bantam Books, 1977): 314.
4. Interview with Gloria Steinem aired by National Public Radio, fall 1991.
5. Rollo May, *The Meaning of Anxiety* (New York: W. W. Norton & Company, 1977): 52–95.
6. Wallace Wilkins, "Desensitization: Social and Cognitive Factors Underlying the Effectiveness of Wolpe's Procedure," *Psychological Bulletin,* 76 (1971): 311–17.
7. John A. Daly and Arnold H. Buss, "The Transitory Causes of Anxiety," in J. A. Daly and J. C. McCroskey, eds. *Avoiding Communication* (Beverly Hills: Sage, 1984): 67–78.
8. Arnold H. Buss and Robert Plomin, *A Temperament Theory of Personality Development* (New York: John Wiley, 1975).
9. Kimberly McEwan and Gerald Devins, "Is Increased Arousal in Social Anxiety Noticed by Others?" *Journal of Abnormal Psychology* 92 (1983): 417–21.
10. Joe Ayres, "Antecedents of Communication Apprehension: A Reaffirmation," *Communication Research Reports* 5 (1988): 58–63.
11. James C. McCroskey, "The Communication Apprehension Perspective," in J. A. Daly and J. C. McCroskey, eds. *Avoiding Communication* (Beverly Hills: Sage, 1984): 27.
12. James C. McCroskey, "The Communication Apprehension Perspective," in J. A. Daly and J. C. McCroskey, eds. *Avoiding Communication* (Beverly Hills: Sage, 1984): 27.
13. Albert Bandura, *Social Learning Theory* (Englewood Cliffs, N.J.: Prentice-Hall, 1973).
14. Joe Ayres, "Perceptions of Speaking Ability: An Explanation of Stage Fright," *Communication Education* 35 (1986): 275–87.
15. Arnold H. Buss, *Self-consciousness and Social Anxiety* (San Francisco: W. H. Freeman, 1980).

16. Joe Ayres, "Situation Factors and Audience Anxiety," *Communication Education* 39 (1990): 283–91.
17. Wayne N. Thompson, *Quantitative Research in Public Address and Communication* (New York: Random House, 1967): 175–76.
18. James C. McCroskey, "Oral Communication Apprehension: A Summary of Recent Theory and Research," *Human Communication Research* 4 (1977): 78–96.
19. Gerald M. Phillips, "Rhetoritherapy Versus the Medical Model: Dealing with Reticence," *Communication Education* 26 (1977): 34–43.
20. Jan Hoffman and Jo Sprague, "A Survey of Reticence and Communication Apprehension Treatment Programs at U.S. Colleges and Universities," *Communication Education* (1982): 185–93.
21. J. Wolpe, *Psychotherapy by Reciprocal Inhibition* (Stanford: Stanford University Press, 1958).
22. Albert Ellis, *Reason and Emotion in Psychotherapy* (New York: Stuart, 1962).
23. Maxwell Maltz, *Psycho-cybernetics* (Hollywood: Wilshire Book Company, 1965).
24. Tim Hopf and Joe Ayres, "Coping with Public Speaking Anxiety: An Examination of Various Combinations of Systematic Desensitization, Skills Training, and Visualization," *Journal of Applied Communication Research* 20 (1992): 183–97.
25. Joe Ayres and Tim Hopf, "Visualization: Reducing Speech Anxiety and Enhancing Performance," *Communication Reports* 5 (1992): 1–9.
26. Joe Ayres and Tim Hopf, "Visualization: A Means of Reducing Speech Anxiety," *Communication Education* 34 (1985): 318–23.
27. Joe Ayres and Tim Hopf, *Coping With Speech Anxiety* (Norwood, NJ: Ablex, 1993).
28. Joe Ayres, Frances Ayres, Alan Baker, Noelle Colby, Camille De Blasi, Debbi Dimke, Lonetta Docken, Janell Grubb, Tim Hopf, Richard Mueller, Diana Sharp, and A. Kathleen Wilcox, "Two Empirical Tests of a Videotape Designed to Reduce Public Speaking Anxiety," *Journal of Applied Communication Research* (in press).
29. The suggestions in the following four sections are based in considerable measure on Winifred W. Brownell and Richard A. Katula, "The Communication Anxiety Graph: A Classroom Tool for Managing Speech Anxiety," *Communication Quarterly* 32 (1984): 243–49.
30. Steven Booth-Butterfield, "Action Assembly Theory and Communication Apprehension: A Psychophysiological Study," *Human Communication Research* 13 (1987): 386–98.

3 Listeners and Listening: Analyzing Audiences and Being a Responsive Audience Member

Chapter Outline

> *For of the three elements in speech making —speaker, subject, and person addressed —it is the last one, the hearer, that determines the speech's end and object.*
>
> *Aristotle*

Consider the following situation: A law enforcement officer is scheduled to give three speeches about drugs—one to an inner city high school audience, one to a youth group affiliated with a local church, and one to a community group of adults. This officer would be foolish to expect the same speech to be effective in all three settings. These audiences differ in terms of age, general attitudes, specific attitudes and experiences with drugs, and attitudes toward police officers. To be effective, this officer should develop three very different presentations in order to take into account the differing characteristics of these audiences.

On the other hand, let us consider this situation from the audience's standpoint. Students enrolled in some inner city schools may have strong attitudes about drugs and police officers and may approach this presentation with their minds closed. Youth group members may wonder why this officer is talking to them when they do not perceive themselves to have the problem. The community group, many of whom are parents, may represent a spectrum of opinions about whether law enforcement has been too stringent or too lax. These attitudes clearly are formidable obstacles for both the speaker and the audience. If they are to benefit from listening to this speech, these audience members should give the speaker a chance to be heard. There is no way for the listeners to tell whether they agree or disagree with what this speaker is going to say until they have listened to the speech.

Speakers and listeners have responsibilities to work together to enhance the communication process. The speaker must consider carefully the characteristics of the audience in order to adapt to the listeners' needs, and listeners should recognize factors that could diminish their capacity to receive a speaker's message.

Listeners: Your Audience

The audience is of major importance in any speaking situation; the nature of the audience greatly influences what a speaker is able to do and how best to do it. This chapter sets forth six areas a speaker should consider with respect to audiences: (1) speaker-audience relationship, (2) audience's level of knowledge about the subject, (3) audience attitudes toward the subject, (4) socioeconomic character of the audience, (5) relating to listeners' needs, and (6) promoting audience unity.

Speaker-Audience Relationship

The speaker is related to the audience in one of two ways. In the first way, the speaker is talking face-to-face with someone or some group; in the second, the audience is physically removed from the speaker, and some means of mass communication is being used to convey the message. These basic relationships affect the presentation in many ways. When speaking face-to-face, the speaker exerts a great deal of control over speech volume, visuals used, interaction between speaker and audience, the length of the interchange, and other variables in the communication situation. In the mass communication situation, someone else often controls these factors. In television, the camera crew films the shots and the director decides which view of the speaker to carry; the sound engineer determines the audio mix; the person sitting at home turns the volume of the television set up or down or decides to go get a snack. The speaker must be aware of these different situations and plan his or her speech accordingly. Presentations made in a speech class will be in the face-to-face setting, so we will concentrate our comments on that area.

It is important to remind yourself that as a speaker, you will *feel* that all eyes are upon you, but really each member of the audience feels as though he or she is at the center of attention—the person to whom and for whom you are delivering the speech. Just as the speaker has a purpose in speaking, so does the audience member who expects to be entertained, informed, or given advice or guidance. If both speaker and audience are to feel fulfilled, it is crucial that the speaker attend to the expectations of his or her listeners.

The two basic things to remember about the audience are that (1) each member is an individual and that (2) the members do not have to listen to you unless they want to. Analyze your own feelings when you are the listener and you will see that this is true.

Although each member of your audience is a unique individual, you can not react to each of them separately. Therefore you ought to find out as much as you can about (1) your audience's general understanding of your subject, (2) the audience's attitude toward your subject, and (3) basic characteristics your listeners have in common that might have a bearing on their reactions to your speech.

In a typical speech course, you often can find out the range of interests of your classmates when they are introduced or introduce themselves. Such information should be very helpful in deciding what topics to select and how to treat those topics when you speak before the class.

You will also learn about your classmates as you listen to their speeches during the semester. If someone talks about various aspects of music, for instance, that will provide you with insight into how that person is likely to see related issues (e.g., support for a series of concerts to be sponsored by the Associated Students). You can then use this information to make

Choose topics that appeal to your classmates' concerns.

predictions and generalizations about the general disposition of the entire group of listeners. Attempt to appeal to your classmates' concerns as much as possible, without compromising your own beliefs.

In non-classroom situations, you may be contacted by a representative of the organization that invited you to speak. Use that opportunity to question the member about the composition of the group, to get an estimate of the number of people who are likely to attend, to obtain a description of the physical setting, to determine the nature of the occasion on which you are to speak, and to ask what the group wants you to speak about. You should also find out what other activities are planned for that meeting, where you will appear in the agenda, and how long your presentation should be. Knowing these things will help you plan your presentation. If, for instance, you are scheduled to appear after an open debate on a controversial issue, you might anticipate the need to spend more time in the introduction of your speech gaining the group's attention than you would if you were first on the agenda.

Knowledge Level

Discover what your audience knows about your subject so you can aim your speech at the right level. If, for instance, you plan to talk about customs in Australia, a young audience might be interested in the differences between games played in Australia and games played in the United States. For instance, bowling in Australia is done outside, on grass, and has nothing to do with seeing how many pins you can knock down, but rather with seeing how close you can come to a target. A more sophisticated audience might appreciate a historical analysis of why most large projects in Australia are carried out by the government rather than by private companies. If the audience appears to have such a low level of information on a subject that "you can't get there from here" or seems to know a great deal more than you know or can learn, choose another topic.

Attitudes

In addition to finding out the audience's knowledge level, you should assess how the audience feels about your topic and how strongly it holds that position. An attitude is a relatively enduring feeling you have about a topic. You may feel that unions are (are not) good for working people. You may feel the United States should (should not) protect its interests by using military force. You may feel that the Equal Rights Amendment provides (does not provide) for the protection of women's rights. You can probably think of any number of issues about which you have formed attitudes. You may hold these attitudes very strongly and be very unlikely to change them (like a belief in God), or you may not feel strongly about the issue and you would change your attitude easily (like whether women should always wear skirts in an office).

Your choice of topic and of how to present it will be helped by knowledge of the audience's attitude toward your subject. If you have chosen the subject "How to Maintain Your Car" for your talk to a group of accountants, you have no reason to assume that this will be a subject that will immediately command their attention. However, almost any subject can be made relevant if you plan your approach thoughtfully and imaginatively. A wise speaker could begin by emphasizing how much money could be saved if the accountants did routine maintenance on their cars themselves. On the other hand, if you are talking to antique car buffs, it might not be effective to open this way since automobile enthusiasts enjoy doing such work and might not mind how much money they spend on their favorite hobby.

To this group you might reveal some unique methods you've devised to maintain a car, building on the attitude they already hold that automobile maintenance is important.

The attitude held by your audience is even more important if you are attempting to persuade, rather than to inform. If a group is already *in favor* of your proposal, you would not approach it as you would if it is *hostile* toward the idea. You would also vary your approach, depending upon whether the group is *strongly supportive* or whether it is only *moderately supportive*. When Franklin Roosevelt addressed the nation during his second term as president, he spoke with great confidence about the steps he was going to take because Americans had given him a strong vote of confidence. Several years later, John F. Kennedy, having won the presidency by the barest of margins, spoke of reconciliation and bringing the country together. You probably will not have the opportunity to address the country after your election as president, but you would be wise to follow the example of Kennedy and Roosevelt and respond to the attitude of an audience.

If the audience is strongly in favor of a proposal, you might talk about how to enact it; if the audience is undecided, you can point out reasons for supporting it. If it is against the proposal, your strategy might be to acknowledge its position as rational and possible, then point out why your own position is different. In all cases, you should speak to the attitudes of the audience as you are able to recognize them.

Research on audience attitudes suggests two conclusions:

1. The more firmly held the attitude, the easier the task will be of strengthening it still further, but the more difficult it will be to change that view.[1] You can ask for some small step-by-step changes; but if you ask for a total reversal of your listeners' position, they are much less inclined to accept your position and they may likely be convinced that *you* are wrong.
2. If an audience's attitude is counter to yours but the attitude is not strongly held, you can safely ask for extensive changes and full acceptance of your ideas; the audience may find that going along with your argument is easier than exerting the effort required to form counterarguments.[2]

Listeners tend to be consistent in maintaining their own attitudinal balance. They tend to protect this balance by the following means:

1. Selective exposure. Listeners attend (or tune in) only speeches with which they already agree, so you have a better than average chance of assuming your audience to be relatively friendly, or at least interested in your subject.

2. Selective attention. For example, you have an appointment at 3 o'clock; you ask what time it is and are told 2:10. Five minutes later you don't remember what time it *was* because you selectively paid attention only to what time it *wasn't*. In the public speaking situation, an auditor chooses to respond only to those ideas that speak to some personal need or interest, screening out everything else that is said.

3. Selective perception. This tendency to distort what is heard (trying to "make it fit" with previously held convictions) can keep those friendly to the speaker unchanged in their attitudes even if the speaker's words challenge previously held notions about the speaker.

4. Selective retention. If all else fails, the listener can simply proceed to forget that disturbing message.[3]

The speaker's only means of overcoming these negative forces is by learning about and understanding the audience and then planning the presentation to be one the listeners will *want* to hear and accept. Chapters 13 and 14 deal more fully with persuasion and the persuasive speech.

Socioeconomic Character of the Audience

In addition to the degree of immediacy of the audience (speaking face-to-face or through mass-media channels), the audience's knowledge level, and its attitude, there are some other general characteristics that provide valuable information to a speaker about an audience. These social and economic factors include age; sex; level of intelligence and of education; social, professional, political or religious group affiliation; occupation; and the commonality of origin of the audience.

Age

Today nearly everyone is aware of the term "generation gap" and the difference in viewpoint to which it refers. In general, young people can be characterized as vigorous, physically active, idealistic, and optimistic, while elderly people tend to be cautious, concerned about security, and more conservative. Middle-aged people usually fall between these extremes; they are best appealed to by arguments of moderation.

If you have an audience that is homogeneous in age you can respond to the specific characteristics of that age group. But if, as is much more likely, your audience contains members of more than one age group, the wise course is to cover as many bases as possible—pointing out the humanitarian aspects of your subject as well as presenting support for its economic and security-assuring aspects.

Gender

If your audience is made up of all men or all women, certain gender-based topics may suggest themselves as most likely to interest the group; in mixed groups, other topics are more likely to be of interest. In recent years, the stereotypes or differences between the sexes have blurred markedly. Many men are good cooks, sports are of equal interest to both men and women, and physical fitness concerns people of every age. Both men and women have become aware that traditional sex-role socialization has limited their avenues of expression and growth. Girls can excel at mathematics, and boys can develop the nurturing attitudes that will make them good fathers in the future. According to recent figures, women comprise a greater and greater percentage of the work force, yet their salaries lag those of their male counterparts. Resentment of such power disparities can cause a large porportion of your audience to be very sensitive to such slights as suggesting that women are interested only in such things as clothes and children, while men are engaged in important events in business and in the world at large. The speaker who refers to women condescendingly or in terms of their physical attractiveness makes a very serious blunder and may arouse animosity toward both the speaker and the subject. Such comments as "It is a great privilege to address a group of such lovely ladies," will persuade your audience of nothing more than that you "just don't get it." Men can be equally turned off by the suggestion that they have no knowledge of the day-to-day problems of managing a household, or that only women can be concerned about issues such as rape or world peace.

Intelligence and Level of Education

People with lower intelligence scores or lower levels of education, or both, do not readily comprehend complex issues and are therefore less persuaded by them. However, when ideas are presented to them in a manner they can understand, their opinions generally are easier to sway. People with higher intelligence or education, or both, grasp ideas more quickly, but they are more skeptical listeners and thus more difficult to persuade. Be careful not to talk down to the audience or use a manner of presentation that is offensive to any portion of the audience.

Group Affiliation

Knowing the beliefs, attitudes, and customs common to the social, professional, political, and religious groups to which your listeners belong can tell you about their probable reactions to a given subject or argument. Stereotypes can be very dangerous and incorrect when applied to *individual* members of a group, but you can often rely on them to make *predictions and*

> Okie useta mean you was from Oklahoma. Now it means you're scum. Don't mean nothin' itself, it's the way they say it.
>
> Grapes of Wrath, *John Steinbeck.*

generalizations on which to base your informative or persuasive appeals. When speaking to a local chapter of the National Rifle Association (NRA), you could assume that most people in the audience would hold the general beliefs of the national association; for example, opposition to gun control. Naturally, a member of the group may disagree with a particular NRA stand, but as a group the local chapter will probably agree with the views of the NRA national leadership.

Occupation

In the earlier example in which you gave a speech on car maintenance, first to a group of accountants and then to a group of antique car buffs, we suggested that their probable *attitudes* toward the subject should influence you in planning your speech. The occupation of your listeners can suggest some general conclusions about the personality types who chose those occupations and what they *know* as a result of having worked at their jobs. It would be wise for you to respect that knowledge and to build on it, recognizing as well the "in-group" feeling they have toward each other as a result of shared problems and experiences. We recognize nurses as being concerned with the health of people, but experienced nurses often develop an emotional distance from their patients in order to endure the daily contact with human suffering. So if you are to talk to a group of nurses about child abuse and want them to react emotionally, you might have to use much stronger material than you would if you were to speak to a group of parents. Also, the group members may hold important attitudes about themselves based on the perceived status of their occupation or their own position and degree of power within that occupation.

Commonality of Origin

Race, nationality, or geographic region can give a group a shared background and special characteristics that you as speaker should know about and for which you should adapt your arguments, language, and cadence of speech. Common experiences or lack of them can establish "in" groups and "out" groups. Often the separation can be caused by speaking different languages, but it also can be based on whether you do or do not know the language of math, of music, of flying or boating, of fishing or skiing.

Just as one cannot make assumptions as to what women and men can do and are interested in, neither can the speaker generalize about members of racial or ethnic groups. Perhaps the only characteristic common to the

> Safety has both anxieties and delights; growth has both anxieties and delights. We grow forward when the delights of growth and anxieties of safety are greater than the anxieties of growth and the delights of safety.
>
> *Abraham Maslow*

experience of non-white racial groups in the U.S. is that they have often experienced adverse discrimination. The speaker should take care not to perpetuate any such attitudes by choice of language, but even more importantly, should cultivate in him or herself a genuine appreciation for cultural diversity that will result in a respect for the dignity and individuality of each audience member. You may want to experience another place and culture first-hand, consciously trying to empathize with people whose background is different from your own.

Mark O. Badger, a 17-year resident of Alaska, tells how his work as producer/cameraman/editor of the PBS series "Make Prayers for the Raven" has helped him look at nature through the eyes of a different culture. The Athabascan Indians, who live on the banks of the Koyukuk River a few hundred miles north of Fairbanks, believe animals know more than they do, and after more than 10,000 years of habitation scarcely a trace of the people can be seen in the wild. Badger tells of how an Athabascan woman once said to him, "When white people look up at a bird, they say, 'Look at that bird!' When we look up at a bird, we think, 'What does that bird see in me?'"

"In other words," Badger says, "these people are always traveling in a watchful world; they are always conscious of how they are behaving towards the environment and towards other animals. I hope I have taken on a bit of that attitude."[4]

Listeners' Needs

We have discussed some of the possible individual attributes of listeners; you can use these to generalize about them as an audience. Your second concern is, How can I get them to listen to me? Broadly considered, you must do the following:

1. Speak to a desire, need, or concern that your listeners already feel or one that they may not have previously recognized. How many times have you "realized" that you really wanted a Coke or a pizza, only after the commercial pointed it out? But this suggestion, no matter how attractively presented, would not have been effective if you had just finished dinner.
2. Provide a means to satisfy that desire or resolve that concern.

> Slogans are both exciting and comforting, but they are also powerful opiates for the conscience. . . . Some of mankind's most terrible misdeeds have been committed under the spell of certain magic words or phrases.
>
> *James B. Conant*

3. Explain and demonstrate the relationship between your subject or the course of action you suggest and some basic human motivation, i.e., motivation that comes from needs ranging from physiological needs to spiritual needs; from love of adventure to desire for security; from selfishness to concern for others; from independence to conformity; from pride to humility. In other words, "How is what you say relevant to me the listener and my concerns?"[5]

In order to speak to the needs of an audience, you should have some understanding of the kinds of concerns its members may have. One of the most useful approaches to the question of human needs was developed by Abraham Maslow. He suggested that human needs range from basic physiological requirements to self-actualization.

Furthermore, these needs progress in stages; that is, needs lower on the hierarchy must be met before the person is free to concentrate on a higher level of need. For example, people who must spend every waking moment in getting enough to eat usually do not think about poetry or music. The five levels of needs identified by Maslow, beginning with the most basic, are:

1. Physiological needs—for air, food, drink, sleep, sex, etc., the basic requirements of the physical body.
2. Safety needs—for security, stability, protection from harm or injury; need for structure, orderliness, law, and predictability; freedom from fear and chaos.
3. Belonging and love needs—for acceptance and approval; need to feel warm affection and lasting devotion with spouse, children, parents, and close friends; need to feel a part of social groups.
4. Esteem needs—for self-esteem based on achievement, mastery, competence, confidence, freedom, independence; desire for esteem of others (reputation, prestige, recognition, status).
5. Self-actualization needs—for self-fulfillment; being true to your self; realizing fully the potential of your capabilities.[6]

As a speaker you should assess correctly the concerns of the audience and be responsive to those concerns. If you oppose nuclear power, you face a different task when you address people who live near or work at a nuclear

Similarity of response produces unity in an audience.

power plant than you do when you talk to people who do not live near enough to feel threatened by nor make their living from the production of nuclear energy.

Audience Unity

Up to this point, we have been discussing the audience as a group of individuals who must be "averaged" together in the mind of the speaker. Let's look for a moment at instances when an audience actually does, for a space of time, function as a single unit. You've all had the experience of being one of the first two or three people to arrive at a social gathering and feeling a little awkward and ill at ease. Then as more people arrived and began to interact, you felt the point at which the gathering became a party. A similar kind of melding can occur when a leader maneuvers a group into taking joint action. A speaker may use humor to get the audience to laugh together or may ask for a show of hands as an expression of approval. A minister may ask the congregation to sing or chant together, kneel together, or rise together. A rock musician may lead the audience in clapping or chanting in unison to heighten the excitement of the concert. Even repeating these procedures again and again may be worth the effort to the speaker; the greater the feeling of unity an audience has, the more likely the speaker is to obtain a favorable response.

When audience members are close together physically, each listener tends to be stimulated more than he or she realizes by the reactions of people nearby. The larger the group and the more emotional the stimulation presented by the speaker, the greater is the impact.[7]

> All speech, written or spoken, is a dead language, until it finds a willing and pre-pared hearer.
>
> *Robert Louis Stevenson*

These types of crowd reaction are like herd behavior in other animals, a kind of social absorption resulting from the natural human desire for acceptance. We have learned to imitate others to gain their approval and to follow implicit suggestions on how to act; we sometimes applaud even if we dislike the performance; we laugh when others laugh, even if we "don't get it." A person who stops on the street and points at nothing at all can soon draw a crowd of other people, all looking and pointing, convinced that they are indeed seeing something.

When used properly by an ethical speaker, these phenomena can suggest useful techniques of persuasion; but the thoughtful listener will resist suspending his or her critical judgment to such a spellbinder. History offers many instances in which the individual alone and the individual in a group are two different psychological beings. Adolf Hitler and Benito Mussolini are examples of unethical speakers who exerted a hypnotic effect on their crowds of followers.

Attention to certain elements in the physical setting can help to achieve the desired oneness of speaker and listeners:

1. Audience unity is best accomplished when the listeners face the speaker and when distractions are slight. Seating the audience in a circle may facilitate discussion, but it is counterproductive to creating a oneness of response.
2. Similarity of reaction is heightened when the audience is densely packed together.
   a. The more compact the audience, the less inhibited it is in responding to the speaker. Lowered lights can also contribute to an audience's sense of anonymity, which frees its members to make overt responses.
   b. The more compact the audience, the more readily responses can be communicated from one member of the audience to the other. A speaker should avoid having an audience scattered around a room too large for the group.
   c. Circular response is intensified when the setting is appropriate to the desired response and allows for a minimum of distractions. The audience responds to all stimuli, including present stimuli and memories of past stimuli, not just to the speaker. Mark Twain once said that he had never yet been able to make people laugh in a church. Space has a particular "feel"; the speaker should check it out ahead of time and make adjustments whenever possible.

By permission of Johnny Hart and Creators Syndicate, Inc.

Listening

There are four basic ways of communicating—speaking, writing, reading, and listening. From research conducted in 1926 and from similar research fifty years later, in 1977, the conclusions are the same: college students spend about 14 percent of their time writing, 17 percent reading, 16 percent speaking, and 53 percent of their time listening.[8] Other research indicates that people retain only about 25 percent of what they hear; considering that we spend such a large proportion of our time in listening, we must lose out on a lot.[9] In a typical lecture, if the average college student retains only 25 percent of what he or she hears, 75 percent of the lecture material is lost! Listening may appear to be very easy, but the fact is that most people are poor listeners and poor listening can have devastating consequences.

In 1977, some 580 people aboard two aircraft in the Canary Islands lost their lives because of poor communication. The pilot of a KLM–Royal Dutch Airlines Boeing 747 was told to stop at the end of the runway and hold for takeoff clearance. At the same time, the pilot of a Pan American World Airways Boeing 747 was told to turn off the runway at the third intersection. Unfortunately, the Pan Am pilot assumed the air traffic controller really meant the fourth intersection since the first intersection was unusable and the third intersection difficult to negotiate. Meanwhile, the KLM plane did not stop at the end of the runway but proceeded to take off. Foggy weather prevented either pilot from seeing the other in time to take evasive action. Traveling in excess of 150 mph, the KLM plane smashed into the Pan Am plane. Investigators concluded "If both pilots and the tower controllers had fully heard—and understood—one another the KLM pilot would never have sent his craft hurtling toward takeoff before the Pan Am plane was off the runway."[10]

Your own experiences in poor listening may never have such devastating consequences, but failing to listen can cause you problems every day. How many times has a friend been talking, then asked you what you thought about what he or she had been saying, and you had to say, "Sorry, I wasn't listening." In class, we often see students doodling, reading the newspaper, or daydreaming. Poor listening is probably as responsible as any other factor in causing students to receive poor grades. In a broad survey of national

Many outside factors can interfere with the ability to hear what a speaker is saying.

THE WORLD'S NOISES

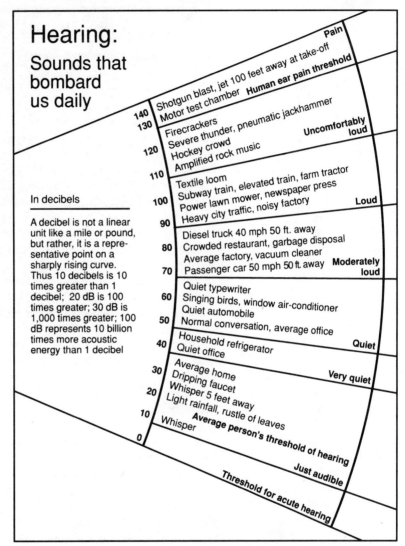

Hearing:
Sounds that bombard us daily

In decibels
___

A decibel is not a linear unit like a mile or pound, but rather, it is a representative point on a sharply rising curve. Thus 10 decibels is 10 times greater than 1 decibel; 20 dB is 100 times greater; 30 dB is 1,000 times greater; 100 dB represents 10 billion times more acoustic energy than 1 decibel

dB		
		Pain
140	Shotgun blast, jet 100 feet away at take-off	
130	Motor test chamber **Human ear pain threshold**	
	Firecrackers	
	Severe thunder, pneumatic jackhammer	**Uncomfortably loud**
120	Hockey crowd	
	Amplified rock music	
110		
	Textile loom	
	Subway train, elevated train, farm tractor	
100	Power lawn mower, newspaper press	**Loud**
90	Heavy city traffic, noisy factory	
	Diesel truck 40 mph 50 ft. away	
80	Crowded restaurant, garbage disposal	
	Average factory, vacuum cleaner	**Moderately loud**
70	Passenger car 50 mph 50 ft. away	
	Quiet typewriter	
60	Singing birds, window air-conditioner	
	Quiet automobile	
50	Normal conversation, average office	
40	Household refrigerator	**Quiet**
	Quiet office	
30	Average home	
	Dripping faucet	**Very quiet**
20	Whisper 5 feet away	
	Light rainfall, rustle of leaves	
10	Whisper	
	Average person's threshold of hearing	
0		
		Just audible
	Threshold for acute hearing	

Chicago Tribune Graphic: Illustrated by Tom Heinz, researched by N. Jane Hunt: Sources: World Book, Rand McNally Atlas of the Human Body, Encyclopedia Americana, "Industrial Noise and Hearing Conversation" by J. B. Olishifski and E. R. Harford.

organizations, "good oral communication ability," which included good listening skills, was the highest-ranked quality among corporate personnel managers when they were asked what they look for in hiring college seniors.[11]

A survey of 1,000 corporation presidents indicated poor subordinate listening habits were the most frequent cause of anxiety in work situations.[12] Another recent study indicated that listening is essential to the success of both superiors and subordinates in the business setting, most notably in (1) meetings, (2) performance appraisals, and (3) superior-subordinate communication. Skills associated with "active" listening are especially needed, more than merely listening for information.[13] Listening is of equal importance in our personal relationships. The ability to relate to others rests in large measure on our ability to be sensitive to their needs, on our ability to be empathetic listeners.[14]

In our society, in which we receive much of our information about the world through the spoken word, we need to be good listeners. We will discuss hearing and listening and the difference between them, the advantages of good listening, factors that contribute to poor listening, and how we can become better listeners.

Hearing and Listening Defined
Hearing

We must first make a distinction between *hearing* and *listening*. The ability to hear is a physical process that happens naturally, while listening requires mental concentration. We hear people talk, but we fail to listen to what they say. Merely "hearing" the communication is not enough to achieve comprehension, but certainly hearing is a necessary first step. Physical barriers that make it difficult for an audience to hear include distractive sounds, poor acoustics, and uncomfortable chairs. The listener can surmount these barriers to some degree by intense concentration, but the typical audience member quickly becomes fatigued from this effort, gives up, and "tunes the speaker out." This pattern of retreat is even more noticeable in people who have a hearing problem; an estimated 10 percent of the population suffers from some hearing loss. If you have reason to suspect that you might not be hearing well, you should arrange to have your hearing tested.

> It is the province of knowledge to speak and it is the privilege of wisdom to listen.
>
> *Oliver Wendell Holmes*

Listening

While hearing is essentially being within the range of and receiving sound, listening is the process whereby the nervous system interprets those sound waves and translates them into understandable messages. Listening in the public-speaking situation requires actively paying attention to the speech; trying to determine the speaker's meaning; and letting the speaker know how you are reacting by nodding, clapping, frowning, and so forth.

Advantages of Good Listening Habits

By listening carefully, you can (1) gain information; (2) perfect your ability to use language; and (3) become more involved in your surroundings. Probably each of you listens to the radio, to television, to lectures, and to friends every day. Besides improving your ability to gather information, paying attention to improving your listening can help you to perfect your own language ability. Listen as others speak well or speak poorly; such modeling is basic to learning any language. In your speech class you have a perfect opportunity to use listening to improve your own speaking. In a typical semester you will deliver six or seven speeches, but you will listen to nearly one hundred fifty speeches—and your instructor may have a word or two to add from time to time as well. As you listen to your classmates, note features of their speaking that seem particularly effective—like strategic changes in the rate of speaking—and pay attention to comments made by the instructor. By listening carefully and using some of the techniques discussed, you will be able to improve your own speaking.

Good listeners may also live more fully. Picture yourself as a friend is trying to tell you about the terrible time she is having in French class while you mentally plan your weekend activities. More than likely your friend will be less inclined to talk to you in the future.

Factors Contributing to Poor Listening
Faking

One behavior that contributes to people's poor listening is to act as if they are listening when they are not. Such fakers look directly at you, nod their heads, but don't hear a word you are saying. Some students, perhaps in necessary self-defense, seem to become very adept at "tuning out" during lectures, even while looking raptly at the professor.

Mental Laziness

Other people habitually avoid situations in which they may have to listen to difficult material. The relatively low number of viewers of educational television is a solid indication of such avoidance behavior in television audiences. One person we know avoids difficult messages by simply deciding, "This is too difficult," and refusing to listen after hearing the first few words.

Listeners and Listening

51

> I think the one lesson I have learned is that there is no substitute for paying attention.
>
> *Diane Sawyer*

We once attended with this acquaintance a speech in which the speaker gave a low-key and interesting presentation on nuclear fusion. Our friend never listened to anything after the title because, "After all, everyone knows that nuclear fusion is tough to understand."

Daydreaming

Another way to avoid listening is to give in to the temptation to daydream. It's easy to imagine yourself out fishing, or out with that attractive person sitting next to you in class, but don't fall prey to temptation. You have to be on guard and remind yourself to be a conscientious listener.

Sometimes, even when we try to listen to what a speaker is saying, we allow ourselves to be distracted. One girl we know talks very fast. It is easy to lose track of what she is saying and become fascinated with the speed with which she talks. Many people dress in unique ways, "talk funny," or walk differently; avoid allowing such irrelevant circumstances to get in the way of hearing what a speaker is saying.

Another way to avoid paying attention is to say, "This is uninteresting." Of course once you label something that way and stop listening, you'll never know whether the rest of the message was interesting or not. As a speaker you should avoid being dull and making it easy for your listeners to tune you out, but as a listener you may have to fight through some pretty dull things and make them interesting on your own.

Preconceptions

Expectations tend to alter perceptions. If you go to a party or a movie expecting to have a good time, very likely you will, but if you expect to be bored, then it is likely you will be bored. If you expect a speech to be uninteresting, it will almost certainly seem so to you. Preconceptions about whether you will agree or disagree with a speaker's point of view are usually borne out.

In one study, people who heard a neutral statement on school busing tended to perceive it as an anti-busing statement when it was attributed to Governor George Wallace, and the same message was judged to be pro-busing when it was attributed to Dr. Martin Luther King, Jr.[15]

Certain words often evoke positive or negative reactions in us, depending on our experiences with such words as pro-life, pro-choice, boy, redneck, women's liberation, reverse discrimination, cop, etc. Once the term is mentioned, we decide what's coming and stop listening. Try to identify the words or phrases you react to as "red flags" and guard against overreacting to them. Conversely, when you are the speaker, put yourself in the other person's shoes and avoid words or a tone of voice that might offend your listeners.

Nobody has ever listened himself out of a job.

Calvin Coolidge, the thirtieth president of the United States, 1923–1929
(nicknamed Silent Cal)

Reprinted by special permission of King Features Syndicate.

Twelve Ways to Improve Listening

It's generally accepted that people can listen at a greater rate than most people talk. While most people speak between 100 and 150 words per minute, the listener can process words at 300 to 400 words per minute, so in effect, we think twice as fast as we talk. The most listenable rate of speech is from 125 to 190 words per minute; this seems to suggest that this slack time between speaking rate and listening rate is not only potentially useful but is actually necessary for the comprehension and retention of information. There are a number of ways to use this time gap while you are listening. We have discussed some of the advantages of listening well and some of the factors that hamper good listening. We turn our attention now to ways to improve our listening ability.

1. Prelistening activities. Before you attend a speech or lecture there are a number of things you can do to improve your ability to listen effectively. Read the available material on all aspects of the issue. Take careful notes; include bibliographic information (author, title, publisher, etc.) so you can find the material again if you need it. Take a few minutes to review your notes before going to the lecture or speech so you will have an overall picture of the issues in mind.
2. Anticipate. As you listen, you can think about what the speaker is trying to accomplish. What is the speaker's goal? How will the speaker try to reach the goal? By posing questions like these to yourself, you can anticipate the direction of the speech and adjust your expectations as the thesis of the speech is developed. This is an excellent way to build your interest in what is being said. It's like mentally putting a puzzle together; you try an arrangement and then see if the speaker confirms it. In person-to-person situations, you can

ask questions directly to help clarify points as the conversation develops; in public speaking settings, remember points you want to have clarified and ask about them at the close of the speech.

3. Listen critically.

   a. Evaluate the evidence presented to back up the main ideas. When you are anticipating, you try to identify the main ideas; in evaluating the evidence, you try to pinpoint the type of information being used to support those main ideas.

   b. Evaluate the speaker's use of reasoning. Is he or she engaging in name-calling? using abstract or general terms? making hasty generalizations? resorting to a "plain folks" appeal to establish common ground with the audience? or using any of the other fallacious reasoning techniques discussed in chapter 14?

4. Be alert. Take advantage of clues to the speaker's meaning and purposes that are available in advance, such as the setting and staging of the event and any printed program notes. Listen in outline form; the choice of material and the position and time given to a particular point can give you a clue as to which ideas the speaker considers most important and which are subpoints. The vigilant listener makes note of the speaker's use of topic sentences, transitions, and summaries. Further clues as to what the speaker considers to be important can be found in inflection, rate, emphasis, voice quality, and bodily action. In written form these points would be set off by bold-face type, italics, or quotation marks.

5. Review. During a speech you will find time in the gap between speaking and hearing time to review the points that have been made. If this chapter were a speech, you might be thinking in mental review that Ayres and Miller have said there are advantages to improving listening and barriers to accomplishing this improvement, and they have offered some techniques for improving listening. Advantages of listening are that you can gain information, perfect your use of language, and become more involved in your surroundings by learning to listen more closely. It is doubtful that you want to be too detailed in your review. People who try to remember too much of a speech sometimes fail to get the message because they tried to get all of the details. Listen for the key ideas.

6. Take notes. You can improve your chances of remembering information by taking good notes on the speech. Note-taking must not be used as a way to avoid listening by doodling, or for trying to write down everything; note only words or phrases that will jar your memory about an important point and reconstruct a detailed set of notes later. Remember, your job is to listen.

> To study persuasion intensively is to study human nature minutely.
>
> *Charles Woolbert*

> Nature has given man one tongue and two ears, that we may hear twice as much as we speak.
>
> *Epictetus*

7. Use good physical position for listening. Good listeners are prepared to listen actively. Focus your attention on the speaker; look directly at him or her and keep watching. Don't slouch and look bored; we often begin to feel the way we look. In face-to-face speaking, provide some feedback while the speaker is talking. If the speaker says something you think is funny, laugh or smile. Nod your head if you agree, or shake it if you don't. Don't be afraid to look puzzled if you are. Feedback like this will help the speaker gauge your reactions and provide an opportunity to alter his or her comments. Providing feedback will also help you to keep alert and focus on the message you are hearing.

8. Be empathetic. Empathy is the capacity to understand how another person feels and to put yourself in that person's place. If you are observing a very nervous speaker, you might recognize that people often get nervous when giving a speech and that this person is trying very hard to make a good presentation. Because you may have been nervous yourself in similar situations, you can empathize with the speaker and offer positive feedback. After you have placed the person's nervousness in proper perspective, you can get on with concentrating on receiving the message. Being empathetic can help you comprehend why you are reacting the way you are and allow you to become a better listener by helping you set aside some of your biases while you strive to hear what the speaker is "really" saying.

9. Listen for ideas. According to Lyman K. Steil, president of Communication Development for the Sperry Corporation, poor listeners focus on the facts while good listeners search for the main themes.[16] Facts are often unrelated bits of information that will make more sense and be easier to recall if you relate them to central themes.

10. Resist prejudging. Reacting to a presentation by thinking of counterarguments often leads to closing your mind to the ideas that follow. Remember the points with which you disagree, but suspend judgment until you are sure of the speaker's position.
11. Post-listening activities. Discuss the ideas that were presented with others who were present. Are you and the others in agreement about what the speaker said? If there are areas of disagreement, you will want to resolve them to be sure you are representing the speaker accurately.
12. Summarize your notes. Again, compare your notes with those of others who attended the presentation. Any areas of disagreement may indicate problems in your listening behavior that you will want to correct. Include bibliographic information on your notes, and file them so you can have access to them later.

Summary

By knowing the type of audience you are addressing (immediate or removed, i.e., face-to-face or via electronic communication), the knowledge level of its members, their basic attitude, and some socioeconomic information about them, you will be better able to adapt your message to the audience and to promote audience unity.

Your listening behaviors determine how well you retain messages that are presented to you. Improving your listening will help you learn, help perfect your own language use, and help you be more involved in communication situations. Faking attention, avoiding difficult listening, labeling messages as uninteresting, daydreaming, and reacting to emotion-laden words are barriers to effective listening. Listening can be improved by anticipating, evaluating the evidence, reviewing, using good listening behavior, and by being empathetic.

Exercises

1. Administer a listening comprehension test. Research by Rebecca B. Rubin and Charles V. Roberts suggests that an excellent test for this purpose is the Watson-Barker Listening Test.[17] Material for this test is available in Watson, K. W. and Barker, L. L. (1987). *Watson-Barker Listening Test* (Auburn, AL.: Spectra, Inc.)
2. Maintain a listening log for two days. Construct hourly time charts divided into ten-minute intervals. Once every hour record whether you were primarily listening (L), speaking (S), writing (W), reading (R), or not communicating (N). Determine the percentage of time you devoted to each of these categories by dividing the total number of categories into the total number of times you said you were engaged in a particular activity. The resulting percentages will give you an idea of how much time you engage in various communication activities. To focus on the times you reported you were listening,

identify those instances when you thought you were an effective listener (E) and those times you thought you were an ineffective listener (I). After you have used some of the advice provided in this chapter, repeat this exercise to see if your listening is becoming more effective.

3. Here is an effective activity for developing good communication skills. Try it one day, keeping the designs simple. Later, try it again several more times, using increasingly more complicated designs each time.

One person is to draw a design (start simple!) on a piece of paper or on the chalkboard, without letting the other person (or persons) see it. Listening to verbal directions given slowly by the person who drew the design (no hands or visual help allowed), the other person tries to reproduce the design on his or her own piece of paper. When the first person is through giving directions, compare the original design with the reproduction. Then, change positions. This way, both people have a chance to practice two vital roles involved in communication—that of the transmitter and the receiver. Each learns the value of clear verbal expression and careful listening.

Assignments

1. Write a brief audience analysis for each of the following situations. Include comments on how the characteristics would influence the way you would approach the speech.
   a. You are a representative of a college school of agriculture. Your topic is "How the market determines food prices." You will talk to each of the following groups:
      1. 50 farmers
      2. 50 college students majoring in agriculture
      3. 50 homemakers
      4. 50 grocery store owners
   b. You oppose the re-election of a member of the school board. You think this school board member should not be re-elected because he or she believes that certain books should be censored. You plan to talk to:
      1. a local group of conservative ministers
      2. a group of high school teachers
      3. a group of students
      4. a group of concerned parents
   Be prepared to discuss your analysis in class.
2. Conduct an audience analysis of your speech class by writing a profile of the group based on an analysis of knowledge level, attitudes, and socioeconomic factors.
3. Attend a speech with another class member; write independent summaries; compare the summaries; discuss how your listening behavior could be improved.

Suggested Reading

Clevenger, Theodore, Jr. *Audience Analysis*. Indianapolis: Bobbs-Merrill Co., 1966.

Floyd, James J. *Listening: A Practical Approach*. Glenview, Ill.: Scott, Foresman & Co., 1985.

Gibson, James W., and Hanna, Michael S. *Audience Analysis: A Programmed Approach to Receiver Behavior*. Englewood Cliffs, N.J.: Prentice-Hall, 1976.

Holtzman, Paul D. *The Psychology of Speakers' Audiences*. Glenview, Ill.: Scott, Foresman & Co., 1970.

Nichols, Ralph, and Stevens, Leonard E. *Are You Listening?* New York: McGraw Hill Book Co., 1957.

Wolff, Florence, Marsnik, Nadine C., Tacy, William S., and Nichols, Ralph G. *Perceptive Listening*. New York: Holt, Rinehart, and Winston, 1983.

Wolvin, Andrew D. and Coakley, Carolyn G. *Listening*. Dubuque, Ia.: Wm. C. Brown Company Publishers, 1985.

Notes

1. Gary Cronkhite, *Persuasion: Speech and Behavioral Change* (Indianapolis: Bobbs-Merrill Co., 1969): 139.

2. Carolyn Sherif, Muzafer Sherif, and Roger Nebergall, *Attitude and Attitude Change: The Social Judgment-Involvement Approach* (Philadelphia: W. B. Saunders Co., 1965); and C. David Mortensen and Kenneth K. Sereno, "The Influence of Ego-Involvement and Discrepancy on Perceptions of Communication," *Speech Monographs* 37 (June 1970): 127–34.

3. Hans Sebald, "Limitations of Communication: Mechanisms of Image Maintenance in Form of Selective Perception, Selective Memory, and Selective Distortion," *Journal of Communication* (September, 1962): 142–49; and Carl H. Weaver, *Human Listening: Processes and Behavior* (Indianapolis: Bobbs-Merrill Co., 1972).

4. Arthur Unger, "An Open-Minded Exploration of an Alaskan 'Forest of Eyes,' " *The Christian Science Monitor,* Oct. 30, 1987.

5. Milton Rokeach, *The Nature of Human Values* (New York: Free Press, 1973).

6. Abraham H. Maslow, "A Theory of Human Motivation," *Motivation and Personality,* 2d ed. (New York: Harper & Row Publishers, 1970).

7. Walter W. Stevens, "Polarization, Social Facilitation, and Listening," *Western Speech* (1961): 168–70.

8. Andrew D. Wolvin and Carolyn Gynn Coakley, *Listening* (Dubuque, Ia.: Wm. C. Brown Company Publishers, 1985): 8.

9. Ibid., p. 19.

10. " 'What's He Doing? He'll Kill Us All!' " *Time,* 109 (April 11, 1977): 22.

11. Thomas Rendero, "College Recruiting Practices," *Personnel* 57 (1980): 4–10.

12. Susan Mundale, "Why More CEO's Are Mandating Listening and Writing Training," *Training* (October 1980): 37–41.

13. Lyman K. Steil, Larry L. Barker, and Kittie W. Watson, *Effective Listening: Key to Your Success* (Reading, Mass.: Addison-Wesley, 1983): 9–10.
14. Gerald Egan, "Listening as Empathetic Support," in J. Stewart (ed.) *Bridges Not Walls* (Reading, Mass.: Addison-Wesley, 1983): 223–27.
15. J. W. Koehler, J. C. McCroskey, and W. E. Arnold, "The Effects of Receiver's Constancy-Expectation in Communication," *Research Monographs,* Department of Speech, Pennsylvania State University, 1966.
16. Cited in Gerald Goldhaber. *Organizational Communication* (Dubuque, Ia.: Wm. C. Brown Company Publishers, 1986): 242.
17. Rebecca B. Rubin and Charles V. Roberts, "A Comparative Examination and Analysis of Three Listening Tests," *Communication Education* (1987): 142–53.

4 Selecting the Topic and Stating the Specific Purpose

Chapter Outline

Selecting the Speech Topic

The first step in preparing a speech is to select a topic. In the world outside the classroom this is seldom a problem because topics are more likely to choose us than we are to choose them. The total communicative situation and our place in it will dictate what is to be discussed. When two business people get together to discuss a deal, neither has to ask, "Well, what shall we talk about today?" The same is true when a committee meets to consider a problem; when a personnel manager interviews job applicants, when a supervisor explains a new sales procedure to employees; when a lawyer advises a client. The purpose of the meeting dictates the general topic. In conversations with your friends you talk about subjects of mutual interest; the public speaking situation has many features of an enlarged conversation. Choose a subject about which you have something to say, one that is of interest to you and of value to your listeners. In every instance, including conversation, some kind of time limit is built into the occasion. This time limit determines how brief or how expansive the treatment of the subject can be. These concerns, then, form guidelines for choosing a topic. It should be suitable to the speaker, relevant to the audience, and realistic in terms of the time limit imposed by the occasion.

The Topic and the Speaker

When you select a speech topic, ask yourself whether this is an appropriate topic for you and whether you are competent to talk about this subject. Topic appropriateness and speaker competence are addressed in more detail in the following two subsections.

Appropriate to the Speaker

Your subject should be interesting to you. Speaking merely for the purpose of "giving a speech" will not be effective either for you or your audience. Choose a subject that you feel strongly about and that you genuinely want to share with your audience. A reporter always looks for the "human angle" in a story; people are news, and getting to know you and what matters to you will be interesting to your classmates. The best place to look for a speech topic is within yourself. Students often overlook things that they know a lot about because they think, "No one would care about that," but don't sell yourself and your audience short. Most people are interested in hearing about many different things as long as the speaker appears knowledgeable and makes the topic interesting and relevant to the audience. International students are often surprised and delighted to find that Americans want to know about their language, their culture, and anything else from their different background.

Most of you won't be able to draw on culture differences for speech topics but will have to rely on other types of experiences. Do you have any hobbies? What kinds of work have you done? Have you done a lot of reading on a particular subject? One woman didn't think she had anything of interest to talk about until she discovered that she could capitalize on her knowledge of mystery and romance novels. She gave a successful talk on the subject "The Literature Professors Won't Talk About." Another student spoke on the differences between foreign and domestic stamp collecting. Still another explained how to extract honey, based on his summer job working for a beekeeper.

Topics for persuasive speeches can be determined in a similar fashion. Have you become involved in some issue, e.g., the budget deficit, women's rights, police brutality, the breakdown of the family, environmental issues, American foreign policy, the plight of the homeless?

If you need help in thinking of a suitable topic, try the following method of assessing your own interests. Take two sheets of paper and head one sheet Personal and one Political. On the page headed Personal, make three columns. These could be called Sports/Hobbies, Convictions, and Occupational. Subdivide the political page into four columns: Local, Regional, National, and International. Then list topics that fit *you* in each column. In the Sports/Hobbies column you might list hiking, boating, scuba diving, gardening, raising animals, model building, candlemaking, sewing, and so on. Once you finish your list, look it over and pick out two or three topics you think might make a good speech.

Here is a different way to brainstorm and come up with a topic: look around you and free-associate. For example, as I write this, it is summer and I'm sitting in the living room of a cabin in northern Idaho. This suggests building by a family or an individual, woodworking projects, construction, interest rates for home-construction loans, well-drilling, and maybe water-witching. I look over at a Franklin stove and I am reminded of recent trends toward using wood for fuel . . . chain-saw safety . . . consumer protection . . . Ralph Nader . . . renewable resources, like wood or solar energy, versus nonrenewable resources, such as oil and coal. I see a rocking chair, which suggests antique furniture . . . oral history . . . problems of the aged . . . Medicare . . . nursing homes. Next, I glance toward the kitchen and I think of coffee . . . South America's geography and people . . . Peace Corps . . . San Salvador . . . Nicaragua . . . cooking of various kinds. I look out at the woods and I am reminded of logging . . . hiking . . . rock climbing . . . kinds of trees . . . tree infestation by the tussock moth . . . to use or not to use the compounds 2,4-D and Agent Orange . . . wild berries and other plants . . . mushrooms . . . hummingbirds and all other birds . . . the food chain and insecticides. The lake makes me think of pure water and anti-pollution standards . . . the effect of dams on fish . . . boats (sailboats, motor boats, and rules for water safety) . . . Polynesian sailors navigating by the waves . . . fishing equipment and tying flies . . . water-skiing . . . geologic formations . . . glaciers and their effects . . . volcanoes and their effects . . . earthquakes . . . the San Andreas fault. I think of wintertime activities here . . . snow skiing and snow ski equipment . . . ski patrol and other rescue organizations . . . football . . . basketball. All of this took me eighteen minutes to note and to type. I found more than thirty-five subjects I could use for a speech and perhaps could be interesting for you to talk about as well. Look around you and come up with some topics suited to your concerns.

Speaker Competence

Once you have a topic, ask yourself whether you are or can become competent to speak on this subject. What do you already know about the subject, based on your own past experiences or those of family and friends; what have you learned in your job, your course of study, or from other reading and listening? If the topic is unfamiliar to you, how available and how good is other information on the subject? A preliminary survey of the information available may prompt you to set aside a topic you might otherwise find interesting because it is not practical to research before your speaking date.

Pursuing new ideas and expanding your interests can be stimulating and worthwhile. Perhaps the ideal topic is one that interests you and that you know a little about; you then can increase that knowledge, and your own competence, through investigation and research.

The Topic and the Audience

In a conversation with someone you try out different topics until you hit one both participants can respond to, perhaps a shared experience or a mutual acquaintance. If a speech is to achieve the desired effect on the listeners—to get them to think or act as you want them to—the topic should establish a common ground between speaker and audience. The speaker must take the audience into consideration in selecting a topic. You should determine if the subject is one that will immediately interest the audience or one that can be shown to be relevant to them.

Factors of Attention

As we consider how to gain and maintain the attention of the audience, let's first define the term we are using. *Attention* is the act of focusing upon one element among many in a situation, to the extent that the other elements are scarcely noticed. Effective learning and retention of information depend largely on how well the listener can be led to concentrate on the speaker's message.

As you analyze your audience members, keep in mind that you will be working to arouse your listeners' interest in your message, and to gain and regain their attention. Although the "factors of attention" are relevant to various stages in the speech-making process, we introduce them here because they are important for selecting a topic. In addition, you should be familiar with the factors early and make use of them throughout the speech-making process.

In general, listeners are attracted to information that (1) fits in with their own needs and motivations; (2) they see as useful to them; (3) is new; (4) is linked to something familiar; (5) is of immediate concern; (6) is in oral style; (7) follows the principles of good delivery; (8) makes use of suspense and conflict; (9) is humorous; and (10) is well-organized.

Audience Needs and Motivations

In chapter 3 we discussed the needs and motivations of your audience members: basic physiological requirements, safety, a sense of belonging and love, esteem, and self-actualization. These *guarantee* that attention will be riveted upon matters affecting the health, reputation, income, property, job, or future well-being of the listener or of someone close to him or her. When you speak on one of these topics, the audience really listens. In a speech on sunbathing, for example, you might wish to appeal to a concern for health. If you want to present information about the hazards of sunbathing, you could appeal to your audience's safety needs by vividly describing people whose skin has become dry and leathery from getting too much sun.

Usefulness

A listener tends to ask, "What's in it for me?" or even, "So what?" Listeners are motivated to listen and to value material that they see they can use. As you talk to relatively affluent people about car care, they might not be primarily concerned with saving money. But everyone has had a car stall at an inconvenient time. If you can give some simple tips about what to do (besides calling the garage) under such circumstances, they would probably find the information useful. If your speech offers a solution to a recognized problem—or sets up a problem and then solves it—you will catch your audience's attention.

Novelty

The listener attends to something new and different. Advertisers find "New, improved!" to rank equally with "Sale!" as a means of attracting attention, but they also recognize the importance of establishing "brand familiarity." The speaker needs to balance these two psychological pulls by: (a) shedding new light, providing new information on whatever is already familiar ("Have you heard the latest about . . . ?"); (b) offering a new point of view or a new interpretation of familiar facts; (c) presenting familiar ideas and facts

THE FAR SIDE

By GARY LARSON

**And then Jake saw
something that grabbed his attention.**

systematically and clearly, bringing them together and giving them structure and continuity, so that the audience recognizes the whole and its parts all in neat order. As your speech unfolds and people become accustomed to your style of speaking and manner of delivery, attention can fade. You can use novelty to regain attention. For instance, using a visual aid toward the middle of your speech will regain attention, in part because it is different from what you have been doing.

Familiarity

"Variety is the spice of life," but nothing is as comfortable as something old and familiar. Using different kinds of supporting material or a different point of view will provide variety in content and pace, but the speaker should point out "links" (signposts that show the relationship of the new material to tried-and-true familiar ideas and attitudes).

Our attention is attracted by examples, by comparisons and contrasts, and by definitions, because each of these devices combines the old and the new, the familiar and the unfamiliar.

For someone who has never seen a zebra but who has seen a horse, describing a zebra as "like a striped horse" can be very useful, but if something is *entirely* new, the mind cannot get started on it. Try, for example, to imagine a color you've never seen, without relating it in some way to a color you *have* seen.

To illustrate the importance of this principle of association of the known with the unknown, read the following passage and try to remember it.

> With hocked gems financing him, our hero bravely defied all scornful laughter that tried to prevent his scheme. "Your eyes deceive," he had said, "An egg, not a table, correctly typifies this unexplored planet." Now three sturdy sisters sought proof. Forging along, sometimes through calm vastness, yet more often over turbulent peaks and valleys, days became weeks as many doubters spread fearful rumors about the edge. At last, from nowhere welcome winged creatures appeared signifying momentous success.[1]

Now, close the book and write down as much as you can remember of what you read.

Very likely, you found this difficult to remember because it seemed like disconnected nonsense. But now, reread the story with this title in mind, "Christopher Columbus Discovering America," and then write down what you remember. Almost certainly, the passage will seem sensible and coherent and you will thus be able to remember it.

Immediacy

That which is located nearby, or which is near in time, will interest an audience. Harold Hill's "We got trouble right here in River City" aroused his audience in the musical *The Music Man,* and many students respond to subjects of campus concern more readily than they do to purely international problems.

The speaker can use this principle of immediacy by such techniques as selecting a topic that is of local interest, referring to the occasion or the setting for the speech, referring to something said by the preceding speaker, or calling that person by name. For instance, it would be easy to arouse interest in the causes of the 1992 riots with residents of Los Angeles. Someone who lives in Yellowknife, Canada, will probably find the topic much less immediate.

Oral Style

The specific and the personal are much more interesting than the general or impersonal. The speaker should talk about real people and events, describing these actual cases in vivid language. Size and contrast also command attention. Devices such as comparison and contrast, repetition and restatement, and examples and illustrations are all part of a lively oral style.

Effective Delivery

The speaker can literally *compel* the listener's attention by his or her own intense physical involvement. If the speaker doesn't show this degree of commitment, it is certain that the audience will not.

Gestures and other visible physical movements can give important emphasis to ideas you want to stress. Poor eye contact reduces listener comprehension, while good eye contact improves it. By using verbal and nonverbal cues you tell the listener which points are most important. Interestingly, if a speaker has poor voice quality, it seems not to affect audience comprehension to any great degree (Abraham Lincoln, for example, is reported to have had a rather thin, raspy voice), but a monotonous, unvaried pitch pattern interferes markedly with the listener's ability to concentrate on meaning.

Repeating the key points two or more times can help the audience focus on the ideas that are essential to remember, rather than on a particular example or illustration. Quotation is a form of restatement; the point is echoed in the words of another person.

The listener will grasp an idea more readily if it is presented to several of the senses at once, and visual aids can be used to very good advantage. A relationship between two facts or ideas may be very clearly shown by a diagram, when that connection would not be clear at all if presented by a verbal explanation alone.

Just as the eye is drawn to a moving object, so is the mind attracted by activity. Use previewing of what is to come—signposts—and clear transitions from one point to another to show that the talk is moving forward. The choice of active, not passive, words will help you to create a sense of movement and vitality.

Suspense and Conflict

Uncertainty, in the form of suspense and conflict, can provoke interest. Suspense and conflict are pleasurable, provided that the resolution of that conflict is satisfying. For example, although stirring an expectation in your audience of information to come may be intriguing, it won't work to your advantage if, when the information is revealed, it's judged not to have been worth the wait.

A controversial topic, one on which opinions may differ, will arouse interest. You've no doubt heard it said, "Never discuss religion or politics," but we would all miss some rousing discussions if we always heeded that advice. And current affairs are the immediate versions of the bigger problems and questions that have always concerned people: religion, love and

> The story is told that General Alexander Smith (who was known in Congress as a long-winded speaker) admonished Henry Clay: "You, sir, speak for the present generation, but I speak for posterity." "Yes," replied Clay, "and you seem resolved to speak until the arrival of your audience."

marriage, divorce, health, education, taxation, war and peace, race relations, and good government, to name a few controversial ones.[2] A specific topic based on one of these human concerns can be made relevant to any audience, and such speech-making performs a vital function in a democratic society.

Humor and Wit

People enjoy humor and wit. It must always be relevant to the point being made, and be in good taste. When properly used, humor can provide a relaxation from tension and decrease listener fatigue. Chapter 15 discusses the use of humor in more detail.

Organization

The listener's interest will be maintained, and she or he also can understand and remember material better if it is well-organized. By showing clearly the structure of the speech, you help the listener to see the total picture and how each part fits into the whole.

The Topic and the Occasion

In the classroom, the time allowed per speech must be very short to provide as many different speaking experiences as possible for each student. But there are program constraints even in other speaking situations, and the considerate speaker adheres strictly to the time limits expected of him or her. As times have changed, so have time limits; the old-time minister thought nothing of sermonizing for two hours, recessing for a picnic lunch, then starting again. Many churchgoers today expect a twenty-minute sermon and a guarantee of being out by noon. An African politician can deliver a two-hour campaign speech and hold attention, but most American politicians confine themselves to thirty-second or one-minute TV spots (and not *just* because of the cost). Perhaps because of our experience with TV commercials, we expect all of our informative and persuasive messages to be short and to the point.

Narrowing the Topic

When you select your topic, you may want to select one that is sufficiently narrow in scope and/or simplicity to fit within the time available, or you may choose to deal with only a restricted portion of a larger subject. In preparing a persuasive speech, you may try to convince your audience of only one proposition among the many possible aspects of an issue. Some subjects are too simple to be worth the time of speaker and audience, and some topics cannot be cut down and still be meaningful. You will need to exercise your judgment here; in any case, avoid saying "too little about too much."

This process of narrowing the subject involves sorting through all the things you *could* say in order to select the one, two, or three points you can present clearly and support well in the time you have available. A teacher cannot thoroughly cover the causes and effects of the Civil War in one class; a politician cannot defend his or her entire record in one speech; the very difficult and troublesome topics of air pollution, consumer safety, the energy crisis, child abuse, and national defense cannot be covered fully in a five-minute speech. The speaker must delimit the subject to cover it adequately and support the ideas specifically, without reducing comments to the trivial. Three to five points are probably the right number for a five-minute speech.

Some subjects are too difficult or sensitive to present orally to a general audience. Complicated processes, highly technical subjects, those subjects requiring a large number of figures and statistics, or highly personal material that might be in poor taste are examples.

One final warning: avoid these two common pitfalls in planning your speech:

1. Don't keep searching and searching for the perfect subject; put forth your best effort to choose wisely, then get on with the next phase of preparation. A reasonably good subject chosen early is much better than an excellent subject that is chosen so late that it cannot be developed well.
2. Don't try to speak on some tired old subject, e.g., "My Summer Job," *unless* you can give it the new twist your audience demands. (Perhaps you were a lifeguard, and someone was "cooperative" enough to nearly drown so you could save him or her.) Don't choose to speak on some unimportant, too-simple subject, like "How to Make a Peanut Butter and Jelly Sandwich"; you will most likely get a bored and insulted audience whose feedback doesn't help your performance at all, and an instructor who yawns and records the grade corresponding to the little amount of effort you have expended.

The Speech Purpose
General Purpose

Now that you have chosen your general subject, you decide what it is you want your audience to do, feel, believe, understand, or enjoy as a result of your speech; do you intend to inform, persuade, move to action, or entertain

> No wind carries those who have no port to sail to.
>
> *Montaigne*

your audience? You inform when you want your audience to understand something. You persuade when you want your audience not only to understand but also to accept your point of view from the many others they could choose. A speech to entertain has a lighter purpose, to please or amuse an audience.

These purposes often will overlap within the same speech; for example, it would be difficult to persuade an audience to give to a cancer research fund without first informing them of the incidence of cancer and the possibilities for discovering a cure through research. However—and this is a crucial point in planning your speech, both in your own thinking and ultimately in the audience's response—if you think you have more than one purpose and do not make a firm decision on what is your *dominant* goal, the entire organization of your speech will be muddy and aimless. Far from accomplishing both goals, you will accomplish neither.

Specific Purpose

The next step in speech preparation is to narrow and shape the general subject and purpose by constructing a statement of *specific* purpose. Other authors refer to the specific purpose as the central thought, central theme, topic sentence, thesis statement, or, in a persuasive speech, the proposition. A specific purpose statement identifies what the speaker wants to accomplish in this speech and indicates the basic material to be covered in the presentation. If the speaker tells someone what the speech is about, the specific purpose statement is the one statement that conveys the essential information about the speech.

To arrive at your statement of specific purpose, begin with your general purpose—for example, to inform—then state exactly what you want the audience to know as a result of your speech. This should be written as a complete thought, one that contains only one idea. In an informative speech, the speaker wants to describe or explain something, or to show how something works. Some specific purpose statements might read as follows:

Specific purpose: To show the audience two differences between downhill and cross-country skis. This statement indicates that the speaker will demonstrate two differences between two different kinds of skis; the goal seems clear and the material to be covered is directly given, making this a good specific purpose statement. Contrast it with the following statement:

Specific purpose: To talk about skis. This vague statement does not sharpen the topic or direct the structure of the rest of the speech.

Specific purpose: To point out two disadvantages of our current social security program for working women. This statement indicates that the speaker will discuss two disadvantages of our social security program. The general goal is clear and the type of material to be covered is shown, making this a good specific purpose statement. Contrast it with the following statement:

Specific purpose: To discuss the disadvantages of social security.

This statement does not sharpen the topic or set up the structure of the rest of the speech. For all we know, the person might be against the entire system, might not like the payment structure, might believe that too many or too few people get benefits, or whatever else.

The following are additional specific purpose statements that suggest the general goal of a speech and basic material to be treated.

Specific purpose: To discuss three things to consider when buying a 35-mm camera.

Specific purpose: To point out the need for insurance and what to look for when choosing a policy.

Note that each of these statements is limited; this narrowing will be necessary if you are to have a precise idea of what your speech is about and also to meet time limit requirements. Even when you are allowed more time to speak, be sure that you have a crystal-clear idea of what you are trying to accomplish.

A carefully constructed specific purpose statement helps you in two ways: it helps you to organize your speech and to avoid taking more time than is necessary to prepare. Write the specific purpose on a card and prop it in front of you while you construct your preliminary outline, then check each main point and piece of supporting material to make sure it fits with the specific purpose and does not take you off on a tangent. Begin from the point of your own knowledge and experience. Decide which points need to be developed further, and spend your research time on only those points.

The specific purpose may be included as a part of the introduction—after an interest-arousing opener—to lead your audience into the body of your speech. The statement most often does not appear in the speech at all, but is implicit throughout; this may be true especially when you give a persuasive speech to an unfriendly audience, because revealing your persuasive intent too early would not be effective. At other times you may directly state your specific purpose after you have developed one or two of your main points.

Summary

You should choose a topic that is appropriate to *you* as the person trying to communicate with a given audience. The speech subject should be timely and significant in the view of the listeners, who say, in effect, "Entertain me, keep me interested, inform me, and persuade me if you can." Whether you inform, advise, persuade, command, question, or amuse, you are encouraging your listeners to shift their thinking along the continuum of possible beliefs, attitudes, and values, toward your goal so that they will think and act as you would like them to. You must be able to say what you need to say about the subject within the time allowed—so be clear, specific, and brief. A clear specific purpose statement will help you organize your speech and focus your research efforts.

Exercises

1. Practice thinking of creative, new and interesting approaches to almost any topic. This might be called a group impromptu. The instructor or a class member should suggest a subject for a speech. Each person should then suggest some new approach to that topic. Pursue one topic until the next student can't think of another new approach, then start a new subject.
2. Have each person develop a list of speech topics. Go around the room and have people analyze one topic listed by each person. Consider whether it is appropriate to the speaker and audience.

Assignments

1. Choose several topics which you could use to prepare a speech for your class. Why do you think these subjects will catch and keep its attention?
2. How might these topics be adapted to other specific audiences you might possibly encounter?
3. Write several specific purpose statements and analyze them in terms of whether the intent is clear and whether the basic information to be covered is indicated.

Notes

1. D. J. Dooling and R. Lachman, "Effects of Comprehension on Retention of Prose," *Journal of Experimental Psychology* 88 (1971): 216–22.
2. Donald C. Bryant and Karl R. Wallace, *Fundamentals of Public Speaking,* 4th ed. (New York: Appleton-Century-Crofts, 1969): 64.

5 Gathering Materials

Genius lights its own fire, but it is constantly gathering materials to keep alive the flame.

Wilmott

It is important to remember that you do not set out to find a speech, but instead you set out to gather the raw material from which to *build* a speech. By far the most difficult and challenging aspect of speech building is the phase of gathering facts, drawing conclusions from them, and molding these facts into a communicative form. But underneath this constructive process there must be research, and any aspiring speaker should be well-versed in knowing how to effectively and efficiently gather material on which to base his or her speech.

The first step in finding material for your speech is to search your own knowledge and experience. Organize what you already know about the topic into outline form so you can see where there are gaps that you will fill in by doing research. First-hand observation and conversations with others can also add to your preliminary store of information and suggest what areas will most likely interest your audience. Be sure to understand clearly what you need to know before you begin to gather materials. In this way you will be able to use the time and energy you have available to do additional research to the greatest advantage.

From the very beginning of this process, three things are most important:

1. Keep an open mind. Do not research a topic merely to confirm what you already believe, but to learn about the topic; be prepared to change your mind in light of what you discover.

    The process of selecting from among the vast array of available materials those items that *best* accomplish the purpose of the speech is called, in classical rhetorical theory, "invention." The speaker makes critical choices, to try to present the best that has been thought and said on the subject, combining these elements in a new way to form ideas that are uniquely his or her own.
2. Read widely. Consult as many sources as time allows. Even if you do not use all your research in this particular speech, this backup information will not be wasted. It may help you to adapt to audience feedback, to answer questions, or simply to feel confident that you are well-prepared. When filming a movie, the director shoots many more feet than are needed; then the editor edits and splices them to come up with the best final product.

"Read as much as possible—and then a little more" is a longtime rule in speech preparation. To accomplish this wide reading for a speech (in fact, to survive in college at all), you must learn to skim read. Pick out the major point in each paragraph, then read more closely those sections that particularly apply.

But if your search turns up little or no information and you conclude that your topic is a "loser," be willing to discard it early. However interesting it might have been, if you can't find the material you need—and *soon* enough to meet the assignment—it is better to choose another topic.

3. Record the information carefully and completely to avoid the frustrating and time-consuming process of going back over what you have already done, checking out the books again to find the source of that good quotation, or the correct information to list in your bibliography. Sloppy or incomplete note-taking is very expensive in the long run, and a student cannot afford to waste time in aimless or frantic activity. When you go to the library, be prepared; take a pen, an ample supply of note cards, your student identification card, and correct change for the photocopying machine.

Put one idea on each note card. If the idea is quoted directly, be sure to put quotation marks around it to remind you that "it's a quote" and be sure to record the page number on which you found the quote. Begin at the top of the card with a heading that explains the contents of the card. In the upper left corner, list the subject, and in the upper right, the section of the speech where it will be used—introduction, body, or conclusion. Next, list the call numbers, in case you need to consult the source again, and bibliographical data, including the following:

For a book: the author, book title, location and name of publisher, publication date, and page numbers.
For an article: the author, title of article, title of journal or magazine, volume and issue numbers, date, and page numbers.

Standard manuals, such as the *Modern Language Association Handbook* (MLA), have detailed guidelines about how to cite various types of reference material. Following are some fabricated examples of book, magazine, and newspaper bibliographic entries, using the MLA guidelines.

Book
Doe, John. *Help with Citations.* New York: Double Trouble Publishing Co., 1984.

Research is an essential element in speech preparation.

Magazine Article
    Doe, Jane. "How to Write Funny Speeches." *North American Journal,* 15, No. 6 (1977), 4–6.

Newspaper
    Doe, Baby. "How to Select Good Parents." *Main Street Times,* 10 Oct. 1989, p. 37, Col. 1.

For another common style of citation, you can look at the footnote and bibliographic entries at the end of each chapter of this book. Those citations follow guidelines of *A Manual of Style* published by the University of Chicago Press in 1982.

Research in Written Materials

Every library develops a system suited to its particular needs, but some general facts are common to most libraries, and a thorough grounding in these basic organizational patterns will facilitate your research as you prepare your speeches. You may need to ask some questions regarding your own library: How is the library arranged? Where are the various types of items located? What are the library hours and the check-out times and procedures? What is the fine policy for overdue books? How does your library operate its interlibrary loan system, and how long may such a loan take? What do you do if a book or other material is not in? Are there other libraries nearby where you can find additional material?

Most libraries have adopted the Library of Congress system (call numbers beginning with letters, i.e., BF) and catalog new books with that system. However, if the library is long established, it probably cataloged its older books using the Dewey Decimal system (call numbers beginning with numbers, i.e., 650.1) and might not have re-cataloged them into the Library of Congress system.

It is often helpful to understand that the numbers and letters refer to general classes of information. For instance, items beginning with 200 in the Dewey system reference materials having to do with religion and items beginning with B in the Library of Congress system contain material related to religion, philosophy, and psychology. We have presented the general categories for each system in figure 5.1.

Do not hesitate to ask for help from reference librarians. They are trained professionals whose job is to assist library patrons, not by doing the research themselves, but by pointing out faster and better ways for you to proceed. Narrow your speech topic before you begin research in earnest; then, with your specific purpose clearly in mind, develop a research plan. Use a subject approach and think in categories. In how many different ways might the information you are looking for be classified?

Specific sources of information include:

1. general reference materials—card catalogs, microforms, dictionaries, encyclopedias, etc.
2. periodicals or magazines and journals; newspapers
3. indexes and abstracts
4. government documents
5. books
6. computerized references
7. experts and organizations.

It is unlikely that you will consult all of these for any one project. You will save time if you always start by consulting the various indexes and catalogs, which will then direct your search to the specific items.

> Anybody who speaks should spend a thousand days on trying to get ideas and knowledge, to every one day they spend on the way to tell it.
>
> *Clarence Darrow*

Figure 5.1 General Reference Categories for the Dewey Decimal and Library of Congress Systems.

Dewey Decimal

000	General works	500	Natural sciences
100	Philosophy	600	Applied science
200	Religion	700	The arts
300	Social science	800	Literature
400	Language	900	History, geography

Library of Congress

A	General works	M	Music
B	Philosophy, religion, psychology	N	Fine arts
C	History, auxiliary sciences (genealogy, archeology, etc.)	P	Language and literature
D	General and Old World history	Q	Science
E,F	History: America	R	Medicine
G	Geography, anthropology, recreation	S	Agriculture
H	Social sciences	T	Technology
J	Political sciences	U	Military science
L	Law	V	Naval science
		Z	Bibliography, library science

General Reference Sources

Use directories, almanacs, encyclopedias, indexes, dictionaries, general reference books and computer catalogs to learn where you will find information on your subject.

You will find some of these resources in the reference section of any library. They are arranged in alphabetical or categorical order, with one or more easy-to-use indexes and ample cross references.

Bibliographies

See if a bibliography has been published that lists materials on your subject. Check a library catalog or recent or back copies of *Subject Guide to Books in Print*, or consult the card catalog and/or the computer catalog.

Encyclopedias

Your library will have one or more of the major encyclopedias—*Encyclopedia Americana, Encyclopedia Brittanica, Colliers Encyclopedia*—that will give background information on your subject and point you toward additional readings.

There are also specialized subject encyclopedias, such as *The Encyclopedia of Associations, Encyclopedia of World Art, The Encyclopedia of Education, Worldmark Encyclopedia of Nations, McGraw-Hill Encyclopedia of Science and Technology*, and *International Encyclopedia of the Social Sciences*.

Indexes and Abstracts

Numerous indexes are available that list and classify the material published in that source or publication. Some of these indexes are general in nature, such as *Reader's Guide to Periodical Literature, Public Affairs Index Service, Index to Legal Periodicals, Social Science Index*, and *Index to Behavioral Sciences and Humanities*. Some are subject specific, such as *Index to Journals in Communication, Business Periodicals Index, Music Index, CBS News Index*, and many others.

If you require more than the title to decide whether the article is worth pursuing, you may want to consult a volume of abstracts, which contains summaries of articles. *Psychological Abstracts, Sociological Abstracts, Language and Language Behavior Abstracts, Communication Abstracts, Child Development Abstracts, Economic Abstracts*, and *Dissertation Abstracts International* are some of the titles of volumes containing summaries of articles. *Resources in Education*, published by Educational Resources Information Center (ERIC), stores documents of all kinds.

One point about scholarly periodicals is that if the name of the journal contains the name of an organization, the journal may be cataloged under the organization's name rather than under "J," for "Journal."

Sources of Facts and Statistics

Dictionaries and almanacs, such as *World Almanac* and *Information Please Almanac*, are good places to find specific facts. So too are collections like *Facts on File*, which provides a brief, factual, chronological account of news events, assembled in annual volumes. Other sources of facts include *The Guinness Book of World Records, The Book of Lists*, the *Congressional Quarterly*, and the *County and City Data Book* (published by the Census Bureau).

I often quote myself. It gives spice to my conversation.

George Bernard Shaw

The following two indexes will be especially helpful as sources for statistics:

1. *Statistical Abstract of the U.S.* (published annually by the United States Census Bureau) summarizes facts and figures that have been collected by the United States government and various private agencies, such as the United States Chamber of Commerce, American Enterprise Institute, the Brookings Institution, and the Carnegie Foundation.
2. *American Statistics Index* provides federal and state governmental statistics.

Polls

We are all interested in what other people think and do about a variety of issues—economics, the arts, politics, health—and you might include the results of a poll on some aspect of your topic. Consult *Gallup Poll Monthly,* published since 1935, or the *Index to International Public Opinion,* published since 1978.

Biographical Information

If you need information about a person, living or dead, consult first a master index, which will direct you to the volumes that include your subject rather than consulting first one, then another of the dozens of biographical dictionaries your library may own:

1. *Biography and Genealogy Master Index* (includes names from 350 biographical dictionaries).
2. *Author Biographies Master Index* (includes names from over 215 biographical dictionaries).

Quotations

Many specialized books are listed under Quotations in *Subject Guide to Books in Print,* but you will most often use the current or back editions of one of these compilations: *Dictionary of Quotations,* by Bergan Evans; *Familiar Quotations,* by John Bartlett; or *Home Book of Quotations,* by Burton Stevenson.

Serial Publications
Periodicals

Periodicals are a basic source of information and are especially useful if your subject is only a year or two old. The two types of periodicals are academic and nonacademic.

> The real purpose of books is to trap the mind into doing its own thinking.
>
> *Christopher Morley*

Magazines and Journals

One of the best-known of the general indexes to periodicals is the *Reader's Guide to Periodical Literature,* which has indexed, by subject and author, articles from over 190 popular magazines, since 1900. *Poole's Index to Periodical Literature* catalogs periodicals published before 1900.

For publications of a less conservative nature, such as *Rolling Stone* or *Mother Jones,* consult the *Popular Periodical Index* or *Alternative Press Index.*

Academic journals are published in every discipline (speech, psychology, agronomy, etc.), and libraries subscribe to many of these journals. The articles in academic journals are often technical, but they may provide information unavailable elsewhere. For example, if you were to look for material on source credibility and ethos in the popular literature, not much information would be available. However, numerous articles on these topics can be found in academic journals like the *Quarterly Journal of Speech, Communication Monographs,* and *Communication Education.*

Newspapers

To find information that has appeared in newspapers, use indexes to individual newspapers or consult *National Newspaper Index,* which indexes five major newspapers from 1979 to the present: *The New York Times, The Christian Science Monitor, The Wall Street Journal, The Los Angeles Times,* and *The Washington Post. Newspapers on Microfilm* lists about 4,600 foreign and 17,000 American newspapers.

Other libraries may provide *Newsbank,* a microfiche clipping service and news digest that selects and organizes newspaper articles according to thirteen broad topical areas.

Government Documents

A government document is anything printed by the government or at government expense. This includes not only official papers, committee reports, hearings and statistics, but miscellaneous material such as park guides, posters, magazines, etc. *The Monthly Catalog of U.S. Government Publications* is an index that provides access to documents by subject, author(s), or title. Other useful indexes include: Congressional Information Service's *Index to U.S. Government Periodicals,* and *UNDOC,* the latest title of the United Nations Documents Index.

When you look for government documents in your library, you may find that they are not filed by either the Dewey Decimal or the Library of Congress subject systems. All documents issued by a particular agency, whatever the subject matter, are usually filed together. This makes it even more imperative that you begin your research by consulting catalogs, indexes, and bibliographies.

Books

Use the subject approach. Browse through the reference shelf where books on your specific subject are grouped. Especially helpful is the reference *Subject Guide to Books in Print (SGBIP),* which offers a panorama of what is available on your particular topic. Also check to see if *SGBIP* lists any bibliographies published on the subject you have chosen.

The Library of Congress receives a copy of every book submitted to the Copyright Office. Books are assigned a Library of Congress number and a Dewey Decimal number; virtually all those same numbers are used by all libraries, which makes it easier for you to find things wherever you are. Once you have either number, you should pick up the book in the appropriate section of the library or give the call number to the attendant if your library does not have open stacks.

If you have trouble finding your topic in the card catalog, in the computer catalog, or in one of these reference sources, try a different spelling or a different wording. Suppose you plan to speak on the subject "The Pit Bull—Menace or Myth?" Where would you look for information? A dictionary check would reveal that there is no information under that term, that "pit bull" is another name for bull terrier. The *Subject Guide to Books in Print* lists many books under "Dogs—Breeds—Bull Terriers."

If a book is checked out or missing, file a recall notice with the librarian to have the book recalled from the user after a reasonable time (perhaps two weeks). If a book is not where it should be, it may be misplaced on the shelf (or stolen, unfortunately). Ask the librarian to initiate a search for it. If the book cannot be found you may be able to obtain it through interlibrary loan.

Microforms and Computerized Resources
Microforms

In these days of low budgets and high costs, many libraries find that microforms are a relatively inexpensive way of increasing the number of volumes they can house. Microforms include: (1) microfilms, which are reels of film; (2) microfiche, or pieces of film containing approximately one hundred frames on a 4-by-6-inch card; (3) ultramicrofiche, which are pieces of film containing up to 1,200 pages on a 2-by-2-inch card; and (4) microcards, which are printed rather than filmed materials. Almost anything may appear in this form—books, periodicals, newspapers, lists of books. Cataloging of these materials, however, has lagged far behind the rate of acquisition, so you may have to do some detective work to find the items that your library does have. Any library that uses microforms will have projection devices to allow you to read and photocopy the material.

Computerized Resources

There are two general types of electronic information services available— on-line databases and CD-ROM. We will consider each in turn.

On-line Databases

A database refers to a service where large amounts of information are stored—usually on a particular topic. On-line databases are usually comprehensive on a given topic and may be of service if your research requires that you unearth a great deal of information. You can access on-line databases through a library or by using a modem and your personal computer through a service like Dialog. Dialog is a vendor of on-line databases and allows access to over 300 online databases. Whether you use your personal computer or the library to access on-line information, you need to use considerable forethought. You proceed by selecting the primary and alternate terms you want the computer to search for in its files. At this point, if not before, you are motivated to narrow your topic, and to carefully plan the entire search in advance to minimize the time spent on the computer and thus the cost. The computer search gives new meaning to the old adage "Time is money."

Computers can aid you by searching through bibliographic references (citations of book titles, book reviews, government reports and publications, dissertations, magazine and newspaper articles, etc.) and also full texts. As more and more published material is originally produced on computers, these full texts are available to be called up by the researcher. One such service, Bitnet, is a network of computers that provides a variety of services to users, both domestically and internationally.

If your topic is in science, technology, or finance, you might need the latest facts and figures that an on-line source can provide. In history, philosophy, literature, theology, and folklore, older materials might be just as useful, but even here the computer can help to identify these sources.

However, the costs and the fees charged by each computer database publisher are the largest single deterrent to more widespread use of on-line database searching. As demand and interest soar, competition will likely bring costs down. In an effort to lower costs, many libraries provide end-user database services such as Knowledge Index or BRS Afterdark. For minimal fees, approximately $5 for five minutes of on-line time, you can do your own information search in over 100 national databases covering many subjects.

CD-ROM

CD-ROM (compact disk-read only memory) is an attractive alternative to on-line databases because libraries provide free searches of this material. These disks allow information to be stored very efficiently. One 5 1/4-inch

CD-ROM disk can store over a quarter of a million pages of material (about as much as you could store on 1,500 normal floppy disks).[1] Many databases are available in this form, and many more are being made available. Another nice feature of these systems is that they can be made directly available to the library patron. Any computer-literate person can run a CD-ROM search (and even a computer-illiterate person can learn to execute a CD-ROM search in a few minutes).

One example of a public-access database that includes statistical quantitative data is *The Source,* which includes both full text and citations. *Encyclopedia of Information Systems and Services* includes both public and private databases in industry and government. As an example of the detailed information available and a suggestion of what lies in the future, *Auto Parts Database* (*Audatex*) lists, for about 1,000 auto models, all the parts of an automobile likely to be involved in a collision, manufacturer's part number, price, and estimated labor hours to repair it. Another, *Bicentennial Inventory,* housed in the Archives of American Art in Washington, D.C., records the title and artist of the piece, the date created, medium, material, dimensions, present owner, and location of each work.

Computers and printed works are two types of the tools available to the researcher. Computers work best for looking information up quickly, and books work best for longer, concentrated study.

Experts and Organizations

Another rich source of information is other people, including public officials, professors, business men and women, and others. This information may be gathered through mailed questionnaires, by telephone, or through face-to-face interviews.

Interviews

The face-to-face interview is by far the most usual and useful means of gathering information from others. Typically, an interview involves two people, although we have all seen interview programs on TV, such as "Meet the Press" or "Face the Nation," in which a panel of reporters questions a celebrity guest.

Interviews can be of many different types, depending on their setting and purpose—to give or to receive information, to persuade, or to advise ·or counsel. We are concerned here with the face-to-face interview that helps you gather information for your speeches.

An interview should be used to augment the material you have found in your library research, not as a first step, but *only* after you have made every effort to find information from other sources. Never approach a potential respondent with, "I have to give a speech tomorrow. Can you tell me everything _____ ?" In order to use the time available effectively, you have to ask questions that allow the respondent to provide the information you need. To accomplish this you need to be an active interviewer.

Know your subject thoroughly, and then trust to luck.

William James

Just as in preparing and delivering a public speech, the interviewer goes through several stages of preparation:

1. Arranging and preparing for the interview
2. Structuring the interview
3. Wording questions
4. Conducting the interview
5. Following up the interview

Preparing for the Interview

Arranging an interview requires much more than simply picking up the phone and requesting an interview with the nearest resident expert. To prepare for an interview, you should:

1. Determine your purpose for conducting this interview. Given what you have learned from prior research, what is it that you need to learn from this particular respondent? After you decide what you want to know, it will be much easier to select the person to be interviewed.
2. Learn as much as you can about the person to be interviewed. What is the respondent's current position and what are his or her qualifications or experience relative to the topic you are researching? What attitudes or possible biases might the person have toward the topic?
3. Arrange in advance a time and place for the interview. The manner in which you request the interview, either from the respondent or through a secretary, may be a crucial factor in the respondent's attitude during the interview, or, in fact, in whether you are granted an interview at all. By being pleasant, accommodating, and precise about the reasons you desire an interview, you improve your chances of being granted an interview. By mentioning what you want to know and why you think Ms. or Mr. X can provide the information, you are capitalizing on some basic public speaking principles; you establish your credibility by displaying your competence and acknowledge the other person's accomplishments at the same time. Everyone likes a genuine compliment (indirect though this might be) from a knowledgeable source. How could she or he refuse your very reasonable request?
4. Once you have the interview arranged, do further research on the subject of the interview to help you frame intelligent and useful questions.

Interviewing an expert in the field provides one source of information for a speech.

5. Pay attention to environmental factors, such as your appearance and grooming and a comfortable setting for the interview.
6. Develop an interview schedule, one that is flexible, but well planned.

Structuring the Interview

An interview, like a speech, has (1) an opening or orientation phase in which purposes are set and both parties learn what to expect of each other and of the situation; (2) a body made up largely of questions and answers, by which the various topics are pursued; and (3) a closing in which the interview is summarized and brought to a conclusion. Central to the preparation for an interview is the goal to be achieved, in this case obtaining the facts and/or opinions needed for the speech that you are preparing.

Conducting the Interview

You have chosen carefully the person to be interviewed, arranged an appointment, conducted preliminary research on the topic and on the person to be interviewed, and planned a schedule of primary and secondary questions. Now the time for the interview has arrived, and you must be aware that as the interviewer, you are primarily in charge. Your responsibilities include opening and closing the interview, keeping the interview moving toward your goals, asking appropriate questions, and providing any necessary follow-up. The interview will consist of an opening, a middle, and a closing phase.

Chapter 5

Opening Phase

The opening phase of the interview is crucial to your success in gathering information. Here you set the tone for the entire exchange. A weak opening may lead to an unsuccessful interview or to no interview at all.

1. To the degree that you have control of the physical setting of your interview, pay attention to such factors as quiet, privacy, and arrangement of the chairs so that you face each other. Try to avoid distractions such as phones and other visitors.
2. Be on time! Greet the person to be interviewed and introduce yourself. A firm handshake, a smile, eye contact, and a pleasant, friendly voice can begin to create a feeling of ease. Then small talk—a reference to a mutual acquaintance or hometowns, or perhaps a sincere compliment—can further help to establish a mutual sense of respect and trust. Be careful not to overdo this phase; if any of this effort at building rapport seems insincere or contrived, the respondent may be antagonized instead; trust is built on truth. The busier and more important the person being interviewed is, the shorter this preliminary phase should be.
3. State the purpose of the interview, establishing a common ground and interest in its goals. Preview the topics to be covered.

Middle or Substantive Phase

You are now ready for the middle or substantive phase of your interview.

1. Your opening question serves as a transition from the rapport-building, orientation functions of the opening phase to the informational function of the body of the interview, and it should be a further warm-up period for both participants. This opening question should not deal with a vital area of the interview or one that is embarrassing or stressful for the respondent. It is best to begin with an open-ended, non-directive question, one that permits an open expression of views with a favorable tone.

2. Draw out the desired information, using a mix of questions—broad, specific, and probing—and avoid unfair tactics, such as leading, loaded, and bipolar questions.

   Be patient and do not interrupt; don't assume that the answer is completed or is not going anywhere. At times, allow pauses to occur; both parties can benefit from a chance to think back over what has been said. Such pauses may seem longer than they are. In research studies in which conversation has been stopped for a brief time, the subjects overestimated the length of time that had elapsed by as much as ten to one hundred times.[2]

3. Keep the interview moving. Do not let it get bogged down or sidetracked. Be considerate of the person's time, and do not prolong the interview needlessly.

4. Be alert to possible feedback. Do not give nonverbal cues that signal how you feel about an answer, but notice and respond to such cues from the respondent. It is especially important that both parties *listen* to each other. Perhaps the most common error committed by interviewers is that of thinking too much about what the next question should be, rather than listening intently to the answer being given.

5. It may be necessary to use a written outline or interview guide, but avoid letting these notes interfere with the close communication between you and the interviewee. It is important that you exhibit a dynamic involvement and be totally engrossed. Record information carefully during the interview. Take notes as inconspicuously as possible, maintaining eye contact while you write. Ask permission in advance if you want to tape record the interview.

6. Strive for accuracy in every aspect of the interview. Do not purposely misquote or misinterpret the respondent's facts, opinions, or attitudes.

7. Be flexible enough to adjust your interview technique if the other person is not as you expected. For example:
   a. If the respondent appears hostile, this attitude frequently can be neutralized by sympathetic and active listening.
   b. If the respondent is talkative, use a majority of closed-ended questions, with statements designed to confine the discussion to the agenda: "Let's come back to this a bit later if time permits."
   c. If the respondent is quiet, use the opposite technique, that of using nonthreatening, open-ended questions, perhaps even reverting to some of the strategies used in the opening phase.

Closing Phase

The closing phase is usually brief and consists chiefly of a summary or restatement of the information gained, to verify its accuracy. It is important to convey a feeling of closure, of wrap-up. Identify mutual understandings, and enumerate any actions you plan to take.

The closing should be well-organized, with no loose ends needing clarification, and yet it must not feel hurried. An abrupt ending could undo the rapport and trust established during the interview. The interviewer may signal the closing phase with a question like, "And one final question: when do you think the administration will announce its decision?"

However, the interviewer does not always have complete control; if the respondent begins looking at his or her watch or stands up, the interview is over, and your obvious move is to express your appreciation and leave.

Following up the Interview

Write up a report of the interview, before your notes get cold. The respondent might wish to receive a copy of your conclusions or a report of how your speech was received. Sending the person a brief thank-you note would be courteous. If you thought the person was extremely helpful, you might consider sending a letter to the person's superior commending him or her.

Summary

Library research and interviews are methods of finding material for a speech. Become familiar with the organizational structure of your library and how to find information in books, periodicals, microforms, and electronically.

Prepare for conducting an interview by selecting the proper person to interview, finding out about the person to be interviewed, making an appointment, and empathizing with the interviewee. In conducting the interview, establish rapport, have a plan, listen attentively, maintain primary control of the interview, and use the types of questions best suited to the particular interview.

Exercises

1. Conduct some practice interviews in class.
2. Arrange to take a guided tour through the library, assisted by a reference librarian.

Assignments

1. Read the information in the following cases to determine what kind of interview structure and questions you would use in each specific situation. What organizational pattern would seem most logical? Chronological, topical, etc.?

A Case of Cheating

A student named Pat Fullmer has been accused of cheating by two instructors at Florida Central College. The instructors questioned a couple of students about the incident and then took the matter to the Student Court. The Student Court has reviewed the evidence and heard testimony by several people. As yet it has not reached a final decision on this case. The interviewer wants to give a speech in class about the case that has captured the attention of students, faculty, and administration. He has made an appointment with Dr. Roy Brown, twenty-nine years old, one of the instructors in the English Department who accused Pat Fullmer of cheating. Pat Fullmer is a junior in history and a C+ student.

A Hero Citation?

Several years ago a natural disaster struck a Scout camp near Queens, Kentucky. A local resident, Sam Browning, has written the national office of Bravery Beyond the Call of Duty, an organization that makes awards to people of all ages who show heroism in coming to the aid of their fellow citizens without an obligation to do so. Browning is forty-nine years old and a lifelong resident of Queens. He is urging that Max Whitmore be awarded Bravery Beyond the Call of Duty's silver medal for actions during the natural disaster. The Bravery Beyond group has sent an interviewer to Queens to interview Sam Browning regarding the facts and community feelings about Max and about whether the silver medal should be awarded to him.

2. Conduct an interview. Turn in your interview schedule and write up the results.
3. Locate at least three books, two popular magazine articles, one academic journal article, and one newspaper article on two of the following topics:

> Horses
> Automobile racing
> Women in politics
> Boer Wars
> Classical music

Indicate the references you consulted to find your material; note which were productive sources and which were non-productive. Be sure to list complete bibliographic data for each source.
4. To become familiar with the reference works in your library, each of you might select one item from the references listed in this chapter and examine it carefully. Prepare a one-page written report; these reports should be reproduced and distributed to the rest of the class.
5. After the class has toured the library, divide it into teams for a library scavenger hunt. Using whatever rules are agreed upon, each group should find as many of the following pieces of information as possible within the given time limits.

> The first capitol of the United States
> The film grossing the largest amount of money and the amount of money it has grossed to date
> The literacy rate for China
> The characteristics of the Impressionist school of painting
> The ethnic population of Texas
> The early years of the Beatles
> The number of votes received by Stephen Douglas from Illinois in the Lincoln-Douglas presidential election of 1860
> The major climbing expeditions on Mount Everest

The profits for Exxon corporation for last year

The political configuration of Europe in 1942

The world's largest library and the number of volumes it contains

The rules for playing "Dungeons and Dragons"

Contemporary speeches on United States energy problems

The number of books published last year by Wm. C. Brown Company Publishers and the categories of books it publishes

Births and deaths in San Salvador over the past 30 years

The actress who won the Academy Award in 1952 for best actress

The text of Dr. Martin Luther King, Jr.'s "I Have a Dream" speech

The amount of money spent for advertising by Procter & Gamble last year

The names and dates of birth of the classical composers referred to as "the three B's"

The historical significance of the slogan "54–40 or fight"

The public figure who said, "If you can't stand the heat, get out of the kitchen."

The prime interest rate for today

The full name of the journals usually abbreviated *QJS, JC, CM, CE*

The principal language spoken in Brazil

The amount of money charged for a thirty-second commercial by CBS during prime time

The birthplace and real name of John Wayne

"Damn the torpedoes, full speed ahead," was said by whom in what battle?

The rate of growth or decline of the GNP this year as compared to last year

Leo Tolstoy's title and most famous work

The first black player in major league baseball

6. Informative Speech—Library Assignment
   A. Books

   To find books, look up your topic in the subject section of the microfiche catalog, computer catalog, and/or the card catalog. Choose two books that might be useful resources for your speech and give the following information for each book:

   1. Author: _____

      Title: _____

      Publisher: _____ Year _____

      Library and Call Number: _____

2. Author: _____

   Title: _____

   Publisher: _____ Year _____

   Library and Call Number: _____

B. Newspapers

   Use any newspaper index discussed in this chapter or elsewhere. Look up your subject and choose one article which might be a useful resource for your speech. Give the following information about the article you select:

   Name of the Newspaper: _____

   Title of Article: _____

   Year: _____ Month: _____ Day: _____

   Section (if given): _____ Page: _____ Column: _____

   If you need them, obtain directions for locating newspapers from the reference librarian.

C. Journal articles

   To find journal articles on your topic use a periodical index or abstract. Indexes and abstracts list citations to articles. A citation gives you information you will need to find the article. Citations are listed under alphabetically arranged subject headings.

   Pick an index or abstract from your library or have a librarian help you find which index or abstract would be best for your topic. Look up your subject heading and select two articles. Using the Sample Citation as a guide, list the following information for the articles you select:

   1. Name of Index used: _____

      Subject Heading: _____

      Article Title: _____

      Article Author: _____

      Abbreviated Journal Title (from citation): _____

      Volume: _____ Pages: _____ Date: _____

      Complete Journal Title (use abbreviations list in front of

      index): _____

   2. Name of Index used: _____

      Subject Heading: _____

Article Title: _____

Article Author: _____

Abbreviated Journal Title (from citation): _____

Volume: _____ Pages: _____ Date: _____

Complete Journal Title (use abbreviations list in front of

index): _____

TO LOCATE YOUR ARTICLES
Bound volumes of journals are often shelved by call number with the books. To find the journals you need, use the section of the card catalog that lists journals alphabetically by journal title. Give the following information:

1. Library location: _____ Call number: _____

2. Library location: _____ Call number: _____

Suggested Reading

Donaghy, William C. *The Interview: Skills and Applications.* Glenview, Ill.: Scott, Foresman and Company, 1984.

Downs, Robert B., and Keller, Clara D. *How To Do Library Research,* 2d ed. Urbana, Ill.: University of Illinois Press, 1975.

Gorden, Raymond L. *Interviewing Strategy: Techniques and Tactics.* Homewood, Ill.: Dorsey Press, 1969.

Goyer, Robert S., Redding, W. Charles, and Rickey, John. *Interviewing Principles and Techniques: A Project.* Dubuque, Ia.: Wm. C. Brown Company Publishers, 1968.

Horowitz, Lois. *Knowing Where to Look: The Ultimate Guide to Research.* Cincinnati, Ohio: Writer's Digest Books, 1984.

Kahn, Robert L., and Cannell, Charles F. *The Dynamics of Interviewing.* New York: John Wiley & Sons, 1964.

Stewart, Charles J., and Cash, William B., Jr. *Interviewing Principles and Practices,* 5th ed. Dubuque, Ia.: Wm. C. Brown Company Publishers, 1988.

Zunin, Leonard, and Zunin, Natalie. *Contact: The First Four Minutes.* Los Angeles: Nash Publishing, 1972.

Notes

1. Gary T. Hunt, *Communication Skills in the Organization* (Englewood Cliffs, N.J.: Prentice-Hall, 1980).
2. Samuel G. Trull, "Strategies of Effective Interviewing," *Harvard Business Review* 22:1 (January, February 1964): 92.

6 Organizing the Speech

Chapter Outline

> *Every discourse, like a living creature, should be so put together that it has a body of its own and lacks neither head nor feet, a middle nor extremities, all composed in such a way that they suit both each other and the whole.*
>
> *Plato*

Importance of Organization

Have you ever misplaced something, and hunted for it for hours? Perhaps you were annoyed with yourself because you weren't "more organized." You can get just as irritated with a disorganized speaker as you search and search, trying to figure out what point he or she is trying to make. The desire for order and organization is fundamental in individuals and in society. To get some idea of how organization affects you, consider how order and structure is necessary to the conduct of your class. Without organization, you might show up for class at 10:10 A.M.; someone else might show up at 3:15 P.M.; and the instructor might decide to hold just one three-hour session per week, on Saturday morning. You might have a speech ready and no one would be there to listen. If you were able to make your speech, instead of proceeding with helping you to improve your speaking, the class might spend much of the time talking about what to do at the next meeting of the class. In short, there probably wouldn't be a class at all. Organization is vital to almost every aspect of human endeavor and to effective speaking, in particular.

Speaker Credibility

Organization is important in making presentations: it reflects on the speaker's credibility; it affects the speaker's self-confidence; and it is important in influencing audiences. If your instructor arrived at class and stated that she or he had no idea of what you would be doing that term, you would not have a very high opinion of that instructor. A speaker who is disorganized is usually not well respected either. Listeners tend to judge such speakers as incompetent, inconsiderate, and unreliable. If the speaker does not respect the audience enough to take the time to get ready for a speech, that

> Order and simplification are the first steps toward the mastery of a subject—the actual enemy is the unknown.
>
> *Thomas Mann*

person appears to be inconsiderate and insensitive. The listener attends the session in good faith, expecting the speaker to be prepared; when the speaker violates this trust, the audience forms an opinion of him or her as being unreliable. The speaker may not actually be incompetent, inconsiderate, and untrustworthy, but simply disorganized. Unfortunately, the only basis the audience has for judging a speaker's character is through the presentation of his or her speech, and the speaker who presents a disorganized message loses credibility with the audience.[1]

Speaker Confidence

The effect of the speaker's disorganization on the audience also affects the speaker because of the interaction between the speaker and the audience. If the audience reacts positively to the speaker, the presentation usually goes well; when the audience reacts negatively, the speaker's performance is adversely affected. Confidence and good organization often go hand in hand. In sports, for example, teams that prepare thoroughly and have a good game plan usually enter the contest much more confident than teams "who make it up as they go along." Speaking is quite similar. When you know how you are going to proceed, you will approach the speech with confidence. You also will be less likely to be rattled by audience reactions because you will know "what comes next."

Audience Interest

Listeners are less likely to accept a message that is poorly organized. Because they have to work harder to understand the speaker, they may become confused and lose interest.[2]

Organization, then, is important in maintaining (1) a speaker's credibility, (2) a speaker's confidence, and (3) audience interest and response. The remainder of this chapter is about how to select a topic, the types of organizational formats, and how to prepare an outline.

To organize simply means to give order to. When you organize your wardrobe you probably put socks in one drawer, shirts or blouses in another, and so on. You put together items that are similar, that belong together. Organizing ideas is the same process; you decide to put things in some sensible order and devise a method for doing so. In the case of socks and shirts, the chest of drawers was a convenient device for arranging clothing. Similar formats exist for arranging ideas.

To appreciate the importance of using a pattern of organization, look at each of the following four lists of words, and then look away and try to recall each list:

1	2	3	4
margarine	dog	apple	eagle
astronomy	donkey	boat	sparrow
sidewalk	giraffe	camera	robin
compass	skunk	dance	skyscraper
smokestack	mouse	elephant	hawk

Very likely, list 1 was hard to recall because you could find no organizing principle in it. The second and third lists were easier because the words on list 2 were all related items, and list 3 proceeded in an order that is familiar to you, alphabetically. List 4 was easy, too, because all the items were similar except the one that stood out as being dissimilar.

Four Basic Organizational Formats for Speeches

Four of the most-used organizational plans for speeches are *time sequence, space sequence, topic order,* and *cause-effect relationship.* (We will discuss *problem-solution* in chapter 14 as an organizational plan for a persuasive speech.) All of these stem from typical thought patterns: beginning to end; what caused it; how to correct a problem; here to there; for versus against; easy to hard; and simple to complex.

Time Sequencing

Time sequencing is moving from an earlier period to a later period in time, or moving backward in reverse chronological order. An example might be the history of aviation from the Wright brothers until now.

A discussion group in one of our classes used time order to talk about the importance of tradition in society. The group began its discussion by taking us back to 1893 and telling us what it was like to go to school at our university then. As this group moved forward, describing what it was like in 1913, 1933, and in 1973, the audience began to develop an appreciation for the contribution made by tradition to the quality of life on campus today. Had the group simply started by talking about whether current traditions should be maintained, it would have been much more difficult to understand the significance of the topic; by using a time sequence, these students added interest and depth to the discussion. Time sequencing seems to lend itself to certain special occasions. Commencement speakers usually use this pattern as they laud the graduates for their accomplishments and urge them to take up the challenges of the future. Martin Luther King, Jr. used this organizational pattern on the 100th anniversary of the Emancipation Proclamation. In his "I Have a Dream" speech, he pointed out the struggles of the past and present, ending with a rosy dream of the future. Organizing material chronologically is a simple but effective technique, useful for a wide variety of topics.

Space Sequencing

Space sequencing refers to ordering points in reference to physical space. You might take your audience on an imaginary tour of the White House, by describing each historic room. Or you might use space sequence for describing lifestyle differences among city dwellers. One of our students used space order effectively by indicating how life is lived in the posh apartments of the inner city, how it is lived in the ghetto areas that sometimes surround the luxurious apartments, and finally, some characteristics of life in the suburbs outside the city. Space sequence could be used to talk about the structural character of a building by pointing out the functions of a foundation, supporting walls, and roof; or it could be used to describe the types of people who choose to sit at the rear, the middle, and the front of classrooms.

Topic Order

Topic order is a useful means of arranging ideas; by examining a subject you will often find it falls naturally into divisions. A ten-speed bicycle, for example, has three different systems—the guidance mechanism, the frame, and the power train; in describing such a bike, you might talk about these three systems. Also, you might use topical sequence for a speech in which you explain the several attributes needed to be a successful football coach.

Bonita Perry, a communicator psychologist for the Sun Company, used a topic order for discussing "Three Career Traps for Women."[3] She pointed out "The Perfectionist Trap," "The Burn-Out Blues," and "The Seduction by Security." The way she labeled these "traps" allowed listeners to infer how each of these topics would be developed.

Cause-Effect Order

Cause-effect organization points out how one occurrence affects later events. When interest rates on borrowed money go up, people tend to borrow less money. When you have a head cold, your eyes get red and your nose gets stuffy. Speakers often use this pattern to illustrate the relationship between smoking and cancer. We once had a student couple this organizational pattern with an extremely powerful appeal. She discussed the well-known links between smoking and cancer, providing all the typical facts. She then electrified the audience by pointing out her personal experience. She had smoked, could tell it was harmful but did it anyway because it was cool. It was cool until she learned one month ago that she had cancer!

These are four basic but effective devices for arranging ideas; any one of them can be used in any of the public presentations described in this book. You might not think of conducting an interview as giving a speech, but here too, you follow a plan, an organized sequence. In structuring questions about a person's involvement in an issue, for instance, you might use a time sequence: "How did you *first* become associated with this issue, Mr. (Miss or Mrs.) X? Did you *then* become the vice-chairperson of the _____ committee?" Some of the exercises at the end of this chapter will help you practice these formats.

A builder needs blueprints; a speaker needs an outline.

Outlining
The Value of Outlining

When your speech is over, what you think you have presented doesn't count for much; it's what the audience remembers that matters. Listeners remember best a few ideas that have been clearly developed and vividly presented, and they remember almost nothing from a shotgun barrage of unrelated bits of information or ideas. As you begin gathering materials for the body of your speech, it is important to learn an organizational technique for these materials. A builder needs blueprints to build a house; a pilot needs a flight plan; a motorist needs a road map; and, similarly, nothing is so helpful to a speaker as an outline.

An outline is a visual representation of how the items of information to be presented are related and the order in which you plan to present your material. Sketching the ideas in an outline is more flexible than writing the speech out word for word. Once you have the ideas in an outline form, you rearrange them until they are in the order that will most effectively accomplish your specific purpose. The outline also helps you to avoid digressions from the specific purpose and tides you over any memory lapses. Having the outline to refer to gives you more confidence and thereby improves your delivery.

Principles of Outlining

Two principles are basic to preparing a speech outline: subordination and coordination. *Subordination* is the grouping of items to be discussed under larger headings. If the major headings in a speech on glass cutting are "Be careful to select glass with good cutting characteristics" and "Put some decorative touches on your product after it's cut," you could discuss the age and thickness of glass under glass selection because those things are relevant to cutting characteristics (i.e., they are subordinate to it). However, you could not talk about these things under item two because age and thickness have to do with cutting, not decorating.

Coordination is making sure that all items under a given heading are of equal weight and importance to the development of that point. For example, if your specific purpose is "To explain three steps in tying flies for dry fly-fishing," you should begin with the first step, "Gathering the necessary materials." In this section you could talk about feathers, glue, string, and pliers. Each of these things is of equal importance and is therefore coordinate with the other subjects under this heading.

Because we tend to think in these patterns already, we find information easier to grasp and to remember when it is presented in accordance with accepted organizing principles:

1. First to last, *not* last to first, such as, "Now that we've finished varnishing our table, let's look at the sanding process that preceded it."
2. Present comparisons positively, not negatively. "The population of Seattle is greater than that of Portland," *not* "Portland's population is smaller than that of Seattle."
3. Proceed from top to bottom, rather than bottom to top. Follow this principle when describing a bridge, a building, or a waterfall, for instance.
4. General to specific. The overall organization of a speech proceeds from general in the introduction to specific in the body, then reminds us again of the general view in the conclusion. For example:
    a. Introduction—Crimes against persons are an increasing problem in the United States.
    b. Body—The incidence of rape on this campus is a cause for concern.
    c. Conclusion—We must redouble our efforts to protect the safety of our citizens, here and throughout the United States.

Outline Divisions

Outlines should contain the following divisions and meet the following criteria:

Item in the Outline

Specific purpose: State what you hope to accomplish.

Introduction: State how you will open your speech (more detailed treatment of introductions is provided in chapter 8).

Body

    I. First main point.
       A. Subhead
       B. Subhead
       C. Subhead
           1. Minor point
           2. Minor point.
   II. Second main point
       A. Subhead
           1. Minor point
           2. Minor point
       B. Subhead

Conclusion

Describe how you intend to end your speech (see chapter 8 for a more detailed treatment of conclusions).

References

List items and/or authorities used in developing the speech.

Criteria

1. Clearly indicate intent.

1. Gain attention.
2. Show the audience that you care about the topic.
3. Lead into the body of speech.

1. State main points and subheads in complete sentences, presenting only one point in each.
2. Use a standard notation and an indentation pattern that shows subordination and coordination.
3. Main points should relate to the specific purpose; subheads relate to the main point they support; and so on.

1. Remind audience of your central theme.
2. Focus attention on items to be remembered.

1. Provide complete data on items used (i.e., author's name, title of work, publisher, place of publication, and date of publication).
2. Provide complete data about people consulted (i.e., who, when, where).

You should use a consistent symbol system to show subordination and co-ordination. A common system of notation uses Roman numerals to indicate main points, capital letters to indicate subheads, and Arabic numbers for lesser points, as is illustrated in the following:

Roman numerals for main points
Capital letters for subheads

I. Main point
  A. Subhead (supporting data)
  B. Subhead (supporting data)

Arabic numbers for lesser points

    1. Details
    2. Details
II. Main point
  A. Subhead (supporting data)
    1. Details
    2. Details
  B. Subhead (supporting data)

Using a system like this forces you to consider what should be talked about, in what detail, in each portion of the presentation. And, as we said earlier, the outline functions as a visual representation of the speech itself: main points stand out in the left margin as superior to the other points; major subheads are indented to show that they are subordinate to the main points, but equal (coordinate) to each other; supports for the main subheads are indented still farther, showing their subordinate relationship to the point under which they appear. If you cannot construct a clear and logical outline of what you plan to say, you probably cannot deliver a speech that your audience will understand and remember.

Balance means to devote a similar amount of time to each main point; if one point is developed less fully than the others, the audience will assume it to be less important. If the speaker thinks it is less important, he or she should give serious thought to eliminating it; again, all the points in a given category (e.g., those with Roman numerals) should be coordinate, equally important.

In 1970 Marvin Karlins and Herbert Abelson reviewed a number of studies and concluded that the first and last points a speaker makes are the points that an audience is most likely to retain. You may want to check this principle for yourself. Study the following list of nonsense syllables. Give yourself three minutes to memorize the list.

GAZ	SIZ
TAY	DOZ
BEK	TAZ
WAD	LUF
FUB	KIB

Now see which syllables you remember best. Most of us will be able to remember those items appearing at the beginning or at the end of the list. This was discovered to be true not only of non-content-oriented items like nonsense syllables, but of items on a news broadcast as well.[4] If the audience is familiar with the subject and is highly interested, the most important argument should be placed first; however, last place appears to be the better place for the key argument when audiences are not well-informed and not very concerned.[5]

Types of Outlines
Sentence Outline

Outlines can properly be constructed by using either words and phrases or complete sentences for all main points and subheads. One may also use complete sentences for main points and major subheads, then words or phrases for supporting details. However, we think that the inexperienced speaker will find it helpful to write a complete sentence outline—it's more work, but more effective. Inexperienced speakers often generate labels for the sections of a speech, but do not have a clear idea of what is in each portion of the speech. Consider the following word outline:

Specific purpose: To provide some facts about the human brain, circulatory system, and strength.

    I. Brain
       A. Weight
       B. Size
       C. Number
   II. Heart
       A. Pump
       B. Work
 III. Strength
       A. Bones
       B. Tendons

Contrast this word outline with the following full sentence outline:

Specific purpose: To provide some facts about the human brain, circulatory system, and strength.

I. Everything we say and do is controlled by the brain.
   A. The brain weighs three pounds.
   B. It has been estimated that an electron tube computer would have to be the size of a New York skyscraper to have the same storage and functional potential as the human brain.
   C. Though small, the brain contains the same number of nerve cells as the number of stars in the Galaxy.
II. Another of the more intriguing organs in our bodies is our heart.
   A. The heart pumps enough blood in one day to fill three tank cars.
   B. It does enough work in one day to lift a one-ton weight five stories high.
III. Some parts of our body, though seeming fairly weak at times, are actually quite strong.
   A. Some bones can resist pressure of over 1,200 psi.
   B. A bundle of tendons one-inch thick can support more than nine tons of weight.[6]

What will be talked about is much clearer in the second outline than in the first. It is easy to assume too much about the first outline, and beginning speakers may deceive themselves by considering word outlines to be complete. The second outline allows you to decide whether everything that needs to be treated is treated, or whether something should be left out. Full-sentence outlines help you clarify your thinking, whereas word or phrase outlines may gloss over deficiencies; when constructing the outline, you should use complete, simple sentences.

Each sentence should contain one single idea, phrased as a statement, not a question.

Wrong	**Right**

I. Building dams can help alleviate the power shortage, but it has adverse effects on fish and other wildlife.	I. Building dams has at least two effects.
	   A. It helps to alleviate the power shortage.
	   B. It has an adverse effect on fish and other wildlife.

Speech Preparation Outline/Speaking Notes

It is important to note that the speech outline is quite different from *speaking notes*. Your outline helps you to prepare the presentation. Speaking notes are designed to help you remember what you want to say in your speech. Such notes vary from person to person depending on his or her needs. One useful approach is to condense your full sentence outline into words or phrases much like the relationship between the word outline on page 106 and the full sentence outline on page 107. One way to approach this is to use note cards. Write a key word or phrase outline in LARGE PRINT and number each card. It may be helpful to write out statistics or quotations in full to ensure absolute accuracy.

Split Form Outline

Robert Ivie has developed an alternative procedure to the use of key phrase note cards, which he calls the *split form outline*.[7] The key word or phrase notes and the full sentence outline are listed on the same sheet. An example of the split form outline is presented in the next section.

The advantage of this split form outline is that the speaker can use the more abbreviated speaking notes on the left entirely, unless for some reason there is a need to be reminded of the supporting details. If the speech is well-rehearsed, then this may never be necessary, but some speakers find it comforting to have the full outline available, just in case.

These full sheet notes are easier to use if a lectern is available, but if one is unavailable you could attach each sheet to a rigid backing, such as construction paper. In any case, the notes must be handled smoothly and effectively, without interfering with the ability to use gestures and other bodily action. That concern must be balanced with the extent to which detailed notes are needed. Remember that your fluency will depend on your familiarity with your material and this will depend on how often and how intensely you have rehearsed. Even though the detailed outline is there, you have no time for sight-reading when your main concern must be to maintain active communication with your audience.

An Example of the Split Form Outline

The following abbreviated outline was prepared by Nancy Lee Ivie[8] for her speech to the Pullman City Council (August 1980), in which she urged the council to reconsider its decision to change the bus route in her neighborhood. Her argument was based on three main points and was supported by two strong visual aids, a petition signed by more than 100 of her neighbors, and a large map of the area with arterials and bus routes clearly marked. We present only the introduction and her first point in order to illustrate the nature of the split form outline.

Introduction
    A. Represent residents

Introduction
    A. My name is Nancy Ivie. I represent the residents of Military Hill in the area north of Larry Street who oppose the change in the Larry Street bus route that was approved by the City Council on August 5.

B. No previous opportunity	B. We are here tonight because we were not previously given an opportunity to voice our concerns. No one notified us of the impending action.
C. Reconsider	C. We would like to voice our concerns and to ask the City Council to reconsider its earlier approval of the change in the Larry Street bus route.
D. Petition	D. You each have a copy of the petition signed by more than 100 citizens, all but two of whom are on the bus route.
E. (Map) New route	E. (Show visual aid, map of the area showing the new and the old bus routes.) Here you see the new bus route in the Larry Street area. We oppose the new transit route for 3 main reasons:

Oppose for 3 reasons:	
I. Unnecessary risks	I. The proposed change poses unnecessary hazards and risks.
A. Children	A. Nearly 150 children under 12 live along the proposed new route; most of these children are 6 and under.
B. Traffic hazards-congestion	B. Bus traffic would add to the already hazardous traffic congestion on the proposed route.
1. street width	1. These side streets are not as wide as the arterial, Larry, the present bus route.
2. 8 turns	2. At eight points along the route, buses would have to turn into opposing lanes of traffic.
3. parked cars—10-ton buses	3. Cars parked along the street cut down still further on maneuvering room for these 10-ton buses.
4. worse in winter	4. The problem is greatly increased in winter.

C. Unnecessary—Larry St. arterial	C. These problems of hazards to children and to property are unnecessary, because Larry Street, the arterial, is conveniently close to all the area to be served.

Nancy Ivie then discussed costs and presented an alternative bus route. The split form outline was useful to her because she included a wide variety of facts that she wanted to be sure were accurate.

Speech Preparation Checklist

The following is a checklist, presented as an outline, for you to follow in preparing a speech.

I. The first stage of preparation includes the following steps.
   A. Analyze the audience.
   B. Choose your topic.
   C. Determine the specific purpose best suited to the topic and occasion.
   D. Conduct research to develop your topic.
   E. Decide on a plan of organization (time, space, topic, or cause-effect sequence).
   F. Write out all the main points of your subject that come to mind. It may be helpful to put each point on a separate card, to allow for easy rearrangement of ideas.
      1. Main points should directly develop each aspect of the specific purpose statement.
      2. Main points should support and explain the specific purpose.
   G. Develop the subpoints to be presented under each main point.
   H. List under each major subhead the information and proofs that explain and develop that point.
   I. Construct an introduction and a conclusion (perhaps more than one, so you can choose among them).
   J. Plan the transitions you intend to use to move from one section of the speech to another (introduction to body, body to conclusion, and at any other points throughout).
   K. If you plan to use visual aids, note at which points in the outline you will use them.
   L. At this point, you should talk through your speech. Listen to the language as you speak. Is it appropriate? Vivid? Oral in style?
   M. As you talk through your speech, time yourself to get an approximate time of delivery and see how it hangs together.

II. Prepare the final outline.
   A. Rearrange the outline to solve any problems that emerged in preparing the rough outline.
   B. You may need to drop some points because they seem irrelevant or because the speech is too long. (It is usually better to drop an entire point than to thin the development of each of the points, leaving only unsupported generalities.)
   C. State each main point and subhead as a complete sentence.
   D. State subpoints either as complete sentences or key phrases.
   E. Refine the introduction, conclusion, and transitions; check to see that they fulfill their purposes.
   F. Prepare the visual aids and practice with them from this point on.
   G. Talk through the speech again, checking for length and ease of flow.
III. Construct a speaking outline.
   A. For your speaking notes, you may use the key phrase format, or you may construct a split form outline. *Number each card or sheet*.
      1. Key phrase—Use 3″ × 5″ or 4″ × 6″ note cards, noting only the key phrases that will remind you of the complete point. Write out completely only those items you want to state exactly, as in a definition or a quotation.
      2. Split form outline—Use a full sheet of paper, divided into two columns. Place a key phrase outline in the left-hand column and a full sentence outline in the right-hand column. (See a fuller discussion of the split form outline and a complete example earlier in this chapter.)
   B. Your speaking notes should help, not hinder you as you speak.
      1. They should be visible at a glance. Type the outline in capital letters, double-spaced, or print large. Number the pages. Add any notes to yourself you think may be helpful, such as "Visual aid here" or "Slow down!"
      2. They should not hinder your ability to move and to gesture. Note cards can easily be held in your hand. The split form outline should be mounted on a heavy backing, such as construction paper; you may wish to place the outline on a lectern, and move back to it as you need to.
   C. Any kind of speaking notes should function primarily as a backup system. Know the main points of your speech and how you plan to support each idea.
IV. Now you are ready to REHEARSE! Practice your speech aloud, referring to your notes only when you need to. It is essential to preserve the extemporaneous quality of the speech, not memorize or

read to your audience. Each time you practice the speech, the actual wording will be somewhat different, but if you talk through your speech several times, you will be confident that you can present it comfortably and successfully. We will go into more detail on oral practice in chapter 11 on delivery.

Summary

If a message is not clearly organized, the listener understands less and remembers less; the speaker may be perceived to be incompetent, inconsiderate, and untrustworthy.

Time, space, topic, and cause-effect sequences are basic ways to organize your speech topics.

Outlining is a means of clarifying ideas, both for the speaker and for the audience. You should use a standard notation system, and clear subordination and coordination of ideas. Attention should be given to balancing the weight given each argument and to the positioning of the argument in the speech.

Outlines may use either full sentences or words and phrases, but full sentences are clearer for beginning speakers. The split form outline can help a speaker feel less worried about forgetting the speech.

Exercises

1. Pick a topic. Develop an outline for that topic in class. Use the criteria raised here to evaluate the outline. Are complete sentences used? Are the items coordinate? Subordinate? Balanced?
2. Prepare speaking notes for the outline developed in item one. Each person should do this individually. Then each person should trade speaking notes with another. These dyads should consider the adequacy of these notes.

Assignments

1. Select a speech topic.
2. Prepare an outline for a one-point speech on the topic.

Suggested Reading

Amato, Phillip, and Ecroyd, Donald. *Organizational Patterns and Strategies in Speech Communication.* Skokie, Ill.: National Textbook Company, 1975.

Haynes, Judy L. *Organizing A Speech: A Programmed Guide.* 2d ed. Englewood Cliffs, N.J.: Prentice-Hall, Inc., 1981.

Thompson, Ernest C. "Some Effects of Message Structure on Listeners' Comprehension," *Speech Monographs* 34 (1967): 51–57.

Thonssen, Lester, and Baird, A. Craig. *Speech Criticism.* New York: The Ronald Press Company, 1948. Ch. 14.

Notes

1. John A. Jones and George R. Serlovsky, "An Investigation of Listener Perception of Degrees of Speech Disorganization and the Effects on Attitude Change and Source Credibility," *SCA Abstracts* (1971): 54.
2. Christopher Spicer and Ron E. Bassett, "The Effect of Organization on Learning From an Informative Message," *Southern Speech Communication Journal* (Spring 1976): 290–99.
3. Bonita L. Perry, "Three Career Traps for Women," *Vital Speeches* 57 (1981): 76–79.
4. R. Wayne Pace, Robert R. Boren, and Brent D. Peterson, *Communication Behavior and Experiments: A Scientific Approach* (Belmont, Calif.: Wadsworth Publishing Co., 1975): 52–53.
5. R. R. Lana, "Familiarity and the Order of Presentation in Persuasive Communications," *Journal of Abnormal and Social Psychology* 62 (1961): 573–77; and "Controversy of the Topic and the Order of Presentation in Persuasive Communications," *Psychological Reports* 12 (1963): 163–70.
6. A condensed version of an outline developed by Jeff Dahl, Washington State University, 1982. Reprinted with permission of Jeff Dahl.
7. Robert L. Ivie, Department of Speech Communication and Theatre Arts, Texas A & M University, College Station, Texas.
8. Nancy Lee Ivie, outline of a speech delivered to the Pullman City Council, Pullman, Washington, in August 1980.

7 The Body of the Speech: Developing Your Ideas

Chapter Outline

> *The mind of the orator grows and expands with his subject. Without ample materials, no splendid oration was ever yet produced.*
>
> *Tacitus*

Strange as it may seem, most of the effort to prepare the introduction and conclusion for your speech should occur *after* you have prepared the body of the speech. You certainly should be thinking of how to handle these two important sections of your speech, the "appetizer and the dessert"; give them some attention as you prepare the preliminary outline, then put them on the "back burner" while you prepare the bulk of the speech, the "meat and potatoes." In this chapter we will discuss types of supporting materials used in the body of the speech to inform the audience.

Supporting Material

The building blocks from which you construct the main body of your speech, called *supporting materials,* add substance and interest to your speech. Supporting materials perform four important functions in the body of your speech: (1) they show the relevance of the topic to the listeners' lives, often through examples or narratives; (2) they clarify your ideas by making them accurate, concrete, easy to understand, and by relating unfamiliar ideas to familiar ideas in specific and illustrative ways; (3) they amplify your ideas to make them bigger, so they will stand out and be remembered; (4) they document controversial statements and claims, thus serving to justify the beliefs, attitudes and values about which you wish to inform or persuade your listeners. This last function, while required in informative speeches, is even more important in speeches to persuade. (Persuasive speeches will be further discussed in chapters 13 and 14.)

The specific devices the speaker uses to develop ideas are factual materials (facts, statistics, and definitions); description; examples; (narratives, illustrations, specific instances, and anecdotes); testimony; comparison, (analogies, metaphors and similes); contrast; repetition and restatement; and visual aids. Ideas are clearer and audience interest is better maintained if you use more than one of these forms of development in a speech, and any one of them may be enhanced by the judicious use of visual aids (to be discussed in full in chapter 9). To be an effective speaker, you must be aware of and develop skill in using and combining these various methods to help your listeners visualize your ideas in terms of their own experiences.

Factual Material

Facts

Facts are verifiable units of information, which may be seen and reported consistently by independent observers. The presentation of facts by a speaker can be enormously influential; scientific facts are especially respected by today's audiences.

> When I was younger I could remember anything, whether it had happened or not.
>
> *Mark Twain*

Statistics

Statistics are examples translated into numbers that describe many observations of size or frequency. The relationship between these instances is analyzed and presented in the form of totals, fractions, percentages, ranges, proportions, or ratios. You may use these statistics to support general conclusions about large groups of people, to infer how or why things happen, or to point out trends across time. The simplest statistics include tallies of items (like the number of cars produced in a month), averages (the average number of cars produced per month over a twelve-month span), and ranges (from the smallest number of cars produced in a month to the largest number of cars produced in a month). Other types of statistics, such as significance tests, standard deviations, and multiple range tests, are used in experimentation, but these more sophisticated statistics are not useful for the typical audience. Our purpose here is to point out the types of statistics most people understand and how they are used.

Statistics are so frequently used that it has been theorized that "if all statistics were thrown out of advertising and government reports, newspapers and magazines would shrink by 56.74 percent and television would program for only 3.782 hours per day."[1]

Guidelines for Using Statistics The statement about the use of statistics that we just quoted might not pass the tests we will give you for authenticity, objectivity, and careful generalization, but it does show how widely statistics are used to support a point. As speakers we must use statistics ethically, and as listeners we should consider them critically. To be an effective means of clarifying and amplifying the speaker's points, statistics should be carefully selected to meet the following criteria:

1. Do they cover a sufficient number of cases to allow a general conclusion? If the number is not large, it must be shown to be representative, by careful attention to sampling to obtain a true cross section. Pollsters are able to use small samples to predict political preferences because they poll a representative set of respondents. Such samples take into account age, education, income, occupation, etc.
2. Is the time frame of the statistics relevant to the point being made? Were the figures gathered over a long enough period of time? Was the time period representative of the total picture? For example, seasonal employment figures gathered in summer might not accurately indicate the rate of unemployment for the entire year.

The Body of the Speech

Are the figures current? Statistical data do not have a very long shelf life. The number of horses shoed per day in 1910 would have little connection to whether one should open a blacksmith shop in the 1990s.

3. Are the statistics being used properly? Do the numbers measure what they appear to measure? Are the units being compared actually comparable? Is ambiguous language used? What does the word *normal* mean? Does *average* refer to mean, mode, or median? Were there shifts in methods of reporting, biased sampling, failure to provide a control group? Is the data complete, or partial and lifted out of context?

4. Is the source of the statistics reliable and objective? Who collected the data and why? Did the data gatherer or the publisher have any special bias or vested interest—"an ax to grind"? The magazine *Consumer Reports* is considered an unbiased source by most people, because the publishers have no connection with the products they test and stand to lose credibility if their reports prove to be inaccurate. A statement from a private oil company as to how much oil remains in their oil fields might be considered to come from a biased source.

5. Were generalizations carefully made? Do the figures support the conclusions drawn by comparing the individual cases? The ethical speaker takes care to avoid the trap suggested by the old saying, "Figures don't lie, but liars can figure."

"More people were killed in airplane crashes last year than in 1910. Therefore, modern planes are more dangerous." Obviously this conclusion does not follow; as we all know, hundreds more people are flying today. Not all such examples of faulty reasoning are as easily refuted from our own personal knowledge.

Extrapolations are useful in forecasting trends. But it is important to remember that while the trend-to-now may be a fact, any prediction of a future trend is at best an educated guess and based on the shaky assumption that present trends will continue. Television can provide an example: The number of sets in American homes increased around 10,000 percent from 1947 to 1952. A statistician in 1952 projecting five years ahead could have demonstrated that by 1957 each household would have forty

Chapter 7

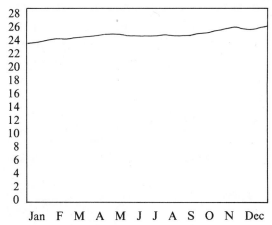

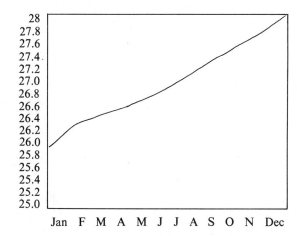

Figure 7.1 By chopping off the bottom portion of the graph and changing the number of dollars represented by each space on the left you have expanded a respectable gain to one that clearly shows prosperity, swelling like the strains of the National Anthem.

television sets, and had anyone been bold enough to extend this prediction to the 1980s we would have been envisioned as drowning in billions of television sets.[2]

6. Even "seeing is believing" can be misused if the intent is to deceive. Notice what a different impression is given by the two graphs in figure 7.1, both conveying the same information: "National income increased 2 percent in a year."

7. Were the questions carefully phrased to be objective, not "loaded questions"?

A southwest area politician sent out a questionnarie to constituents with the following question about a controversial dam being considered for the area: "Assuming there is no other way to stop floods in Phoenix, are you in favor of Orne Dam?" He later stated that he supported the dam because 85 percent of his constituents favored it. However, polls with more objective questions on the same issue showed a much lower level of support.

Techniques for Presenting Statistics To be effective supporting material, statistics must not only relate clearly to the point they develop but should be easily understandable and meaningful to the listener. To this end, we present the following "do's and don'ts" for statistics:

1. Do state the figures as simply as possible, but still be accurate. Round off the numbers whenever possible. In comparing the length of rivers, you probably don't need to say that the Amazon River is 3,987 miles long and the Mississippi River is 2,378 miles long; it's better to say that one is about 4,000 miles long and the other about 2,400 miles long.

Example is not the main thing in influencing others. It is the only thing.

Albert Schweitzer

By permission of Johnny Hart and Creators Syndicate, Inc.

2. Don't use statistics alone, without an accompanying illustration. As a rule, they're not very interesting, and many people have difficulty handling figures mentally. Compare them to something the audience can visualize. In discussing the inflation rate you might say that at a 10 percent inflation rate, a dollar will lose half its value in five years. That means that the pair of jeans you paid twenty dollars for today will cost you forty dollars five years from now. Or: In one area in Washington state, erosion is ripping land away at the rate of three tons per acre. In one year that's enough soil to fill a line of railroad cars that would encircle the world three-and-one-half times. These statistics are made more meaningful by being translated into concrete terms that are more easily understood.

3. Do use visual aids to add interest and clarity. Presentation of a large number of statistics is often hard to follow, and visual aids, such as charts and graphs, make the information easier to grasp as well as more interesting. Visuals showing tallies, averages, and ranges may be used by themselves, or they may be compared with another figure. For instance, you might want to compare the number of automobiles produced in Japan, the United States, Great Britain, and West Germany during a twelve-month span by using a line graph.

4. Don't overuse statistics! If you group too many statistics together or present them too quickly, you might tire and confuse your listeners.

5. Do cite the source and date of your statistics, so your audience can judge the authenticity of the statistics.

Definitions

Definitions of basic or important terms, phrases, or concepts enlarge, compare, or restrict the terms to make the meaning clear. They should be brief and stated in words the audience understands. You must provide a definition if you have reason to believe that the listener is completely unfamiliar with the word; if the word is obscure, ambiguous (i.e., no clear referent), or if it may have more than one meaning.

Words that refer to concrete items are easier to define than those that refer to abstract principles. Techniques for defining unfamiliar words rely heavily on relating the unknown to the known. You may give a definition in one or more of these ways: (1) list synonyms that are likely to be familiar to the audience; (2) give an operational definition of what its purpose or function is (e.g., an oscilloscope measures electrical impulses); (3) compare or contrast it with a known object or concept; (4) give examples; or (5) indicate the special sense in which you will use the word.

Often you can combine these methods to enhance clarity, by listing synonyms, for example, and then contrasting these with antonyms. By combining these definitional techniques you improve the chances that your audience will appreciate the special way in which you are using the term.

The following illustration employs familiarity and example to define communication apprehension:

Communication apprehension combines two relatively familiar terms to create a new meaning. Communication is talking with someone else; apprehension is being afraid or anxious about something. Thus, communication apprehension is being afraid to talk with others in various situations like job interviews, first dates, or public forums.

Description

Description is an explanation or exposition of a scene, place, object, experience, or process. You can show the relationship between the whole and its parts, or tell how something works. Based on your own observations and impressions, and by using vivid, descriptive words that appeal to the senses, you paint verbal pictures for your audience. For example, rather than simply saying that you were cornered by a bull, you could bring the situation alive with a vivid description of how you felt.

"When I looked up, I was horrified to see a raging, two ton, black bull coming straight at me."

Description used with some of the other techniques of support, such as visual aids, can be an extremely effective form of development.

Examples

The several different types of examples are all useful in clarifying an idea. Examples may be real or hypothetical; they may be a long narrative or short specific instances, or they may be anecdotes.

The universe is made of stories, not of atoms.

Muriel Rukyser

Narratives

Narratives are extended examples, a re-creation of an event, with a story line. These are used when you don't think the audience will grasp the point by a brief reference and will need to hear the whole story. In talking on the subject "The Other Side of the Renter's Story—A Landlord's View," you might use a narrative to make the point that some problems that are blamed on landlords really derive from ignorance on the part of the renters:

> I am reminded of the case of two tenants who felt they had been deceived by the landlord. In this instance, their heat bills had been running almost twice what the landlord had suggested they would be. Even with rising heat costs, these renters didn't think the heat bill should be that far off. After a couple of bills and many derogatory remarks to their friends about the nasty, evil, money-grubbing landlord, they brought the matter to the landlord's attention. The landlord was duly perplexed since the heat bills had been much lower in the past, and he agreed to check out the furnace. While inspecting the furnace, the landlord happened to notice that the storm windows hadn't been installed. The tenants had been shown the storm windows earlier and told to install them when the weather turned cold. They had forgotten—presto, high heat bills—but due to neglect and ignorance on the tenants' part, not due to a rotten landlord. Of course, not all. . . .

This is a long account, but no one would understand the point if the case was not developed in some detail. Because narratives may be long, they should be carefully chosen to develop a particular point and to help accomplish the specific purpose of the speech.

Illustrations

You may say, "Cognitive dissonance occurs when two incompatible cognitions come into contact with one another," then use an illustration such as the following to help people make sense out of the statement.

Let's say you have just bought a new car with which you are tremendously pleased, and you happen to read an article that says this car is "unsafe at any speed." You now are in a state of cognitive dissonance and will need to do something to rid yourself of that condition. You might sell the car or ignore the article. Dissonance theory attempts to predict what you will do when two incompatible cognitions (I like the car versus it's a bummer) are present at the same time.

By using illustrations, you can enliven even the most difficult material. An illustration is a detailed example presented in narrative form, recounting a happening or telling a story (which may be real or hypothetical).

Anecdotes with a humorous twist can be used to illustrate points in a speech.

Specific Instances

Specific instances are brief illustrations; you assume that the audience members know the details of the case and it is only necessary to remind them by a brief reference to the instance to make your point immediately apparent. The point will be stronger if the audience is familiar with the examples, and close attention to audience anlaysis can help you choose examples that fit the listeners' experiences.

Anecdotes

Anecdotes are illustrations, either short or long, that have an entertaining, humorous flavor.

Abraham Lincoln tells the story about the man who was tarred and feathered and ridden out of town on a rail. When asked to react to the experience, the man replied, "Well, if it wasn't for the honor of it, I'd rather have walked."

Anecdotes are often well-received by an audience, but any example must be an aid to making a point and not become so interesting for its own sake that speaker and listener forget what is being exemplified. The vivid, dynamic quality of humor does more to elicit interest than it does to provide rational support for an idea. Not everyone is skillful at using humor, and if you're one who can't tell a story effectively, then don't. Also, take care not to use jokes, however funny, that offend particular members of the audience.

Some Pointers about Examples

Examples are the simplest, most common method used by a speaker to support an idea. Following are some important points you should remember about using any type of example.

1. Use extended examples to illustrate main points, perhaps followed by one or more undeveloped specific instances; use only short examples for minor points, so your audience does not get bogged down in too much detail.
2. Examples should meet the following criteria:
   a. Is the example clearly relevant to the point it supports?
   b. Is the example you offer a typical case and not one that misrepresents the total picture?
   c. Do you give enough examples to support your general conclusion?
   d. Do you account for any negative instances that exist?

Testimony

Testimony can be either a quotation or a paraphrase. A quotation is a direct statement of another's opinions or conclusions, given in the exact words of the person being quoted; a paraphrase is a close restatement of the words of another. In both cases, the speaker should give credit to the source of the material. When used well, the testimony of others can add attention value and can clarify and give added credibility to your ideas or information; you can verify the accuracy of a point by citing authoritative persons who agree with your statement.

A quotation from an expert in the field will add to the audience's perception of you as a credible speaker; the quotation suggests that this speaker must have done some homework or she or he wouldn't have known about this supporting statement. Literary quotations are often useful because the author has said something in a unique way and no other phrasing will do quite as well. We might, for example, quote Mark Twain to dramatize this point, "The difference between the right word and the almost right word is the difference between lightning and the lightning bug." In addition to using such expert opinions, the opinions of your peers may be used as support as well, perhaps in the form of the compiled results of a survey.

You should follow certain guidelines in selecting persons to be quoted in your speech:

1. Is the quoted statement clearly relevant to the point being discussed?
2. When, where, and to whom was the statement made, and has any change occurred since that time to make the statement obsolete?
3. Is the statement quoted consistent with the overall intent of the source? Quoting out of context can be false and misleading.
4. Is the person being quoted a recognized authority? The person cited should qualify by training, experience, or special position as an expert on your subject.
5. Is the person one whom your listeners will recognize as being an authority? If the person is unknown to your audience, you will need to present his or her credentials.
6. Is the expert unbiased, not unduly influenced by personal interest in the matter? If the opinion stated runs counter to the natural interests and biases of the person who is being quoted, such "reluctant testimony" is especially strong. For example, if a prominent military person speaks out against a strong military posture, one would consider that the position was not merely a reflex reaction but was thoughtfully, perhaps even grudgingly, arrived at.

Comparison

Comparison is the act of pointing out the similarities between what you are talking about and something with which the audience is already familiar. Comparison is a useful device for clarifying your ideas and making them interesting. You might have experienced such a "renewing of attention" when a lecturer said, "This is really very much like. . . ." and proceeded to illustrate a vague concept by bringing it within your experience. It is essential that one of the two paired ideas be known to the audience and that the similarity or distinction between them be made clear. We shall describe some basic comparative devices here.

Comparison may be short or long; an extended comparison is called an analogy. There are two types of analogies: literal and figurative.

A *literal analogy* compares two members of the same category, pointing out their similarities and reasoning that since they are alike in these ways they may be assumed to be alike in other as yet unproven ways.

Officials of a university that is establishing branch campuses might argue that governance structure and funding should be patterned after other universities that already have established branch campuses. If the comparison is to be valid, the speaker should make sure the institutions being compared are quite similar.

To measure the validity of a literal analogy, test it against the following criteria:

1. Are the essential features of the two items or ideas being compared more alike than unlike? Your audience must be able to see enough points of similarity to establish a logical connection.
2. Are the items being compared sufficiently familiar to your audience that the comparison helps to clarify your point?
3. Does other evidence point to a relationship between the known and the unknown and thus support the conclusion you have drawn from the analogy?

A *figurative analogy* compares unlike objects, often in highly picturesque and imaginative ways. Such a comparison is not useful to support a logical conclusion but is drawn largely for clarification or for interest value.

Author William Catton speaks of his uncle, the noted Civil War historian Bruce Catton. In *Waiting for the Morning Train, an American Boyhood,* Bruce Catton chronicled the end of Michigan's lumbering era. William Catton has memorized the opening sentence of a chapter: "We lived in Indian summer and mistook it for spring. Winter lay just ahead when we thought June was on the way," he recites.

"It really grabbed me," William Catton said. "My area is human ecology, and that sentence very nicely describes the state of the world. We are devastating the planet. There are many ways in which industrial civilization is into its declining phase."[3]

Metaphors and Similes

Some shorter kinds of comparisons are called *metaphors* and *similes*. "He's a rock," is a metaphor. By making this comparison, you suggest that a person has the qualities of a rock—immovable, solid, and enduring. Metaphors make a point in a quick, lively way; they can provide a subtle and interesting way of introducing a comparison.

Similes differ from metaphors in this way: similes always include the words "like" or "as" or "as if." Here are two examples:

"Alimony is like pumping gas into another guy's car," observed Mickey Rooney.

When makers of billiard tables decreed that tournament players had to wear black ties, Minnesota Fats said, "Dressing a pool player in a tux is like putting whipped cream on a hot dog."

Contrast

Comparison and contrast are often used together. Comparison states that objects or ideas are like one another, and contrast points out the ways in which they are different.

Many people have suggested that the brain and a computer are similar, that the on/off function in a computer's memory is like the firing or failure to fire of an individual brain cell. Nothing could be further from the truth. The on/off function in the computer is an electromagnetic process; electricity charges an electromagnet to be in the on or the off position. The firing of a brain cell is a chemical process and has nothing at all to do with electromagnets. This fact makes a major difference in the matter of memory, for instance. If you assume that the brain retains information on a magnetic base, you will have a faulty understanding of how memory functions in the human brain. The retention of information seems to be based on chemical patterns, and whether a cell fires or not, the brain cell still retains the chemical pattern. However, if electricity is shut off in the computer, the memory trace is gone, and if you don't have some other record of it, you will not be able to retrieve the information.

Audience members may, of course, contest the speaker's viewpoint, but the contrast used here makes it clear that the speaker thinks that computers and brains are not similar. This process of explaining what a thing is by telling what it is not is sometimes called *definition by negation*. Despite their somewhat negative tone, you will find many instances in which contrasts are effective ways of making points.

Repetition and Restatement

Repetition is repeating something in the exact words used before; restatement is repeating the same idea, but using different words. Both are devices for emphasizing, regaining attention, and helping your listeners to understand and to remember. Because your ideas exist in "aural space" rather than on the printed page where they can be reread, you often need to repeat them for your audience. This technique is like providing an instant replay for your audience, stopping the action just long enough to let the hearer grasp the idea completely. Repetition is especially useful for strong emphasis. Repeat up to three times, not one after the other, but throughout your speech.

Restatement is less likely to be monotonous, so it can be used both sequentially and distributively. Some listeners may understand an idea expressed in one set of words better than in another, so it helps if you immediately restate it in another way for clarity. Or you may reword your idea in several ways throughout your speech.

Dr. Martin Luther King, Jr. used repetition and restatement in the conclusion of his "I Have a Dream" speech, delivered August 28, 1963, to some 200,000 people gathered at the Lincoln Memorial in Washington, D.C., in celebration of the 100th anniversary of the Emancipation Proclamation.

> And so let freedom ring from the prodigious hilltops of New Hampshire.
> Let freedom ring from the mighty mountains of New York.
> Let freedom ring from the heightening Alleghenies of Pennsylvania.
> Let freedom ring from the snow-capped Rockies of Colorado.
> Let freedom ring from the curvaceous slopes of California.
> But not only that.
> Let freedom ring from Stone Mountain of Georgia.
> Let freedom ring from Lookout Mountain of Tennessee.
> Let freedom ring from every hill and molehill of Mississippi, from every mountainside, let freedom ring.
> And when this happens, and when we allow freedom to ring, when we let it ring from every village and hamlet, from every state and city, we will be able to speed up that day when all of God's children—black men and white men, Jews and Gentiles, Catholics and Protestants—will be able to join hands and to sing in the words of the old Negro spiritual, "Free at last, free at last; thank God Almighty, we are free at last."

Guidelines for the Use of Restatement and Repetition

You may follow these guidelines for the use of restatement and repetition when you are speaking:

1. Use restatement to clarify each main point.
2. Use repetition if the exact wording needs to be retained.
3. Use repetition to forcefully drive home a point as in Martin Luther King, Jr.'s "I Have a Dream" speech.
4. Close a unit of thought with a restatement or repetition of the sentence that began the unit.
5. Use restatement or repetition in the conclusion of the speech to summarize the substance of the specific purpose and of each main point. The material on transitions in chapter 8 provides further insight into the use of internal reminders, like repetition and restatement, in speeches.

Visual Aids

Visual aids are graphic forms of support and are very useful in presenting material that is difficult to talk through or exceedingly boring if you do. We will discuss fully the kinds of visual aids and how to use them in chapter 9.

Variety in Development

Each form of development—factual materials (facts, statistics, definitions); description; examples (narratives, illustrations, specific instances, and anecdotes); testimony; comparison (analogies, metaphors and similes); contrast; repetition and restatement; and visual aids—is one way of clarifying and amplifying ideas, and of maintaining attention. Plan to use more than one method of development to provide a change in the point of view from which you present your ideas. Just as a television program filmed by only one camera would be static and uninteresting, a speaker should use a variety of developmental strategies. Each of these developmental devices must be (1) factually accurate; (2) relevant to the point being developed; (3) specific and concrete; (4) clear and understandable to the audience; and (5) interesting.

In preparing the body of the speech, you should select from among these basic building blocks those that will have the most meaning and impact for the specific audience to be addressed, and combine them in varied and interesting ways. You should then apportion the number of supporting materials according to the importance of each point, emphasizing and arranging all to accomplish best the goal of the speech, the specific purpose.

Summary

To clarify and amplify the main points of your presentation, you can use factual materials—facts, statistics, definitions, description; examples—narratives, illustrations, specific instances and anecdotes; testimony; comparison—analogies, metaphors and similes; contrast; repetition and restatement; and visual aids. Facts are verifiable units of information, which may be seen and reported consistently by independent observers. Statistics are numbers and interpretations of numbers that are used to show how much of something there is, the typical amount of it, or the range of material included. Defining important words or concepts might be necessary to make them clear to the audience. In using description, you describe a scene or an object or explain a process. Examples are instances of that to which you refer. They may be brief, as in specific instances, or extended references, as in the case of narratives. Humorous stories based on personal experiences are called anecdotes. Testimony consists of quoted comments of noted authorities or uniquely phrased statements that are repeated word-for-word or paraphrased, and that are used to support points. Comparison means showing the similarities between known and unknown things; such comparisons may be long, as with an analogy, or short, as with similes or metaphors. Contrast is pointing out ways in which items are unlike. Repetition or restatement of a point helps to clarify and to emphasize an idea. Visual aids are graphic means of describing and explaining; they present a pictorial representation of your point.

Exercises

1. Present examples of various types of development while other students identify the types of development contained in those examples.
2. Practice presenting the same idea using different types of development.
3. Listen to a speech (on television, in class, or outside class) and bring to class two examples of development you thought were well done. Be prepared to share your examples with the class and to explain why you thought they were good.

Assignments

1. Develop a five- to seven-minute informative speech, including at least three different forms of development.
2. Develop a speech of description. Describe a commonplace object without naming it or showing it to the audience. When you have finished your description, have the audience guess what the object was. Discuss how the audience members arrived at their conclusions.

Suggested Reading

Clark, Ruth Ann. "Making Ideas Impressive," in *Persuasive Messages*. New York: Harper & Row Publishers, 1984: 67–85.

Kellerman, Kathy. "The Concept of Evidence: A Critical Review," *Journal of the American Forensic Association,* 1980: 159–72.

Lane, Leroy L. *By All Means Communicate*. Englewood Cliffs, N.J.: Prentice-Hall, Inc., 1987: 244–52.

Seiler, William J. *Introduction to Speech Communication*. Boston: Scott, Foresman, and Company, 1988: 161–74.

Notes

1. Edwin Cohen, *Speaking the Speech* (New York: Holt, Rinehart & Winston, 1980): 95.
2. Darrell Huff, *How to Lie With Statistics* (New York: W. W. Norton & Co., Inc., 1954): 140.
3. Peter Harriman, "A Literary Legacy," *Daily News,* Moscow, Idaho, April 26 and 27, 1986.

8 Introductions, Conclusions, and Transitions

"Have you ever lived on an iceberg? I have, and . . ."

This introductory line was used by a woman whose subject was "The Rigorous Conditions Scientists Sometimes Have to Endure to Gather Data." As she talked, she phrased her supporting data vividly to keep attention riveted on her subject. "I suppose most of you think doing laundry is tough enough at the local laundromat. Imagine doing it when you have ice instead of water and a bucket instead of a washing machine." She ended this presentation by summarizing the points she had made, but in such a way as to remind her audience clearly of her major point. "Try doing laundry in a bucket, using an outdoor toilet when it's 20° above, melting snow for drinking water, and doing without the other comforts we take for granted, and you'll soon appreciate the hardships scientists endure to gather information we read about in a warm, comfortable library." By having a unique approach to an interesting subject and varying her appeals throughout, this speaker was able to arouse her audience's attention and to keep its attention on her subject for the duration of her speech. This chapter discusses how you attract attention in the introductory portion of your speech, focus attention on the things you want the audience to remember at the conclusion of the speech, and move easily from one portion of the speech to another with the use of transitions.

Introductions

Just as first impressions are important in social settings, the first impressions an audience forms of a speaker are vital and often lasting ones. As Benjamin Franklin wisely noted, "Well begun is half done." Your chances of making a good first impression in a speech will be better if the introduction (1) gains attention; (2) creates a favorable impression of you, the speaker; and (3) directs the audience toward the purpose of your speech. We will discuss several guidelines for accomplishing these goals.

Gaining Attention

Your primary concern in your opening remarks is to arouse the audience's interest specifically in *this subject;* some techniques, such as irrelevant jokes, insults, silly behavior, or a statement or action that is *too* startling, might attract attention, but actually direct it away from the subject of your speech. Sometimes your listeners are already so strongly interested that you can begin immediately by announcing your topic. But most often, you will have the task of motivating your audience to pay attention. Audience members must become involved; they must be convinced that this subject is important to *them* and one they want to hear about. Some commonly used methods for arousing audience attention are novelty, stories, quotations, humor, references to the audience or the occasion, questions, and suspense.

What holds attention determines action.

William James

THE FAR SIDE   By GARY LARSON

"Fellow octopi, or octopuses ... octopi? ... Dang,
it's hard to start a speech with this crowd."

Novelty

Psychologists have demonstrated that people become heedful of events around them. If someone yells in the hall while you are reading this, you will probably stop reading and listen closely to learn what the yelling is about. This human tendency to respond to novelty can be very important; if the person in the hall is yelling "Fire!", responding would be important to your very survival. In order to take advantage of this natural response to novelty, a speaker may begin his or her speech by saying or doing something out of the ordinary. One student appeared before one of our classes with sheets draped around him to pique interest in his speech, "The Real Story Behind Hallowe'en"; another student arrived at class with a ball and chain strapped to her ankle as a means of graphically illustrating "How Those Extra Pounds Drag You Down."

In another speech, a speaker opened by asking the class if it "knew that the United States government engaged in legal counterfeiting." He went on to point out that, in his mind, printing money to pay for services not covered by current tax revenues was little different from counterfeiting. Another student shocked the class to attention when she opened her speech by stating: "I have always believed that actions speak louder than words. Judging by their collective inaction it seems evident that students, faculty, and administrators at this university do *not* believe in the constitutional guarantee of equal opportunity." Her thesis was that women's sports didn't receive equal treatment at the university, thus women were deprived of the opportunity to participate in them.

It is important, though, that in being novel you don't become outlandish. One student we encountered was deeply worried about the increasing incidence of cigarette and marijuana smoking among young people. In his zest to convince people of the folly of smoking, he overstepped the bounds of propriety and enraged people, rather than simply capturing their attention. He opened his speech by taking a small white mouse from a cage and injecting the mouse with nicotine; the mouse went into convulsions and died. Students in the class were so angry they hardly allowed him to speak. In the comments afterwards, the only thing the class wanted to talk about was how someone who treasured life so much could so callously take it. In this case, the student got attention but couldn't direct that attention to the thesis of the speech. He could have held up the mouse, told the class what would happen if he injected it with nicotine, and then put the mouse back in the cage unharmed; this would have aroused the class's attention and directed it appropriately. If you use a novel approach to gain attention, be careful not to do something that commands such attention itself that it detracts from your thesis rather than leads into it.

Stories

Everyone likes to listen to a good story, and, consequently, stories make excellent attention getters. Stories can be about things that have happened to you or something you have read; they can be humorous or serious. *Stories* is a broad term that covers anecdotes, narratives, and illustrations. Anecdotes are usually humorous stories; narratives are stories about a personal experience; and illustrations are more detailed examples of the point being made.

As attention gainers, stories must be prudently used. Certainly the story should be in good taste and not be offensive to any members of the audience; the story should also be pertinent to the subject and purpose of your speech. Once your story has gained attention you should be able to transfer the audience's attention to the subject of your presentation.

M. Euel Wade, Jr., a senior vice president of Southern Company Services, Inc., used this device in a speech entitled "The Lantern of Ethics: Custom and Character in Corporate America."

> Before beginning prepare carefully.
>
> *Cicero*

Thank you, Dr. Crask. It's a pleasure to be here. More than two thousand years ago, Diogenes walked down a dusty road in ancient Greece. According to legend, as he walked, he carried a lighted lantern in his hand. He carried the lantern because—even in broad daylight—it wasn't easy to find what he was looking for: an honest man.

Today—after all the passing centuries—we read the morning paper or listen to the evening news and wonder if Diogenes would find the search any easier. "Iran-Contra Affair Rocks the Presidency," reads a headline. "Another case of insider trading on Wall Street," begins a newscaster. Scandal has become so much a national preoccupation, there's even a new board game that tests a player's ability to make ethical decisions—it's called "Scruples."

With so many signs of unethical behavior in society at large, we may wonder if ethics has *any* place in the business world. We may question if "business ethics" hasn't become a contradiction in terms. And we may even ask ourselves if Diogenes would stand a chance if he walked down the country roads, along the city streets, or through the corporate corridors of America today.

To explore some of these issues, I'd like to borrow a couple of concepts from Diogenes' time. The Greeks who lived around that period—philosophers like Plato and Aristotle—spent a lot of their time arguing about ethics and virtue.[1]

In addition to telling a story, this speaker uses the story to prepare us for the remainder of his speech.

Quotations

Provided that they are relevant and provocative, quotations from individuals or from articles recounting recent events can also be used as effective ways of getting audience members to pay attention. If you're interested in gaining the attention of a group of college freshmen you might do something like the following:

Congratulations on choosing X College (or University)! It's the best! Or is it? Arthur Levine, in a September 1980 article in the *Chronicle of Higher Education,* claims you really have no way of telling how good our school is. In fact, according to him, "The situation is at once laughable and sad. If a person wants to buy a $200 camera today, there are any number of consumer guides to turn to. However, if that person wants to invest four years and $20,000 in an education, the rule is: Let the buyer beware. Restaurants, movies, hotels, and even running shoes are divided into quality classes, why not colleges?" When I thought about it, I realized Levine was absolutely right. I decided to come here because a friend did and I had no idea whether it was a quality school or not. I decided I'd better find out before I got much further into this thing. So I spent the last couple of weeks looking into it and I want to share what I've found with you.

Quotations, like other devices to gain attention, should allow the speaker to arouse interest in his or her topic. Care needs to be taken to avoid using quotations that are so interesting in themselves that the audience continues to dwell on them long after the speaker has moved on. In the example above, the quotation piques one's interest in the quality of education in general, then interest is quickly shifted to a particular school. (Perhaps even now you are wondering about the quality of *your* school.) When you use a quotation as an opener, strive for a similar pattern.

Humor

Telling a funny story or personal experience can be a very good way to relax yourself and establish rapport with your audience. Some words of caution are called for:

Avoid telling jokes or a series of one-liners whose only purpose is the obvious one of warming up the audience. The story should be relevant—to you, your topic, or to the audience or occasion. Further, be sure that the story is in good taste. Humor is not funny if it is offensive to any individual or group.

In the introduction to his graduation address to Vassar College graduates, Garry Trudeau, creator of the comic strip "Doonesbury," used humor very effectively and with complete relevance to the occasion, the audience's expectations of him as a humorist and his major theme, "pertinent and impertinent questions."[2]

The Value of Impertinent Questions
—Garry Trudeau

Ladies and gentlemen of Vassar:

My wife, who works in television, told me recently that a typical interview on her show used to run ten minutes. It now runs only five minutes, which is still triple the length of the average television news story. The average pop recording these days lasts around three minutes, or about the time it takes to read a story in *People* magazine. The stories in *USA Today* take so little time to read that they're known in the business as "News McNuggets."

Now, the average comic strip only takes about ten seconds to digest, but if you read every strip published in the *Washington Post,* as President Bush claimed to, it takes roughly eight minutes a day, which means, a quick computation reveals, that the Leader of the Free World has spent a total of eleven days, three hours and forty minutes of his presidency reading the comics. This fact, along with nuclear meltdown, are easily two of the most frightening thoughts of our times.

(Trudeau begins in a humorous style by referring to Jane Pauley, the prominent news anchor, in an understated way as "my wife, who works in television . . ." He goes on to take irreverent jabs at such social and political institutions as *USA Today* and President Bush, both favorite targets in "Doonesbury.")

There's one exception to this relentless compression of time in modern life. That's right—the graduation speech. When it comes to graduation speeches, it is generally conceded that time—a generous dollop of time—is of the essence. This is because the chief function of the graduation speaker has always been to prevent graduating seniors from being released into the real world before they've been properly sedated. Like all anesthetics, graduation speeches take time to kick in, so I'm going to ask you to bear with me for about a quarter of an hour. It will go faster if you think of it as the equivalent of four videos.

(Here the speaker makes reference to the occasion and to his role in the ceremony.)

I want to speak to you today about questions. About pertinent questions and impertinent questions. And where you might expect them to lead you.

I first learned about pertinent questions from my father, a retired physician who used to practice medicine in the Adirondacks. Like all parents racing against the clock to civilize their children, my father sought to instruct me in the ways of separating wheat from chaff, of asking sensible questions designed to yield useful answers. That is the way a diagnostician thinks. Fortunately for me, his own practical experience frequently contradicted his worthiest intentions.

Here's a case in point: A man once turned up in my father's office complaining of an ulcer. My father asked the pertinent question. Was there some undue stress, he inquired, that might be causing the man to digest his stomach? The patient, who was married, thought about it for a moment and then allowed that he had a girlfriend in Syracuse, and that twice a week he'd been driving an old pick-up down to see her. Since the pick-up frequently broke down, he was often late in getting home, and he had to devise fabulous stories to tell his wife. My father, compassionately but sternly, told the man he had to make a hard decision about his personal priorities if he was ever to get well.

The patient nodded and went away, and six months later came back completely cured, a new man. My father congratulated him and then delicately inquired if he'd made some change in his life.

The man replied, "Yup. Got me a new pick-up."

(Here Trudeau announces the subject of the speech to follow, then illustrates the title with a pertinent [and impertinent] story.)

So the pertinent question sometimes yields the impertinent answer. In spite of himself, my father ended up teaching me that an unexpected or inconvenient truth is often the price of honest inquiry. Of course, you presumably wouldn't be here if you didn't already know that. I'm confident that your education has been fairly studded with pertinent questions yielding impertinent answers.

(The relevance of the story is again driven home, and Trudeau compliments his audience and the school from which they are graduating.)

References to the Audience and to the Occasion

Speeches can be opened by saying something about the audience and/or occasion. Janice Shaw Crouse, associate vice president of Academic Affairs at Taylor University, does both in the following introduction.

It is with a tremendous amount of gratitude and to be honest just a few pinches of regret that I stand here today and officially close the first year of the Marion-Grant County Career Women's Council. I hope that you all share in the sense of satisfaction at what has been accomplished this year. There is a summary of the year's activities at your place setting. Here you see the joint product of the hard work of this year's officers and committee chairs as they worked to launch this organization and to plan challenging and interesting programs. I am proud of the growth and development that has occurred in our founding year and I know that you join me in expressing appreciation to each person who made this year such a success.[3]

It is desirable to include the audience as quickly as possible, and asking a question is one good way to elicit an immediate verbal or mental response.

Robert K. Oldham, director of the Biological Therapy Institute, combined questions with an example to create a powerful introduction in a speech he delivered in Cleveland in the summer of 1987.

> She traveled thousands of miles because we were her last hope. She had been rejected by the National Cancer Institute (NCI), and major university cancer centers at Johns Hopkins, Sloan Kettering and M. D. Anderson. She had advanced colon cancer in the liver, lungs, and bone. Government and university research centers were right in rejecting her. They wanted to give their studies the best chance to succeed. She and her family were searching for help. They had no place to turn. We rejected her, too.
>
> Could we have helped? Should we have tried? Probably her disease was progressing too fast for our research laboratories. Our efforts take time and she had precious little. But, they wanted us to try. We said no.[4]

By providing a specific example, Mr. Oldham stimulates the audience's desire to *want* to know the answers to the questions he poses.

The use of suspense can be an effective way to attract interest in topics an audience has heard before or would rather not attend to. Consider the following:

> As one born in the shadow of Spencer's Mountain (which became Walton's Mountain in the TV series) and raised in rural Virginia in the '30s, I grew up with a shared belief in America as an isolated community. I, and everyone I knew, was an isolationist, a protectionist, and an America-firster. We raised and grew what we needed; free trade to us meant buying our staples on the cuff at the general store.
>
> Today I can vividly recall the publication more than four decades ago of Wendell Willkie's book *One World,* a plea for international cooperation which galvanized all of us jingoists and protectionists into fervent denunciation of "one worlders."
>
> The debates I grew up with in rural Virginia centered around the isolationists and protectionists versus the "one worlders." Now in 1987, the debate is framed in much the same way. The debate is much the same, but the world is different. In political and diplomatic terms, one world has never been more than a dream. But in economic and financial terms, global trading and global investment have created the global marketplace—a one world marketplace. The Asian and European enemies of Wendell Willkie's time are now vital lifelines to our own domestic economy. Our stocks and bonds are traded twenty-four hours a day in Asian and European markets, and when investors lose confidence in their governments, or our government, the market crash will occur on Wall Street and in Asia and Europe.[5]

By keeping the listeners guessing as to whether he is an isolationist or free trader, Norman L. Dobyns, vice president of Public Affairs for Northern Telecom, Inc., aroused interest in his discussion of free trade.

> Our judgments, when we are pleased and friendly are not the same as when we are pained and hostile.
>
> *Aristotle*

Establishing Credibility

We said in chapter 1 that credibility rests on a perception of the speaker as competent, trustworthy, and having an attitude of goodwill toward the audience.

Competence

If the chairperson who introduced your speech didn't describe your credibility, you might establish your competence by briefly stating your qualifications to speak on the topic. This should be done tactfully and without bragging. Consider the following:

Bragging: I spent ten years working with the best flyers in the world, so I know what I'm talking about.

Tactful: During my ten years in the Navy, I had the opportunity to work with the Blue Angels, the Navy's crack precision-flying team.

One thing you should never, ever do is to destroy your own credibility by apologizing: "I'm really nervous because I'm not very good at public speaking . . ."; or, worse yet, "I've been pretty busy, so I'm not really prepared. . . ."

Competence is also established as you continue with your speech. If you are organized, and thorough with your information and documentation, you will be seen as competent.

Trustworthiness

To determine whether you are trustworthy, an audience will watch you. If you have an open and direct manner, show a clear interest in and warmth toward your listeners, and speak honestly with them, the audience will consider you to be trustworthy.

If your next-door neighbor, whom you have known for years, tells you that someone you know less well drinks too much, whether or not you believe that claim will depend on how much trust you have in your neighbor. If in the past this neighbor has been scrupulously honest about things said about others, you will probably believe the statement about drinking. However, if you have found the neighbor to be a gossip and often wrong about such statements, you will likely be skeptical of the information. Trust in a public-speaking situation works in much the same manner. An audience may already know some information about the speaker and treat his or her statements accordingly. It may also be guided by the person who gives the introduction. If the speaker is introduced warmly by someone the audience trusts, some of that trust will transfer to the speaker. The audience also watches carefully those speakers whom they do not know and who are introduced by someone they do not know. If the speaker says things that the audience knows to be true, it will begin to develop a basic trust of the speaker. This is, of course, one of the reasons a good speaker sets out to establish common ground with an audience as early and as often as possible.

Goodwill

By minimizing distracting differences and establishing a common ground, you can develop a bond of goodwill between you and your audience when you speak. Sincerity plays an important part in establishing goodwill with an audience. You should look the listeners directly in the eye and take on an attitude appropriate to the subject—don't joke if the subject is serious or make apologies for being unprepared. In essence, you need to act in a manner that convinces the audience members of your respect for them.

Point out or imply as many similarities as possible between yourself and the audience, especially your common interest in the subject of your speech. If you are talking to a college class about abortion, you might present statistics showing how many young adults have had to face this issue. If your topic is buying skis, point out how many people today ski and how this group might find the information on buying skis to be useful.

If you suspect that your audience might not have a favorable opinion of you or your subject, you might use a technique called "positive association." This tactic has long been used by speakers to establish an atmosphere of warm acceptance before launching into rougher persuasive waters.

> Such strategy was illustrated a number of years ago when Senator Robert F. Kennedy spoke to the student body of Brigham Young University. The speech he gave was made about two weeks after he had announced his candidacy for the presidency. He knew at this point in the campaign that his main opponent was President Johnson and was also aware that his own predominantly liberal views would probably conflict with the rather conservative views held by the students. Therefore, he spent his first ten minutes discussing an army—called Johnson's Army—that was sent against the Mormons in Utah in the early history of the territory. After establishing his knowledge of the history of Utah, he stated he felt just like one of the Mormons who was forced to fight against Johnson's Army. This remark brought a great roar of approval before Kennedy launched into discussing why the troops should come home from Vietnam, a point of view his audience did not necessarily hold. But attitude scales administered before and after his presentation indicated a significant shift of opinion toward Kennedy's position.[6]

Direct the Audience Toward the Theme of Your Speech

It may be necessary to provide background for your speech to help the audience understand that which follows. This may include definitions, if they are required, and confining the topic to the portion of it you intend to cover. What specifically are you going to explain or suggest that the audience do? An important feature of the introduction is to provide a bridge to the body of the speech, moving from the preliminaries to fulfilling the speaker's specific purpose. This transition device, often called a partition, takes you from where you have been to where you are going. For example:

> From your reaction to the problems I had on my cross-state bike trip, I think you'll understand why I'm going to turn my attention to how to maintain the brakes and shifters on your bike.

This speaker has previewed the two main points in the speech. She will talk about (1) maintaining the brakes and (2) maintaining the shifters on a bicycle. Incidentally, the speaker mentions that she bicycles a lot so she might be competent and experienced.

Points Made about Introductions—Summary

Besides the part it plays in the overall structure of the speech, the introduction performs another important function for the speaker. It gives the speaker time to get past the initial nervousness and gain confidence from the audience reaction to the getting-acquainted remarks. We'll talk more about this in chapter 11 on delivery.

The speaking situation may demand certain brief formalities, acknowledging the introduction given by the chairperson and including, perhaps, a reference to the occasion. Beyond that, the introduction should be long enough to accomplish the three goals we have discussed and no longer. You may want to get the audience into a frame of mind that urges it to hear you out. Just as it takes longer to get a conversation going with strangers than with old friends, the actual length varies, but the introduction should comprise about 10 to 12 percent of the total speech, the conclusion 4 to 5 percent, and the remainder of the time should be devoted to the body of the speech. This means that in a five-minute speech, your introduction will be about a minute in length, your conclusion about one-half minute, and the body about three-and-one-half minutes.

The introduction gains audience attention, establishes the speaker's credentials, and previews the speech. It also contributes to your own ease as the speaker and helps get you into the swing of your presentation.

Maintaining Attention

Research indicates that most people do not continually focus on one stimulus for longer than about eight seconds. Therefore, speakers do not "hold attention"; they constantly regain it.[7] A speaker has to work hard to compete with distractions—noise, or the possibility that the listeners are tired or distracted by personal problems.

Many of the things we have talked about are useful in helping you to maintain attention. Briefly, if your presentation is well-organized, the audience will be able to follow what you are saying. Using a variety of development helps enormously. Think about how absorbing television is; it maintains interest by changing images very rapidly. You can refer to your introductory appeal to recapture attention. In later chapters we will discuss other factors that are helpful in maintaining attention, such as vivid language and dynamic delivery.

Conclusions

We have talked about the goals of the introduction and how to achieve them. Let's look now at the conclusion. Although the introduction and the conclusion are at opposite ends of the speech, they actually have much in common. (Besides, having gotten yourself into this speaking situation, you need to know how to get yourself out of it!)

The speaker begins on a general note in the introduction, narrows the topic to the specifics he or she wants to discuss in the body, then again broadens the theme to make a general wrap-up in the conclusion. All of the techniques for gaining interest in the introduction are useful in the conclusion as well—an illustration or story, quotation, question, a startling statement, or statistic. Two important functions of a conclusion are (1) to remind the audience of the basic purpose of the speech, and (2) to bring the speech psychologically to a close for the speaker and the audience. The most successful methods for accomplishing these goals are a summary, emotional appeal, logical appeal, and challenge. Most conclusions will employ more than one of these techniques. We will discuss each in turn.

Summary

A summary is just that. In the final moments of your speech, you briefly restate the central idea of your speech and sum up the main points that clarify or prove that idea. These points can be in the same order as before or in reverse order. John L. Mason used the following summary to stress the main points he made in a speech, "Investing for Results: Corporate Philanthropic Activities:"

> In summary, Monsanto Fund follows a philosophy of focused philanthrophy—or investing for results—to support the corporate mission.
> In the future, I see no change in this philosophy or our priorities. What I do see is that our focus on results will continue to sharpen. We will continue to work to make our investments more productive.
> How will we do this? By funding more catalyst projects and fewer maintenance programs . . . by helping create more partnerships . . . and, to some degree, by increasing the size of grants while reducing the number of recipients.
> By continuing to sharpen our focus on results, we believe Monsanto Fund will better serve not only our shareholders, employees and neighbors in our communities but also society at large. It's a substantial agenda. And it will take time. But that is our aim. . . . And we will settle for nothing less.[8]

The summary conclusion is one of the most effective in all kinds of speeches, and *every* informative speech should have a summary element, perhaps with another device. You need to keep the summary brief. It is easy to get carried away at this stage and go right on past a good potential ending; such tangents confuse and frustrate your audience.

Emotional Appeal

If you want to leave your audience in a particular mood—angry, fearful, anxious, happy—you might conclude with an emotional appeal (see chapter 13 for a more detailed discussion of emotional appeals). Jonathan Cutler uses this appeal in concluding a speech on youth participation.

> The bottom line of youth participation is about deepening our faith in the potential of young people. There is a wonderful story that Leo Buscaglia tells. It is about a study called "Pygmalion in the Classroom." People from Harvard came in to a school and said to all the teachers, "We are going to go in your classroom and we are going to be giving a test to be called the Harvard Test of Intellectual Spurts. It is going to measure which kids in your classroom are going to grow intellectually during the year that they're in your class. And it will pick them out. It never fails. We'll be able to tell you, and think of what a help this will be." So they went in and they gave some old obsolete IQ tests. Then they threw it in the garbage and just took five names at random from roll books and sat down at an interview. They said to a teacher, "Now these are the kids that are going to spurt this semester: Juanita Rodriquez." "Juanita Rodriquez couldn't spurt if you put her in a cannon!" said the teacher. "Nevertheless, the Harvard Tests of Intellectual Spurts never fail," said the bigwigs. And do you know what happened? Every name that they had put on that list spurted all over the walls. Which shows that you get what you expect. Inspire youth to give, and you can expect great things from them.[9]

This ending expresses optimism about today's youth and stresses the need for the audience members to have faith in the potential of young people.

Logical Appeal

In ending with a logical appeal, you stress how reasonable your case is. You might conclude a speech on inflation in this way:

> I've shown you the basic relationship between the government's spending more money than it takes in and inflation. The relationship is of a cause-effect nature. If the government spends more than it receives, and prints more dollars to cover that difference, it is expanding the number of dollars in circulation, but those dollars don't have any support base. Each dollar, then, is worth less. When each dollar is worth less, you have inflation. Deficit spending by government is the cause of inflation.

This type of conclusion stresses the reasoning that was developed in the speech. Conclusions of this nature are usually most effective when briefly presented. If you plan to use a logical conclusion, identify your reasoning clearly and work on presenting it simply and directly. It is quite possible that you will want to add a stirring emotional element as well.

Challenging the Audience to Achieve a Goal

In challenging your audience to achieve a goal, you finish the speech by telling the audience of something that needs to be done and challenging it to do it—perhaps to join you in doing it. For example:

> There is a lesson there for all of us in the Marion-Grant County Career Women's Council. Like Mary Lou Retton on the eve of the 1984 Olympics, we stand today on the threshold of unlimited opportunities. Through determined preparation, when Mary Lou reached her opportunity she was ready to shine. She performed to her full potential and proved that she was made of solid gold. Her success was a joy and an inspiration. There was no question that she earned her position; she belonged there and she handled the role with incredible aplomb.
> Let it be true of all of us![10]

This kind of ending works well when speaker and listeners share a common cause. Speakers whose conclusions are clearly stated and who call for a specific course of action create more attitude change than those who let the audience figure out for itself what belief to adopt or action to pursue.

Other Considerations

We said earlier that the introduction and the conclusion have much in common. You can often use that fact to good advantage by pointing out that relationship for the audience. You may restate an apt quotation used in the introduction; restate or answer a question posed earlier in the speech; or finish a story that was begun in the introduction. All of these techniques for concluding a speech are aimed at leaving the audience with a favorable impression and helping them remember what you have said.

After all this effort to finish on a strong note, don't weaken it by saying, "Thank you" or "Are there any questions?" If you've done your job well, they should thank you with their response and applause, and if there are questions, they'll ask them.

Transitions: Moving from Where You Are to Where You're Going

We spoke earlier of the role of the transition in bridging the gap from the introduction to the body of the speech. Now we will further examine this important element in the organizational pattern of the speech. You must use transitions to move smoothly from one main point to the next and from one section of the speech to the following section or your presentation will seem awkward and disjointed. Transitions link the completion of one idea and the start of another idea. They also serve to remind you of your sequence of thought. Good transitions help the audience to anticipate and to remember.

Linking

Transitions make clear the thought patterns of the speaker and allow the audience to anticipate the nature of the forthcoming material. As the speaker, you know already the ideas to be presented and the order in which they will occur, but the listener must pick them up and assimilate their meaning as they go by just once. You can guide the listener by frequent use of summarizing, linking, reminding, and forecasting. Some examples of transitional words and phrases that let the audience know you are about to provide additional material are "In addition"; "Next . . ."; "It follows that . . ."; "Now let's move on to . . ."; "Not only . . . but also . . ."; and "Now that we've . . . , let's look at . . .".

Expressions that let the audience know you are going to draw a conclusion include: "Therefore . . ."; "Thus . . ."; "In summary . . .".

Words and phrases like "However . . ."; "Although . . ."; and "On the other hand . . ." point out that you are about to speak of an exception or return to an original position.

Expressions like "In other words . . ."; "For example . . ."; "In fact . . ."; and "More specifically . . ." lead the audience to expect a restatement of earlier material or an example.

Signposts are a particularly useful type of transition. They usually consist of a number: "First, . . ."; "My second point is . . ."; "Third, . . ."; "The fourth step is . . .", but they may be such words as, "Finally, . . ." and "The last point is . . .". One speaker used signposting by saying:

> *And secondly,* with respect to conventional armaments, I believe that new emphasis must be given to those talks which will greatly reduce the threat between the poised NATO and Warsaw Pact armed forces. As I stated earlier, the greater reduction in nuclear armaments must not have as its goal the increase in conventional armaments and armed forces. We must not make the world safer for such armaments.[11]

Certain of these linking devices are most commonly found in speeches with a particular organizational pattern: Such terms as "first, second, third . . ."; "next, then . . ."; "after . . ."; and "following . . ." are appropriate to a chronologically arranged speech, while "so, since, thus . . ."; "due to . . ."; and "because . . ." denote a cause-effect organizational pattern.

Reviewing and Previewing

Summary transitions, those that review that which has gone before and preview that which follows, are excellent memory aids. Through repetition they help the audience to remember the material. The use of emphasis— "Now I want especially to emphasize this point"—is another way to regain and focus audience attention and help others retain your message.

John Temple, a student in one of our classes, used the following summary transition in a speech given during the 1980 presidential contest between Ronald Reagan and Jimmy Carter. This student had just discussed the economic theory underlying each of the candidate's approach to the issues of unemployment and inflation.

Signposts are transitions that usually consist of numbers.

So you see the Kemp/Roth approach to stimulating the economy differs from the Keynesian approach in one basic way. Kemp and Roth feel that the government should cut both spending and taxes at the same time to stimulate the economy. Keynesian economists feel that you should cut taxes but not decrease spending to accomplish that goal. Kemp and Roth further argue that Keynesian economics have created an enormous governmental structure that pervades all of society. What I intend to do in the second portion of this speech is to point out one historical situation in which Keynes' economic theory was successfully applied and one in which the Kemp/Roth plan was used. From that, perhaps you can better judge which suits the tenor of our times: the Keynes' approach taken by Carter or the Kemp/Roth approach backed by Reagan.

This internal summary worked to restate concisely the essence of two economic theories and then prepare the audience to receive additional information.

Use plenty of transitional devices in your speech. Summarizing, previewing, signposting, and emphasizing will help your audience to follow and to remember your ideas, and they will help you, the speaker, to maintain organization and control as you make your presentation.

Summary

It is important to gain, maintain, and focus audience attention and interest throughout your speech. In the introduction, a speaker gains attention, establishes credibility, and leads into the body of the speech. Novelty, stories, quotations, references to the audience or the occasion, questions, and suspense are ways to gain attention. To create a favorable impression of you as a speaker, and thus a more favorable hearing for your ideas, first establish respect for yourself as a credible speaker on this subject, then build rapport with your listeners and show them you are trustworthy. The third function of the introduction is to set the stage for what is to follow in the body of the speech. The conclusion of the speech is the portion of the presentation that refocuses attention on the purpose of the speech, emphasizes what you want the audience to remember, and brings the speech to a satisfying close. Summaries, logical appeals, emotional appeals, and goal challenges are ways of ending speeches. Transitional techniques—reviews, previews, signposts, emphasis—move speaker and audience from one point to another in the speech and help the audience understand and remember your material.

Exercises

1. Present several possible strategies for introducing an informative speech.
2. Repeat exercise 1, focusing on conclusions for an informative speech.
3. At the close of a speech, have two or three members of the audience say what they believe was the specific purpose of the speech. Then tell what you intended as the specific purpose. If you and the audience agreed, discuss whether the introduction, conclusion, and transitions helped develop this mutual understanding. If you are in disagreement, discuss whether the introduction, conclusion, and transitions contributed to the lack of understanding.

Assignments

1. Develop several possible introductions and conclusions for a speech you have been assigned.
2. Practice using various transitional devices to move from the introduction of a speech to the body; to move from one main point to the next main point of that speech; and finally, to move from the body of that speech to the conclusion.
3. Identify transitional devices used in a speech appearing in a recent issue of *Vital Speeches*.

Notes

1. M. Euel Wade, Jr. "The Lantern of Ethics: Custom and Character in Corporate America," *Vital Speeches,* March 15, 1988: 340–41.
2. Garry Trudeau, "The Value of Impertinent Questions," *Representative American, Speeches 1986–1987,* ed. Owen Peterson (New York: H. W. Wilson Co., 1987): 133–45.
3. Janice Shaw Crouse, "The Managerial Woman: Settling In, Branching Out, Moving Up," *Vital Speeches,* November 1, 1986: 57.

4. Robert K. Oldham, "Patients as Research Partners: The Privatization of Cancer Research," *Vital Speeches,* October 1, 1987: 763.
5. Norman L. Dobyns, "In This Us Versus Them World: Be Sure You Know Which Is Which," *Vital Speeches,* February 15, 1988: 274.
6. Jon Eisenson, J. Jeffrey Auer, and John V. Irwin, *The Psychology of Communication* (New York: Appleton-Century-Crofts, 1963): 251.
7. R. Wayne Pace, Robert R. Boren, and Brent D. Peterson, *Communication Behavior and Experiments: A Scientific Approach* (Belmont, Calif.: Wadsworth Publishing Co., 1975): 55–56.
8. John L. Mason, "Investing for Results: Corporate Philanthropic Activities," *Vital Speeches,* April 1, 1988: 375.
9. Jonathan C. Cutler, "Youth Participation: Teaching Youth to Give," *Vital Speeches,* October 15, 1987: 13.
10. Janice Shaw Crouse, "The Managerial Woman: Settling In, Branching Out, Moving Up," *Vital Speeches,* November 1, 1986: 59–60.
11. Roger Mahony, "Summit III: A New Hope, A New Faith," *Vital Speeches,* February 15, 1988: 273.

9 Visual Aids

We prefer seeing (one might say) to everything else. The reason is that this, most of all the senses, make us know and brings to light many differences between things.

Aristotle

Example is always more efficacious than precept.

Samuel Johnson

Using Visual Aids

Any technique that presents a stimulus to one or more of the five senses (sight, hearing, touch, taste, and smell) can provide a dramatic way to clarify, make vivid, or support an idea. Audiences are not usually as single-minded as the young lady in the Alan Jay Lerner song from *My Fair Lady:*

Sing me no songs. Read me no rhymes.
Don't waste my time.
Show me.[1]

Visual aids, when properly used, can enhance informative and persuasive speeches. One study found that when a person was given information orally, he or she recalled 70 percent of the information three hours later, but only 10 percent of that information was remembered three days later. However, when the person was given information both orally and visually, 85 percent of the information was retained three hours later and 65 percent still remembered three days later.[2] Another study confirmed that showing while telling enhanced the comprehension of lecture material.[3] And speakers who used visual aids were perceived as more credible and persuasive than those who did not use visual aids.[4] As a speaker, you can communicate more effectively and gain more acceptance from your audience if you use pictures, graphs, charts, and other aids to augment your ideas.

When to Use Visual Aids

Use visual aids to reinforce the verbal message and to illustrate points that are difficult to imagine or that are beyond the experience of the audience. Aids should be used when they help present ideas more effectively and more efficiently. How something is done, how it works, or the relationship of its parts can often be made clearer and more understandable to the audience if you employ visual aids.

Analyze your audience to find out how much it already knows about your subject to help you decide if an aid would be appropriate. You don't need to show an audience of American college students what a football looks like unless you plan to use the football to demonstrate something else.

Another question for analysis is whether your audience can easily grasp your information aurally; a poster that lists the three main points of your speech is a needless visual aid. For a longer speech or a more complex topic during which the audience might lose its concentration, visual aids can provide a welcome change of pace. Each audience member has a unique background, and if you want each one of them to see a scene or a group of people in a certain way, you may want to provide specific visuals to help establish the desired mood.

Visual aids are especially useful in presenting lists of facts or statistics. They help listeners grasp information, and they provide an additional sensory stimulus that helps to maintain attention. Taxes, profits and losses, and population trends, for example, are easier for listeners to comprehend if they are presented both orally and visually.

In spite of the advantages of pertinent and well-used visual aids, you should not drag them in indiscriminately or use them as a crutch and possible distraction. You should use visual aids only if you need them, if they add something, and if they are well-prepared and well-used.

Types of Visual Support

Many different kinds of visual aids are available to the speaker. We are using the term *visual* aids broadly throughout this text because most, but not all, aids typically used by speakers appeal to the sense of sight. These "visual" aids include the speaker himself or herself, actual objects, models, diagrams, maps and globes, schematic charts, graphs, photographs and drawings, handouts, chalkboard and other kinds of boards, audiotapes and records, videotapes and motion pictures, slides, and overhead or opaque projections. We will describe each of these and suggest how to prepare the aid with some special "do's and don'ts" for using it.

The Speaker (or Helper)

By using body and gesture as well as wearing traditional attire, you might demonstrate a stroke in golf, what to wear when running, or with a helper, methods of self-defense. If you plan to use a volunteer, make your arrangements ahead of time and practice your speech at least once with the volunteer present.

Actual Objects

If the size and character of the object is appropriate, an object itself can be a very effective visual aid. To discuss the characteristics of a particular style of art, you might bring a few select examples to class. Avoid bringing objects that are too unwieldy to use, like the student who once arrived at class with a huge motorcycle. Since some of the items he wanted to show the class were on the side of the bike away from the students, he spent most of his time struggling to turn the bike around rather than talking to the class. A picture, model, or drawing would have served much better.

Models

If the object or process used as a visual aid is too small to be seen or too large to be portable, a model of it may be constructed—either in complete, cutaway, or mock-up form. In using either objects or models, your hands will be occupied and you will need to anticipate how to hold or where to place your speaking notes while taking apart or pointing to the various parts of the object or model.

One student clearly demonstrated construction techniques involved in building log homes by using a small model. He had carefully laid out the various pieces and then showed us how the pieces fit together in much the same way the actual home is built.

Chalkboard

You can use the chalkboard, as well as other kinds of board, including magnetic, flannel or felt, hook and loop or Velcro, and metallic or plastic surfaced. The chalkboard is readable, erasable, cheap, and convenient. It can be used to show step-by-step development without giving attention to forthcoming steps before you are ready to discuss them. However, its very availability can tempt you to use it impromptu, and the best visual aids are always those that are carefully planned and rehearsed. Furthermore, you are in danger of losing contact with your audience while drawing or writing. If you use the chalkboard, be sure that you are skillful at drawing, that your writing is legible and in a straight line, and that your audience can see what you write. You might want to go early to the room where you are speaking, clean the board and remove any distracting material, draw the figure, and cover it up until you are ready to use it. In general, anything that can be done with a chalkboard can be done just as effectively with the following other types of aids.

Diagrams

Objects and models have the advantage of being three-dimensional, but sometimes the various parts or the functions of the object you are using can be seen better in diagram form. Also, flip charts or diagrams on posterboard usually are more portable and easier to handle than the original item.

Maps and Globes

Using maps and globes is particularly helpful if those used show only the data you plan to discuss, without introducing distracting information. A student speaker used a rough drawing of the state of Washington on which she marked locations of small breweries that produce limited quantities of premium beer. By the time she finished, there were stars in every area of the state. Her point was that such interesting features are easily accessible if you just know where to look.

The visitor to London can tour the War Cabinet Rooms, from which Winston Churchill and his staff directed England's fight against Adolf Hitler. You can see the actual maps used, peppered with pinholes where pins had shown the locations of supply ships and their escorts. Each time a ship was sunk, its pin was removed, and the sight of all the pinholes in those maps brings home the magnitude of the terrible loss of men and materials more forcefully than words alone could do.

Figure 9.1 Line Graph. *[U.S. Department of Agriculture, March 1988,* Fruit and Tree Nuts: Situation and Outlook *(TFS 245). EC-10 refers to the ten countries in the European Common Market before Spain and Portugal joined the market.]*

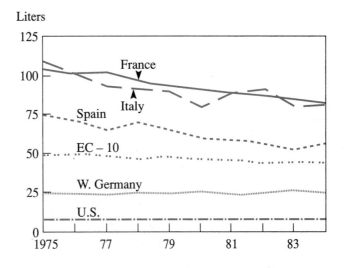

Figure 9.2 Bar Graph. *[U.S. Department of Commerce, June 1988,* Technology Intensity of U.S., Canadian, and Japanese Manufacturers Output and Exports *(DTR 012–88).]*

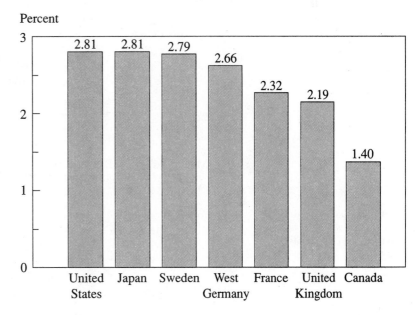

Schematic Charts

Graphs

Charts can be used to show relationships clearly, as do, for example, organizational charts or genealogical charts.

A graph is a visual device for presenting facts, especially facts involving numbers and quantities in relation to time. The *line graph* can show a general trend over a period of time. The line graph in figure 9.1 traces wine consumption over an eight-year period. The *bar graph* is useful for showing comparisons. The bar graph in figure 9.2 compares the amount spent on

Figure 9.3 Pictograph.

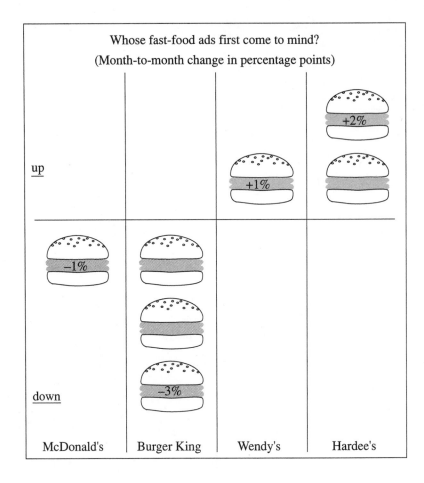

Whose fast-food ads first come to mind?
(Month-to-month change in percentage points)

up

+2%

+1%

−1%

−3%

down

McDonald's   Burger King   Wendy's   Hardee's

Figure 9.4 Pie Graph. *[Bureau of Census, March 1988,* The Hispanic Population in the United States *(p-20#431).]*

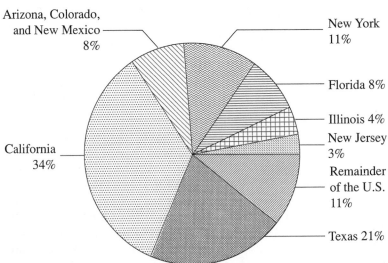

Arizona, Colorado, and New Mexico 8%

New York 11%

Florida 8%

Illinois 4%

New Jersey 3%

Remainder of the U.S. 11%

Texas 21%

California 34%

research and development vis-à-vis the gross domestic product for several countries. *Pictographs* present such comparisons in picture form. The pictograph in figure 9.3 shows the relative effectiveness of fast-food ads by using representations of hamburgers. The *pie graph* shows how a whole is divided into parts. The pie graph in figure 9.4 illustrates the distribution of the Hispanic population in the United States. The availability of user-friendly computer graphics programs makes the production of such material easy. Take care not to overdo it and clutter the aid with distracting material.

Charts like these are suitable for giving information that might be dreary if presented only orally, and in clarifying complex relationships.

Posters

Posters showing charts, diagrams, and graphs like those in this section, have some advantages over other types of aids, such as the chalkboard:

1. They can be prepared ahead of time; thus they are more easily available at the proper point in the speech. Sometimes it is better to prepare the poster partially, then fill in the missing parts with stick-ons or a marking pen during the speech.
2. Displaying a poster containing these aids make it easier to maintain eye contact with the audience than it is while drawing on the board.
3. Posters can manipulate color, wider and narrower lines, shading, and cross-hatching to add variety and clarity.

Some tips for preparing and displaying posters for greatest visibility include:

1. **Size.** For ease of handling, twenty-four inches by thirty inches is a good size for a poster. A poster of this size can be held and manipulated easily, yet is still large enough to be seen. If you plan to prop up the poster, be sure it is stiff enough to support its own weight. If you plan to display it on a chalkboard or an easel, be sure to have the necessary tape, tacks, or whatever is needed to secure it.
2. **Lettering.** Poster lettering should be at least one inch high to be seen at a distance of thirty-five feet, two inches high to be seen at seventy feet, and so on. Block letters are the most visible. You should label all parts clearly.
3. **Color.** To achieve a strong contrast, light on dark, or black on pastel or brightly colored paper is desirable. The color of the graphics should not be too close to the color of the background. Many different colors combined may be pretty, but they are not as clear and easy to see. When you prepare a flip chart, use a magic marker that will dry quickly and will not "bleed" through to the back of the page.

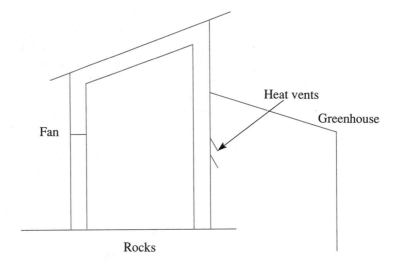

Figure 9.5 An energy-efficient home.

Heat vents

Greenhouse

Fan

Rocks

4. **Simplicity.** Since you are providing explanatory material verbally, present only the pertinent and necessary details on the poster. Use as few key words as possible, leaving lots of space around the words and the design. Use arrows, lines, and other graphics to save space and reading time. Avoid cluttering; use a separate aid for each point.

Photographs

If it is important that the audience see a place or an item in a particular way, a picture may accomplish this end. Photographs pose certain problems: they must be large enough to be seen from the back of the room, and this usually requires making an expensive enlargement or projecting the picture. Pictures should not be used if they include detail that is extraneous to your subject, and they should not be handed around the room; either of these could distract the attention of your audience.

Drawings

Many times a poster, drawing, or other object can substitute for a photograph. A student who trained exotic animals showed a picture of the first animal she had trained—a fox. Unfortunately, the picture was much too small to be seen except by those in the front row. If no enlargement was available, a sketch would have served much better. Related research suggests that simple drawings are often superior to pictures.[5]

Whether or not you do them yourself, drawings should contain only the essential material you want to get across in your speech and should not include any more details than you plan to talk about. One student used a straightforward drawing of an energy-saving device as a visual aid (figure 9.5). Since he wanted only to point out how a greenhouse could be used to

Chapter 9

produce heat for an adjacent room, a professionally drawn set of blueprints would not have worked nearly so well. The audience could have got lost in the maze of numbers and lines that were designed to provide detailed information for a builder. A simple drawing such as this needs to be done carefully, but it need not be done by an artist to be effective.

Handouts

Duplicated material can be useful as a follow-up in certains kinds of settings. The speaker giving the annual report to the board of directors of a company, presenting the church budget, or participating in a discussion of comparative salaries of workers can often make a more efficient presentation if a copy of the material is given to each member of the audience. On most other occasions, such handouts would prove a distraction and should be distributed, if at all, at the close of the speech; for example, a card that tells what to do in case of accidental poisoning, or one that informs the citizen of his or her rights in the event of arrest.

Aids Requiring Machinery
Audiotapes and Records

Audiotapes can bring actual sounds and voices into the speech setting. Such recordings are often quite useful to demonstrate types of music, speaking styles, special sounds (birdcalls), and so forth. Equipment for this method of demonstration is often light and portable. However, be sure you have practiced using it so you can do so easily.

Overhead Projector

An overhead projector shines a bright light through a clear or tinted plastic sheet, projecting whatever is drawn or printed on the sheet onto a screen or wall. You can prepare the transparency ahead of time or write on it as you talk.

This machine is cumbersome, but the overhead has certain advantages in that the room need not be darkened and the speaker can face the audience while the visual aid is being presented. You should practice using the overhead projector so you can focus it quickly, so you will know where the switch is, and so you will learn to avoid putting your notes on the side of the machine where they may be blown around by the cooling fan. Always have an extra bulb because when you use any machine, Murphy's Law states: "If anything can go wrong, it will, and at the worst possible time."

Machines Needing Dark Rooms

When using any of the following machines, the room must be darkened. This can present problems to the speaker. You must make the usual physical arrangements—get the machine, make sure it is in operating condition, make sure an electrical outlet is available, that the room can be darkened, and so forth. In addition, you face a difficulty in maintaining close contact with the audience while the room is darkened, not to mention the fact that you cannot see to use speaking notes.

Most often the screen is in a fixed position in the room, but if you are using a portable screen, try to place it in a corner of the room; in this position the screen is visible to a maximum portion of your audience. The screen should be placed so the bottom is even with the tops of the heads of the people seated in the front row. For good visibility, the front row should not be closer than two-and-one-half screen widths from the screen, and the back row should not be farther than seven screen widths from the screen.

Videotapes and Motion Pictures

Videotapes and movies can be effective, but besides the problems inherent in using any machinery, they require close editing, and even then they might require an amount of time that is disproportionate to the total length of the speech.

Motion pictures can be used to show an item or a process that is either too large or too small to illustrate in another way. They may also be used to compress time—e.g., a series of shots taken over a period of time can give the effect of seeing a flower open up. Or time can be stretched out, as when a fast-film picture is taken of a bullet shattering a piece of glass. Motion pictures may also prove invaluable for illustrating a complex activity that is otherwise difficult or impossible to describe. One of our students wanted to illustrate how you could get special effects when making home movies. She first described how to set up a special effect—in this case a bomb blowing up—then showed a short film of the process. When using a videotape or a movie, you should always prepare the listeners for what they are to note in the film or videoclip to follow.

Opaque Projector

The actual image of a page in a book, a typed page, or a diagram, no larger than twelve inches by twelve inches, is projected on a wall or screen. To be able to project directly from a book obviously is a time-saver, but you must beware of presenting more than is needed to make your point. A senior engineering student who used the opaque projector to present some material from one of his textbooks discovered that the text, which seemed simple to him, was incomprehensible to a class of nonengineering students.

Slide Projector

Pictures or other visuals in the form of mounted transparencies may be projected on a screen or wall; you may use them one at a time or in a series. A good rule of thumb is to include on any one slide only as much information as you could comfortably put on a three-by-five-inch card, leaving a good border and space between the letters. If a person with normal vision can read a two-by-two-inch slide with the naked eye, it should be readily visible when projected. Remember that the pictures should illustrate what you say, but they should not be the main point of focus. One student used slides to explain that Singapore was truly an industrialized country but lost some of the effect by including slides of unrelated scenery.

Guidelines for Using Visual Aids

Visual aids can be very helpful in presenting your ideas to your audience more effectively and efficiently, but there are some "do's and don'ts" for using them that you should remember. It helps to keep in mind that any visual aid, to be effective, should be simple, serviceable, and easily seen.

1. The aid should be an integral part of the subject and a needed form of support. You can use a model, map, or graph to help describe the operation of a machine, the geographical location of an unfamiliar place, or a statistical trend, thus presenting the information much more clearly and effectively than by relying on words alone. You should avoid using an audiovisual aid for its own sake. Aids should be used to support important points you wish to emphasize; if everything is emphasized, nothing seems important.

2. The aid must fit the subject. If you want to talk about the characteristics of leaves, long-distance pictures of forests won't work. We had a student who wanted to talk about English saddles, but brought a Western saddle as an aid. The two types of saddles have almost nothing in common, so she spent most of her time telling us how the Western saddle was different from the English saddle. A drawing of an English saddle would have done the job much better.

3. The entire audience must be able to see or hear your visual aid. A wallet-sized picture of a hang-glider would undoubtedly be too small to be effective. As John Hancock signed the Declaration of Independence in big, bold letters he declared that those signatures should be able to "be seen by the King of England without his glasses." Your visual aids should make your message just as loud and clear. It is a good idea to pretest sight lines and sound levels from all points in your audience.

Be careful not to stand in front of the aid or obstruct the view of the aid for any part of your audience. You might want to use a pointer to help you avoid this problem and direct attention to various parts of the aid. Depending on the size of the audience and the shape of the room in which you are speaking, you might have to pan from side to side when showing a picture or object to be sure it can be seen in all areas of the room.

4. Do not allow the aid to interfere with the speaker/audience relationship. Talk to your audience, not to the aid. The visual aid should support your use of language, not serve as a substitute for it. As speaker, you must still use vivid description and maintain fluency. First, say what your listeners are supposed to see, hear, and understand from the audiovisual resource, introduce it, then restate what the listeners should note and how it is relevant to the point being made.

5. Don't allow the visual aid to be a distraction to your audience, sending their thoughts away from your specific purpose. Don't fiddle with the aid or look at it as you talk. Show it only while you are talking about it; it should not be visible either before or after the point it serves to illustrate. Place posters face down on the desk or covered on an easel. Keep small objects in an inconspicuous box until you use them, then put them away again. Almost never should you circulate anything around the room; inevitably some audience members will still be looking at the aid after you have gone on to another point. A technique called *revelation* can be employed. This involves covering a portion of your poster, then revealing it when you are ready for it; or perhaps placing additional transparencies over the original transparency if you are using an overhead projector. By timing the presentation of your aid to coincide with the time when you are talking about the material illustrated by your aid, you can capitalize on the attention value of the aid and use it to underline what you are saying rather than detract from it.

6. A visual aid should be simple and clear.

7. As speaker, you should never make the audience feel uncomfortable by your handling of a visual aid. For example, if the speaker waves a gun around, the audience won't be able to think about anything except, "Is it loaded?"

8. Be careful about using live aids, like pets and small children, because they are notorious "scene stealers." One of our students learned this when the dog she brought along to demonstrate proper training techniques got so excited by the attention from the class that he ignored every command.

Trifles make perfection, and perfection is no trifle.

Michelangelo

9. Practice with your visuals many times. Determine when, how, and where you will use them. Ideally, you should rehearse with the visuals every time you talk through the speech, including having a dress rehearsal in the room where the speech will be held. You should be familiar enough with the aid that you need only glance at it to point out what you are talking about. Other than these occasional glances, you should be looking at your audience and talking directly to them.

These practice sessions are doubly important if your aids require audiovisual machinery. Make sure the device is available on the day you want to use it and that it is in good working order. Practice operating the equipment. You might enlist a helper to operate the machine for you. Make sure that the electrical outlet is live and that your cord is long enough. Note where the light switch is and how to operate the window shades.

Summary

Audiovisual aids can generate interest and provide aesthetic appeal, and they can also instruct and inform the audience. You should use aids only when they are relevant and appropriate to your subject. They can reinforce the verbal message, stimulate or renew interest, and illustrate factors the audience might find difficult to see or imagine. Above all, you the speaker should remain in charge and should maintain the closest possible relationship with your listeners.

Exercises

1. Draw a map of your state (and other places) on the chalkboard while describing it to the audience. Discuss the effectiveness of your presentation in relation to eye contact and understandability. Consider alternative visual aids for presenting this map.
2. Select three different visual aids to clarify the following items. Assuming you could use only one of these aids, which would be the most suitable? Why?
   - Fire Safety Systems in High-Rise Apartment Buildings
   - New Advances in Automobiles
   - The Key to Successful Sales
   - New Art Forms

3. Form small groups and discuss the types of visual aids that might be appropriate for the following messages:
   a. Much progress has been made in diagnosing and treating sports injuries.
   b. The national park system should be expanded.
   c. Current movies rely more on special effects than on substantive plots.
   d. These are the procedures you should follow if your car will not start.

Assignments

1. Use a visual aid in an informative speech.
2. Visit the audiovisual center nearest you. Make a note of the services available. Try to obtain a catalog of materials that are available for use through the center.

Notes

1. Copyright 1956 by Alan Jay Lerner & Frederick Loewe, Chappell & Co., Inc., owner of publication and allied rights throughout the world.
2. W. Linkugel and D. Berg, *A Time to Speak* (Belmont, Calif.: Wadsworth, 1970): 68–69.
3. Emil Bohn and David Jabusch, "The Effect of Four Methods of Instruction on the Use of Visual Aids in Speeches," *The Western Journal of Speech Communication* 46 (Summer 1982): 264.
4. W. J. Seiler, "The Effects of Visual Materials on Attitudes, Credibility, and Retention," *Speech Monographs* 38 (1971): 331–34.
5. G. L. Wilkinson, *Media in Instruction: 60 Years of Research* (Washington, D.C.: Association for Educational Communications and Technology, 1980): 16.

10 Language Use

> ". . . words and language are not wrappings in which things are packed for the commerce of those who write and speak. It is in words and language that things first come into being and are."
>
> *Martin Heidegger*

The Importance of the Words You Use

There's a wonderful promotional ad that compares public radio to television: a little boy says, "I like radio because the pictures are better." This imaginative feature of language is at work every time you talk to an audience. Listeners form an impression of your total person on the basis of how you talk, your verbal style. Word choices and the way those words are combined into sentences and paragraphs make up the speaker's *style.* This style should not be merely decorative but should stem from a genuine desire to communicate particular ideas to a particular audience. Your choice of language should reflect the best attributes of an enlarged conversation. Many good speakers swear by the KISS method—Keep It Simple, Stupid! Good oral style should exhibit clarity, vividness, and appropriateness. You can make your presentations more effective by doing the following three things:

1. After first forming a clear idea in your own mind of what you want to express, choose language that presents your thoughts clearly and precisely.
2. Search for vivid words and constructions that arouse your listeners' interest.
3. Choose language that is natural and comfortable for you to say and appropriate to the speech occasion and setting. Select words and sentence structures with the target audience in mind.

Clarity

One way to achieve clarity is by choosing simple, familiar words that are concrete and specific instead of abstract and general. Concrete words represent actual objects, events, or experiences in reality. Abstract words refer to theoretical ideas that cannot be directly experienced or observed through our senses. Abstractions are vague; they blur individual characteristics in order to incorporate many specifics under one heading. This leaves the listener the task of deciding which of the many possible meanings was meant. "A great many" is vague and could convey many different meanings to different people, while "eight out of ten" or "nearly 80 percent" gives a much more specific message. "The house on the hill" is much less precise than "that beautiful new colonial-style house on Beacon Hill near the library." Cultivate the habit of consulting a dictionary or a book of synonyms, such as *Roget's International Thesaurus,* to suggest precise ways to express your meanings.

> The speaker's goal in the choice of words is "not that language may be understood, but that it cannot be misunderstood."
>
> *Quintilian*

> Speak so that the most lowly can understand you, and the rest will have no difficulty.
>
> *Abraham Lincoln*

A regular feature in the *Columbia Journalism Review* is its column "The Lower Case," a collection of bloopers that have appeared in newspapers across the country. The humor in these headlines comes from possible misinterpretations of language that is not clear and from the manner in which words are put together. Some of the choicest of these appear in a book called *Red Tape Holds Up New Bridge* and are shown in figure 10.1.[1]

It is desirable to build a good vocabulary so one can choose exactly the right word to express a thought, but the sincere speaker should avoid using "words for words' sake," especially complex words. The Gettysburg Address consisted of only 272 words, of which 190 had one syllable and 56 had two syllables.[2]

Although technical terms are specific and concrete to an audience that understands them, they do not create interesting sensory images in the minds of a general audience. Slang is equally ineffective in a public speech because, although it may create a special effect with a specific audience, it is generally imprecise and quickly obsolete. If everything is "nice" or "cool," then no distinctions are made between the various things being described.

Listeners want efficiency and, thus, economy of their mental energies. If the speaker's language is unclear and listeners have to sift through the utterance to decipher the meaning, they will have less energy left for understanding and remembering the ideas expressed. The speaker who has some concern that a word might be unfamiliar to the audience may employ synonyms, restatement, comparison and contrast, examples, or other means to clarify the thought. By observing audience feedback, you can evaluate how much is enough amplification.

Vivid Language

Vivid language can be described as active, energetic, compelling, urgent, forceful, exciting, lively, and involving. We will discuss twelve prominent devices you can use to make your language more vivid. Some of these techniques we have mentioned previously in relation to creating interest and attention in an introduction to a speech (see chapter 8). Vivid language will also help to maintain a high interest level throughout the entire speech.

Figure 10.1 Ambiguity in headlines.

Within the image:

Baseball Talks in 9th Inning
Philadelphia Daily News 5/22/80

Red Tape Holds Up New Bridge
Milford (Conn.) Citizen 7/12/82

Sisters reunited after 18 years in checkout line at supermarket
Arkansas Democrat 9/29/83

'Nagging' wife critical after hammer attack
Trenton (N.J.) Times 9/29/82

Give the Palestinians a homeland -- Ottawa
Toronto Star 7/31/82

Eye drops off shelves
Tri-City Herald (Pasco, Wash.) 8/5/82

Police kill man with TV tuner
The Blade-Tribune (Oceanside, Calif.) 6/3/86

Man shot in back, head found in street
Worthington, Minn., Daily Globe 12/08/84

White House Kills Fund Raiser After Complaints About Tactics
Newsday 3/19/81

British left waffles on Falklands
The Guardian 4/28/82

19 Feet Broken in Pole Vault
Wichita (Kan.) Eagle-Beacon 6/21/81

Silver Objects Often Taken — Police Units Seek Pattern
The New York Times 2/16/86

Rebel threats keep traffic light in El Salvador
The Atlanta Journal and Constitution 1/20/85

Abraham Lincoln and Stephen A. Douglas at one of the Lincoln-Douglas debates. Lincoln's simple straightforward style of speech contrasted sharply with Douglas' florid oratorical style.

Active Verbs

Active verbs are more vivid than passive verbs; avoid the words *have, to be,* and *got.* By using active verbs you can create a sense of "You are there" in your audience, not a bland, "You are listening to someone else who was there."

Contrast the following descriptions:

"The sun seemed to press on the roadway, and inside the truck, hot light bounced off chrome, flickering like a torch."[3]

The sun was shining on the road and reflecting inside the truck.

The first uses active verbs while the second uses passive.

Personalization

It is also true that the more a listener feels that you are talking directly to him or her, the more likely it is that you will keep his or her attention. Just as you find it easier to pay attention in a conversation with some interesting person than to pay attention in a large lecture session, so will your audience find your speech more interesting if you seem to be talking directly to each person in it. Personal pronouns such as *I, you, we, us,* and *our* are more direct than *one, a person, an individual, people,* and so forth. Contrast the statement "when a person straps a parachute on for the first time, a chill passes up and down the spine," with the one, "when you strap your parachute on for the first time, a chill passes up and down your spine."

Imagery

You should choose language that helps the listeners to experience your ideas. To achieve this goal, use words that evoke strong sensory images, creating moving pictures in the minds of your audience. Words that describe size, shape, color, and movement are effective, as in the following passage from James Michener's *Hawaii.*

> [Listeners] . . . like words that set an event before their eyes; for they must see
> the thing occurring now, not hear of it in the future.
>
> *Aristotle*

Millions upon millions of years ago, when the continents were already formed and the principal features of the earth had been decided, there existed, then as now, one aspect of the world that dwarfed all others. It was a mighty ocean, resting uneasily to the east of the largest continent, a restless ever-changing, gigantic body of water that would later be described as pacific. Over its brooding surface immense winds swept back and forth, whipping the waters into towering waves that crashed down upon the world's seacoasts, tearing away rocks and eroding the land.[4]

Parallelism

Parallelism gains impact by the repetition of a definite pattern of words, phrases, or sentences. Winston Churchill inspired freedom-loving people in every country when he declared during World War II: "We shall not flag or fail. We shall go on to the end, we shall fight in France, we shall fight on the seas and oceans, we shall fight with growing confidence and growing strength in the air; we shall defend our island, whatever the cost may be; we shall fight on the beaches, we shall fight in the fields and in the streets, we shall fight in the hills."[5]

Repetition

The quotation from Winston Churchill also points up the mounting intensity that can be generated by repetition of a key word or phrase. From the repetition of "For Brutus is an honorable man" in Marc Anthony's funeral oration (*Julius Caesar* by William Shakespeare), to the emotion-laden phrase "I have a dream," repeated again and again by civil rights leader Martin Luther King, Jr. in his 1963 speech in Washington, orators have made good use of the power of repetition in speech construction.

Rhetorical Question

A rhetorical question is a question asked by the speaker that she or he does not expect the listener to answer out loud, but rather, to answer the question mentally. In this way the audience becomes actively involved. Edward R. Murrow used this device in his 1958 speech to the Radio and Television News Directors Association: "So the question is this: Are the big corporations who pay the freight for radio and television programs wise to use that time exclusively for the sale of goods and services? Is it in their own interest and that of the stockholders to do so?"

Metaphor

The language of poetry (and of advertising, which has been termed *sponsored poetry*) frequently uses *metaphor*—the transfer of a term from the object to which it usually refers to another object, to show an implied relationship—such as *the evening of life* to represent old age. The Greek word

Metaphor has been called "the window in an argument," because it lights up reason.

Henry Ward Beecher

meta means *across* and phor means *carry*; thus, carry meaning across, transfer it, apply it in a fresh way. The public speaker has as much need for fresh, new approaches to utterance as does the poet, and certainly as much need to communicate feeling.

Metaphors are imaginative comparisons that illuminate an idea. They intrigue the listener by offering a fresh way of looking at the subject.

Some famous examples of metaphors are seen every day in advertising slogans, as well as in such famous statements as the biblical quotation used by Abraham Lincoln, "A house divided against itself cannot stand." or Harry Truman's "If you can't stand the heat, get out of the kitchen." Ambrose Bierce spoke wryly of lawsuits:

Litigation is a machine which you go into as a pig and come out as a sausage.

Aristotle said that the use of metaphor indicated an eye for resemblances. If we keep firmly in mind that an implied *resemblance* is not the same as saying that two things are the *same,* we can avoid some of the problems caused by ambiguity in language. We can use metaphors when our purpose is to build emotional bridges from one mind to the next, and employ the hardworking language of reports, statistics, and reasoning when we need to use arguments based on logic.

Simile
A simile, like a metaphor, is a type of comparison. The difference is that a simile always includes "like" or "as." Again from King's "I Have a Dream" speech: " . . . we will not be satisfied until justice rolls down like waters and righteousness like a mighty stream."[6] T. H. White, in *Seasons of the Angler,* uses this simile: "The fisherman fishes as the urchin eats a cream bun—from lust."[7]

From *National Geographic,* "As 'the shrimp among whales,' Korea has managed to play off the major powers contending for the peninsula—China, Japan, Russia, and, most recently, the United States."[8]

In Jesse Jackson's stirring speech to the Democratic Party's 1988 convention in Atlanta, he likened the blending together of the many different factions in America to the quilt his grandmother made from patches of many different colors and fabrics.

Antithesis
A parallel construction that opposes or contrasts one idea with another is called *antithesis.* One example is this statement made by Daniel J. Boorstin: "It's the duty of a newspaper to comfort the afflicted and afflict the

> Language is not only the vehicle of thought; it is also the driver.
>
> *Ludwig Wittgenstein*

comfortable."[9] In a speech to the National Press Club, Norman Lear, creator of "All In The Family" and numerous other television comedies, combined antithesis with a play on words: "The government must do more to protect the commonweal against the common wheel of fortune."

And none can forget John F. Kennedy's 1961 inaugural address and his stirring words, "Ask not what your country can do for you—ask what you can do for your country."

Alliteration

Alliteration is the repetition of the same sound, usually at the beginning of a word. Thomas Jefferson used alliteration when remarking on the effectiveness of centralized government in his comment, "When we must wait for Washington to tell us when to sow and reap, we shall soon want for bread." More recently, on a similar theme, Hubert H. Humphrey used alliteration as well, "Shall we sit in complacency, lulled by creature comforts, until we are engulfed in chaos?"

Quotations

The speaker or writer can borrow from the vivid writings of others to illustrate his or her ideas. Some good sourcebooks for such quotations are:

Bartlett's Familiar Quotations, Little, Brown & Co., 1934.
Five Thousand Quotations for all Occasions, Lewis C. Henry, ed. N.Y.: Doubleday & Co., 1945.
The Macmillan Book of Proverbs, Maxims, and Famous Phrases, Burton Stevenson, ed. N.Y.: Macmillan Co., 1948.
The Concise Oxford Dictionary of Quotations, Oxford: Oxford University Press, 1981.

Lists of synonyms may be found in a dictionary or in a thesaurus, such as *Roget's International Thesaurus.*

Avoid Clichés

Colorful language is pleasing to the reader's or the listener's ear, stimulating to the imagination, and easily retained by the mind. The speaker or the writer should avoid clichés, trite expressions that have been so overused as to have lost most of their original meaning. *Cold as ice, smart as a whip, without further ado,* and other such expressions are no longer colorful.

Appropriateness

The language used by the public speaker should be appropriate to the speaker, to the audience, and to the occasion. By taking care to choose appropriate language, the speaker can reduce distraction, distortion of his or her ideas, and loss of credibility as a speaker.

> Speak properly and in as few words as you can, but always plainly; for the end of speech is not ostentation but to be understood.
>
> *William Penn*

Wordsmiths

Drawing by W. B. Park; © 1988. The New Yorker Magazine, Inc.

As we stated before, you as speaker must analyze the character of the prospective audience. What are the special interests and attitudes of the audience, and its level of knowledge? What does the nature of your subject and of the occasion lead it to expect, and what does it expect of you?

As a speaker, you should avoid using language your listeners will not understand, but you still should not talk down to them. An audience that is already sympathetic to you and to your point of view can be approached more casually than an audience that is hostile. It is important that you adapt to the audience, but still not be untrue to yourself—your language should be consistent with your own background and status.

To be appropriate means in essence to exercise good taste. A serious or formal occasion requires a more dignified and restrained style of speech, while a more informal and joyous occasion calls for language that is light and lively. Listener expectations would be violated by slang in a funeral service, as it would by ponderous formal language in an after-dinner speech. The public-speaking occasion most often calls for elevated conversation, language that is more careful than everyday conversation, but less formal than a serious essay.

Some types of language that are always inappropriate are vulgar language, improper grammar, and bigoted or intolerant remarks about any person or group. Excessively strong or shocking language that may be intended merely to prod an audience toward or away from an idea can backfire and create hostility toward the speaker instead.

Sexist and/or Racist Language

Benjamin Lee Whorf, a noted linguist, argued that language shapes thinking. That is, the way we talk reflects the way we think. If we refer to doctors as "he", we begin to think you have to be male to be a doctor. When you refer to a person whose gender is known, then by all means refer to that person by the appropriate pronoun. If, however, the referent is unclear, refer to the person as he or she. Further, if your audience is of mixed gender, use examples that include people of both genders and try to avoid stereotyping women as secretaries, homemakers, and the like, while characterizing men as breadwinners, bosses, and so on. In this day and age, men's and women's roles are so diffuse that these stereotypes are no longer appropriate. We know a married couple who are both employed as teachers. One teaches home economics at a high school and the other is a basketball coach at a university. The man holds the former position and the woman the latter.

Similar comments apply to racist language. Stereotypes we hold for Hispanics, whites, blacks, and other groups are seldom accurate. Avoid making blanket claims about an entire ethnic group or race of people.

Differences between Writing and Speaking

We have been discussing some attributes of language that are common to both spoken and written communication. Attention to and practice in either speaking or writing will have a helpful effect on the other. Good writing should have the vitality of spoken language, and the speaker can benefit from making a conscious effort to improve his or her vocabulary and to use correct grammatical construction. For both speaking and writing, language should be clear, vivid, and appropriate.

However, there are some significant differences between writing to be read and writing to be heard. These differences arise from factors implicit in the communication setting:

1. The writer does not aim at specific members of a visible audience, while the speaker directly addresses an audience. That is, speaker and audience share the same speech setting; each is visible to the other, thus allowing the speaker to create a more direct communication dynamic; meanings are different when expressed by a living, breathing person.

> Does it read well? Then, it's not a good speech.
>
> *Charles Fox*

2. Written communication can be read and reread for understanding. Oral communication occurs in acoustical, aural space so the meaning of spoken words must be grasped the first (and only) time the listener hears it.

3. The speaker tends to use more personal pronouns—*I, we, us, you, they*. The writer is more formal, less direct—*one might say, this writer believes*. Abraham Lincoln's Gettysburg Address provides an excellent example of the effectiveness of direct discourse. Even though he was speaking on a solemn occasion, the dedication of a national cemetery, Lincoln breathed life and humanity into his speech by using personal nouns and pronouns in every sentence: *our father, we, us, they, the brave men, living and dead, of the people, by the people, for the people*.

4. The speaker uses more short, simple, familiar words than the writer. Contractions, such as *don't* and *won't* (frowned on in formal writing), are widely used by speakers. The average adult has a reading vocabulary of 80,000 words, nearly one hundred times as many as in his or her speaking and listening vocabulary. The speaker must carefully space and repeat technical information, especially numbers, and explain any foreign phrases or unusual terms.

5. Words with concrete meanings are easier to understand orally than are more abstract words. In speech, you should make use of figurative language, picture-producing words that are connotative and not merely denotative.

6. Speakers use sentences that are varied in kind and in length, more often simple sentences, and frequently fragmentary. Such sentences might appear faulty and inaccurate in written form, but they are perfectly acceptable when spoken aloud. That's the way people talk, so they understand these constructions.

7. Many more exclamations, commands, and questions are used in direct discourse than in written. Rhetorical questions are particularly useful; they stimulate active involvement as the listener answers internally.

8. Repetition and restatement are very important devices for the speaker. The reader of written material controls the pace; he or she can pause to reread, review earlier passages, look up unfamiliar words. But the listener in a speaking situation has no such control over the rate at which the message is presented, so the speaker must use language the listener can grasp immediately and may need to repeat a point or elaborate it with illustrations or examples.

9. The writer can deal with subjects that are more complex or abstract than can the speaker. Listener expectations are different, and the reader is not stimulated and distracted by the other people in the audience.
10. The speaker can also add inflection, pause, emphasis, rate, and gestures to supplement his or her words. These verbal aids are necessary to substitute for the punctuation marks that help to clarify written discourse.
11. The immediacy of the situation allows the speaker to respond to feedback from the audience and to amplify any points that appear to be unclear. In short, the speaker enjoys a major advantage over the writer because of the direct relationship between the speaker and the audience. However, the speaker must be alert to the problems that may arise from the fleeting nature of the speech act; many of these difficulties can be overcome by learning to interpret and respond to feedback provided by the audience.

The following examples provide a contrast between a passage constructed for oral presentation and one for the written medium.

Oral Version

Do you know how your automobile works? Perhaps you do your own repair work? If you do, you will recognize that these (holds up wires) are spark plug wires. But even those of you who are not into do-it-yourself automobile maintenance may like to save money by knowing what to ask for from your mechanic.

These spark plug wires appear to be just alike but if you cut into them (speaker cuts the wires), you can tell right away that one actually has a wire in it (speaker strips enough of the insulation to reveal the wire) but the other doesn't (speaker shows the graphite in the second wire).

I'd like to explain to you how this wire (holds up graphite wire), which doesn't seem to *be* a wire, in certain circumstances can help your car perform better and put money in your pocket.

Written Version

Spark plug wires serve to carry a current of electricity from the distributor to your spark plugs. These wires are constructed in different ways. One way is to wrap a core of copper metal in insulation; another way is to wrap graphite, a conductive material that is usually used as a lubricant, in a similar blanket of insulation. These two types of wires have different qualities. This manual describes the conductive qualities of these wires, the respective advantages of each type of wire, and recommends which wire should be selected under which conditions.

There are obvious differences in these passages; the first is livelier but much less precise than the second. The first takes advantage of the presence of the audience (holding up the wires, etc.), and the target group is known. The second is directed to a more general audience.

How to Improve Your Oral Style

There are a number of ways to improve your oral style. We will list some here for your consideration.

1. Listen and read widely. Observe how good writers and speakers use language in speeches, plays, poems, novels, and essays. Ann Tibbetts, a college teacher and business consultant, advises students and executives to "everyday, read some great writing: fiction, poetry, drama, essays, speeches . . . you need to gain a feel for words: the weight, shape, sound, and taste of them."[10]
2. Make a conscious effort to improve your vocabulary. As you read, look up unfamiliar words to add them to your bank of word choices, then make an effort to use them in conversation, in writing, and in your speeches.
3. Practice speaking in all sorts of situations, formal and informal, listening critically as you speak. It is very helpful to use a tape recorder as you talk through your speech. Record the speech several times, noting words and phrases you particularly like or others that are awkward or unclear.
4. Reading aloud from literature is especially effective in the training of a public speaker. Vivid language and well-crafted sentences can serve as models of composition, and saying them aloud can have excellent transfer value for the speaker. We first learned our speech through hearing and speaking, and the most effective way to improve our speaking style is also through hearing and speaking.

Summary

By careful word choice your speech can have greater clarity, vividness, and appropriateness. You can strive for clarity by selecting those words that say precisely what you mean and avoiding those words that say almost, but not quite, what you mean. You can make your statements more vivid by using active verbs, personal terms, and words that carry clear images (e.g., by saying, "a bright-eyed, hawk-nosed, weathered, demanding man of seventy" rather than saying, "an old man"), parallelism, repetition, the rhetorical question, metaphor, simile, antithesis, alliteration, and quotation. Appropriate language is language that is suited to both the audience and the speaker. Sexist and/or racist language tends to rely on stereotyping and usually is offensive to large numbers of people. Language style for speaking is different from that for writing. Speaking is more spontaneous and flexible than is writing. Listeners have to be able to understand what the speaker says as it is being said. Use the flexible nature of speech to keep your audience's interest high so it will attend to your message and remember it.

Exercises

1. Describe the following scenes in clearer, more vivid, and appropriate language.

    The little girls were surprised to find a small puppy under the Christmas tree.

    The railroad seemed to be in need of repair.

    Jack is a complete basketball player. He plays hard on both ends of the court.

2. Identify why the descriptions you provided in exercise 1 were more vivid, more appropriate, and clearer than the statements you were given. What stylistic devices did you use to breathe life into these scenes?

Assignments

1. Read a speech printed in the most recent issue of *Vital Speeches* and analyze it for style. Be sure to remark on its clarity, vividness (provide examples of active verbs, personalization, imagery, parallelism, etc.), and appropriateness.

Suggested Reading

Anderson, Wallace L., and Stageberg, Norman C. *Introductory Readings on Language*. New York: Holt, Rinehart & Winston, Inc., 1962.

Hayakawa, S. I. *Language in Thought and Action*. 4th ed. New York: Harcourt Brace Jovanovich, 1978.

Sontag, Susan, "On Style." *Against Interpretation*. New York: Dell Publishing Co., 1967.

Tibbetts, Ann, "Ten Rules for Writing Readably," *The Journal of Business Communication* 18 (Fall 1981): 56.

Notes

1. *Red Tape Holds Up New Bridge,* ed. Gloria Cooper, Vol. 166, No. 41, (New York: The Putnam Publishing Group, 1987).
2. G. G. Williams, *Creative Writing for Advanced College Classes* (New York: Harper and Brothers, 1954): 106.
3. William Least Heat Moon, *Blue Highways* (New York: Ballantine Books, 1982): 7–8.
4. James A. Michener, *Hawaii* (New York: Ballantine Books, 1982): 1.
5. Winston Churchill, speech to the House of Commons, June 4, 1940.
6. Martin Luther King, Jr. address at the civil rights march on Washington, August 28, 1963.

7. T. H. White, *Seasons of the Angler,* ed. David Seybold, (New York: Weidenfeld and Nicolson, 1988).

8. Boyd Gibbons, "The South Koreans," *National Geographic* 174 (August 1988): 246.

9. Daniel W. Boorstin, speech to the Associated Press Managing Editor's Association, Chicago, October 18, 1965.

10. Ann Tibbitts, "Ten Rules for Writing Readably," *The Journal of Business Communication* 18 (Fall 1981): 56.

11 Delivery

Chapter Outline

Introduction

We have been talking about how to select and organize your ideas in a speech. And now comes the moment of truth, the point at which you deliver your speech to the audience. Delivery is *how* you say what you say to convey your thoughts to your audience. Just as with every other speech element we have discussed, good delivery is that which is appropriate to the speaker, the subject, the audience, and the setting or occasion. Even outstanding delivery cannot rescue a poorly planned speech, but poor delivery can ruin even a well-constructed speech.

The speaker seeks a desired effect on an audience—to inform, to entertain, or to persuade. The subject of a speech and its specific purpose have a direct bearing on the style of delivery that is most appropriate. A persuasive speech typically will require a more energetic and emphatic style of delivery than will a speech to inform. In both instances, the speaker's effectiveness hinges on his or her acceptance as a credible source. Numerous studies point to the fact that skilled delivery helps audiences understand and retain messages better because the speaker is perceived as being more credible.[1] Fortunately, speech studies also indicate that by observation and practice, a speaker can improve the vocal and bodily skills necessary to achieve effective delivery.

From the standpoint of delivery of the speech, audiences are influenced to believe and to be persuaded by you:

1. When you are enthusiastic and dynamic. In what ways have you sought to learn more about the topic, to find information that could 'lead to a solution to some problem the audience can see exists? Have you actively addressed the problem yourself? By pointing out how involved you have been with this issue and showing your enthusiasm for the subject, you can do much toward delivering your speech in a manner that will be well-received.
2. When you are similar to the audience. Are you interested in your listeners, and do you share the same goals and needs? You, of course, need to point this out through dress, action, and references to such similarities.
3. When you are competent. Does your background and experience in this area qualify you as an expert on the subject? Have you extended this background by doing research, finding evidence that experts agree with your opinions, and finding that facts and statistics from reliable sources back up those ideas? It is often a good idea to point out your credentials in the speech.

However, credibility building must be done subtly so you do not appear to be bragging. Evidence of the speaker's competence can often be more appropriately presented by another person; the speaker may be introduced by someone who is already perceived by the audience as credible. The introducer then serves as a sponsor who builds up the speaker so that the audience perceives him or her as competent also. If there is no third party available to introduce you, you can tactfully indicate your credentials for talking about the issue. In discussing whether campus police officers should wear firearms, one of our students used the following strategy to mention his speaking credentials:

> I suppose some of you can recall the incident last month when a student stole a police car, as a prank. The campus police officer did not see it as a prank and fired a shot at the fleeing vehicle, just missing the driver's head. Fortunately no one was injured and the vehicle was abandoned.
> The student who took the police car is a good friend of mine, and the incident shook us both up. It caused me to spend a lot of time looking into the issue of whether campus police officers should carry firearms.

Conversational Style

There is no such thing as one perfect style of speech delivery, an ideal form into which every speaker should be molded. Each speaker is different; each subject and special purpose, audience, and occasion is different; and all may be combined in an infinite number of ways. In the eighteenth and nineteenth centuries, speakers tried to be great orators. They viewed the speech as a performance, rather than as a shared communication. This attitude won't go over with today's listeners. They prefer to be spoken *with,* not *at,* and they are quick to label as "phony" anyone who "comes on too strong." The speaker who employs the conversational mode, enlarged to meet the needs of the setting and the occasion, is rated as significantly more personable and trustworthy than one who is overly dramatic.[2] It may be helpful, in fact, for you to think of public speaking as an enlarged conversation. In a good conversation, the participants are interested in the subject and reveal their interest through direct, spontaneous, animated, and emphatic delivery styles.

Strive for a conversational tone.

Consider the contrast between the following two speeches. First, Thomas Henry Huxley, a nineteenth century scientist famous for his defense of Charles Darwin's theory on the *Origin of Species,* introduces his sixth lecture to an audience of workers and, second, our rewrite of that introduction in today's more conversational style:

> In the preceding five lectures I have endeavored to give you an account of those facts, and of those reasonings from fact, which form the data upon which all theories regarding the causes of the phenomena of organic nature must be based. And, although I have had frequent occasion to quote Mr. Darwin—as all persons hereafter, in speaking upon these subjects, will have occasion to quote his famous book on the *Origin of Species*—you must yet remember that, wherever I have quoted him, it has not yet been upon theoretical points, or for statements in any way connected with his particular speculations, but on matters of fact, brought forward by himself, or collected by himself and which appear incidentally in his book. If a man *will* make a book, professing to discuss a single question, an encyclopedia, I cannot help it.
>
> Now having had an opportunity of considering in this sort of way the different statements bearing upon all theories whatsoever, I have to lay before you, as fairly as I can, what is Mr. Darwin's view of the matter and what position his theories hold, when judged by the principles which I have previously laid down, as deciding our judgments upon all theories and hypotheses.[3]

The same subject might be introduced as follows today:

If you will recall in the past several lectures we've been discussing some of the facts reported by Charles Darwin in his book on the *Origin of Species.* We pointed out, for instance, that in the relatively isolated Galápagos Islands he noted several varieties of similar animal species. However, we haven't talked about how all these facts fit together. How they all make sense. That's what we're about to do tonight. Tonight we consider how Darwin's theory explains the facts we've been discussing.

The second passage is less formal and uses more understandable language. In any speech, you must take into account and adjust to the physical and psychological aspects of the setting and the occasion. The size of the room, the presence or absence of a speaker's stand, whether you are using a microphone, the size of the audience and the seating arrangement—all are factors dictating your decisions about delivery. Also important are psychological motivating factors, such as the occasion that brings the group together, the mood projected by the surroundings, and the motivations of the listeners. Any professor will tell you that addressing a class of students who are required to take a course presents a very different challenge from one in which the students have elected to take the course out of interest.

> The passions are the only orators who always convince. They have a kind of natural art with infallible rules; and the most untutored man with passion is more persuasive than the most eloquent without.
>
> *La Rochefoucauld*

Communicative Thrust

Some general guidelines can be used to promote a sense of conversation in any speech setting. The speaker should show a strong desire to talk with *this* audience about *this* subject—a communicative thrust. The speech situation is not like delivering a newspaper—toss it on the porch and leave. Nor is it like serving a hamburger—set it in front of the customer and go away. The speaker goes the next step to coax listeners to "read—it's interesting," or "eat—it's good for you!" then observes with interest how they like it so she or he can improve the product on the spot or in the future.

Focus on Ideas

If you can successfully get into the ideas you are presenting, a conversational delivery style will naturally accompany this involvement in the idea. When you are talking to your friends about the wisdom (or folly) of using nuclear power, you don't worry about whether or not to bang your fist on the table; you do it naturally to emphasize a point. Similarly, when you focus on ideas in a speech, you will find that your means of expressing those ideas will flow naturally. Your instructor, of course, will point out elements of delivery to enhance the effectiveness of this natural style. However, if you can achieve a natural mode of expression you will be over the biggest hurdle in learning effective delivery techniques.

Directness

When you speak, your delivery should be physically direct. During the preparation phase, you have chosen a subject of interest to a particular audience and you have used language that is direct, including personal pronouns and active verbs. You have chosen illustrations and supporting materials that will appeal to this audience. Now, don't "blow it" by looking out the window or at your notes. Look directly at your audience and make good use of eye contact and facial animation to show that you believe what you are saying. Physical and vocal animation show interest and generate enthusiasm.

The Speaker as a Visual Aid

You yourself can be a visual aid to provide punctuation and emphasis. In speech-making, facial expression, gestures, walking, pauses, and variations in pitch, rate, and volume are used to focus and refocus the listener's attention. They take the place of commas, exclamation points, paragraphs and underlining, which direct the reader of a written text.

> The world is already full of speakers who are too busy to prepare their speeches properly, and the world would be better off if they were also too busy to give them.
>
> *William Norwood Brigance*

Spontaneity

Spontaneous expression gives the impression that the idea is being formed at the time the words are spoken. *Spontaneous* and *rehearsed* might seem to be contradictory terms, but in reality you can seem relaxed and spontaneous in a public-speaking situation *only* if you have the confidence that comes through preparation. You should rehearse the speech until the ideas are thoroughly in mind, using slightly different wording each time. When the time comes to deliver the speech, you can then virtually go on automatic pilot so far as the ideas and the order of the speech are concerned. Then it becomes important to show fresh enthusiasm for the subject, remembering the interest that caused you to speak about it in the beginning. Just as it does in a conversation, an animated, emphatic style of speech will demonstrate your interest in the subject and arouse the audience.

Delivering a public speech can be compared to hosting a party. If you invite people to your home, you may feel a little nervous about whether the house is thoroughly clean, the food is all right, and the guests will hit it off with each other. But you wouldn't hide in a corner or stand looking out the window while your guests are there. It's your party, and it's up to you to make it a success. Then after everyone's gone and you look back on a successful evening, you feel good about it, and you're motivated to clean up and look forward to giving another party. You may be surprised to discover that giving a speech can give you the same sense of pleasure and a desire to repeat the experience.

Modes of Delivery

The speaker must choose among the several modes of delivering a speech: extemporaneous, manuscript, impromptu, and memorized. Although extemporaneous delivery is preferable in most speech circumstances, you will find one of the other modes useful in some situations.

Extemporaneous

In the extemporaneous mode of delivery, the speech structure is thoroughly prepared in advance, but the greater part of the wording of the speech is created as the speech is being delivered. The speaker may use notes, but only to remind him or her of the main points of the outline, or to provide an exact quotation or set of figures.

The extemporaneous speech has certain advantages, including:

1. Extemporaneous speech is carefully prepared, organized, and rehearsed, so the speaker can maintain direct eye contact.
2. No attempt is made to memorize exact wording, so it is largely spontaneous.
3. With only a note card or two in your hand, you are free to move about and interact with the audience.
4. An extemporaneous speech shows more of the elements of good conversational style than does any other mode of delivery. Although you have practiced the speech earlier, you will be using your own words as you do in conversation. These natural phrasings and rhythms are easily understood by an audience.
5. In speaking extemporaneously, you can adjust to the speech situation—you can vary the length of the talk, for example, by cutting out a subpoint or adding an example or two.

Disadvantages

The extemporaneous speech has these possible disadvantages:

1. The speaker may occasionally search for words and choose language that is not very precise.
2. The speaker may develop a particular point more than was intended, thus deviating from the planned outline and creating time problems.
3. If the speech must be repeated, some variations will occur from one presentation to the next.
4. An insecure speaker may overuse notes.

Preparing for Extemporaneous Delivery

The extemporaneous mode of delivery is favored for most speech situations; it provides the best compromise between the stilted artificiality of a rigidly learned talk and the desperate groping for something to say that can characterize impromptu speaking. You will be most successful in *conversing* with your audience extemporaneously if you follow these procedures in preparing and delivering your speech:

1. Prepare the speech itself thoroughly. Careful attention to a logical succession of ideas will make the points you wish to make easier for you to remember and easier for your audience to remember also.
2. An oral style of speech composition will highlight a direct relationship between you and the audience. These characteristics of oral style make ideas clearer the first (and only) time the audience hears them, and they have greater effect by making the audience feel personally involved: shorter, simpler sentences; statistics that are rounded off; words with fewer syllables; more personal pronouns; more rhetorical questions; and fragmentary sentences.

> Delivery, I say, has the sole and supreme power in oratory; without it a speaker of the highest mental capacity can be held in no esteem; while one of moderate abilities, with this qualification, may surpass even those of the highest talent.
>
> *Cicero,* De Oratore

3. Rehearse many times, using the following guidelines:
   a. Rehearse *aloud*, not silently.
   b. Practice under conditions that approximate the speech setting.
   c. Many short practice sessions over a period of several days are better than one or two long sessions because your speech needs time to "jell."
   d. For the early practice sessions, use your speech outline. Read through your outline once or twice before you begin, then put your outline away. Go through the entire speech several times without stopping, checking the outline from time to time to see if you are leaving out any important points. Polish a particularly troublesome section if necessary; then go back to delivering the speech from start to finish. Allow the exact wordings to vary, but if you come upon a way of expressing a thought that you particularly like, note that wording and use it again next time. Plan a beginning and an ending sentence that you will virtually memorize, still allowing other wording to vary.
4. After the first two or three times you talk it through, time your speech. Add, delete, or rearrange if necessary to stay within your time limit. Some say, "The best speeches are those that have good beginnings and good endings—close together."
5. Printing the key phrases that form the bare bones outline of your speech clearly on note cards is an effective way to prepare your speaking notes. You may also write out quotations or materials that have to be stated exactly in their entirety.
6. Continue to practice daily, using the speaking notes you have prepared. Three-by-five cards are not bulky or noisy; they can be held in the palm of your hand and brought to eye level if you need to refer to them. Your notes should be unobtrusive, but don't try to hide them.

If you can move on to the next step, that of discarding your notes entirely, you will find that this gives you a tremendous psychological advantage with your audience. And after all, if you want your audience to remember these few key points, you should be able to remember them also.

When you speak extemporaneously, you may experience a few "ums" and "ahs," but your own speech personality is allowed to come through. If you practice a lot, it is unlikely that you will forget large important sections of your speech, and you will gain the ability to respond to feedback from your audience.

Manuscript

When reading from a manuscript, the speech is completely written out in advance and read to the audience. Even when the speech is to be delivered extemporaneously, you may read a quotation or a short passage to illustrate a point within the speech. Techniques for such oral reading are discussed in the Appendix.

Advantages

Some advantages of reading your speech from a manuscript are:

1. You can select words judiciously and rework and polish your speech, perhaps with the help of others.
2. You do not have to worry about forgetting the ideas or stumbling over the words, because the script is right there in front of you.
3. Some situations call for exact wording or adherence to time limits. If the president of the United States is delivering a major address, an incorrect word or phrase might lead to serious repercussions; if a scientist is reporting technical data, she or he needs to be accurate; if an address is being given on radio or TV, it must not run over or under the time allotted.
4. It is possible to distribute copies of the address, for example to news editors and reporters.

Disadvantages

Some of the disadvantages of reading your speech are:

1. The word-for-word approach limits flexibility and spontaneous adaptation to feedback. You may be reading and notice that several audience members appear puzzled. If you have practiced delivering the written text only, you may find it difficult to add information that clarifies the material.
2. Many people do not read well, causing their delivery to be stiff and mechanical.
3. Unless you are skillful as a reader and very familiar with the material, eye contact may be inhibited, and this violates the principle of directness. When speakers read to the manuscript rather than to the audience, listeners often wonder why they came to hear the speech instead of writing for a copy of it.
4. Movement and gesture is inhibited; if you place the manuscript on a stationary lectern, you can scarcely move around at all.
5. It takes a lot of time to write a speech completely, to polish and rework it to be sure it is in oral style. The time spent writing the speech might be better spent in repeated oral rehearsal of an extemporaneous speech.

Delivery Techniques for Manuscripts

For the occasions when the public speaker does use the manuscript mode of delivery, the following techniques will prove helpful. Realize, too, that even if your entire speech is not written out, you may apply the techniques of manuscript reading in those parts of a speech where quoted material is being used.

1. The script should look good to the audience, not be tattered or folded, and should be in a rigid folder. It should be typed neatly, double- or triple-spaced, with no inked-in corrections, so it will be as legible as possible. You may wish to highlight certain portions, but take care not to clutter up your manuscript. *Number the pages.* A quotation or short passage to be included in an extemporaneous speech should be typed or clearly printed on a note card.
2. Practice reading your script aloud *many* times. Reword any awkward phrases and note how long it takes to read aloud. Make necessary changes, retype, then do the bulk of your practicing from the final draft. Don't retype at the last minute so that your eye doesn't know where to find things.
3. If you plan to use a lectern when you speak, use one when you practice. Using a speaker's stand is the usual way to deliver a manuscript speech, but if the pages are firmly clipped into a rigid folder, it is possible to hold it in your hand, and you might want to do so in order to be freer to gesture and to move.
4. Work for eye contact as you read. Practice until you are so familiar with the speech that you can look at the audience *most* of the time. But do not go that next step and attempt to memorize it. Hold the note card or script (in its rigid folder) about chest high, so you do not have to bob your head up and down to maintain eye contact.
5. Work for an alert, dynamic, enthusiastic delivery. Practice using appropriate gestures, especially head and upper body movements and facial animation.
6. Pay attention to vocal aspects of your delivery. Vary your vocal pattern, and especially make good use of pauses for attention and emphasis. Advertisers use white space to make their printed copy stand out, and speakers should remember to use pauses to emphasize the ideas when reading. Pauses are especially important to set off main divisions of a speech and to highlight major points.

Jack Valenti, president of the Motion Picture Association of America and a prominent former speech writer for President Lyndon B. Johnson, offers important advice for drafting and delivering a speech manuscript. He recommends working on the *thought* to be conveyed, the *theme* of the speech, and the *mood* to be expressed.[4]

> It usually takes more than three weeks to prepare a good impromptu speech.
>
> *Mark Twain*

Impromptu

When speaking impromptu, the speaker has little if any advance notice of or time for preparation and must speak off-the-cuff, relying on personal knowledge and speaking skills to get him or her through.

Advantages

The only advantage of speaking impromptu is spontaneity and, of course, the preparation time you save.

Disadvantages

Disadvantages of impromptu speaking include:

1. You may panic and freeze entirely, or at best have a halting delivery.
2. You may ramble and repeat yourself in a disorganized way.
3. You may make inappropriate statements or express immature judgments. (You may be surprised at what you hear yourself saying!)

Impromptu is less a mode of delivery than it is a method of dealing with a crisis situation. Never *plan* to speak impromptu!

However, you might be called upon to speak impromptu (1) in a class, for information, or to evaluate the previous speaker; (2) at a meeting, to share your expertise on a particular issue; (3) in an interview, where every question you answer requires a short impromptu speech.

Practicing giving impromptu speeches will help you to gain confidence in your ability to maintain control and achieve your speech purpose under fire.

Advice about Speaking Impromptu

We recommend the following for dealing with an impromptu situation:

1. Prevention is your best defense. Experienced public speakers (like Mark Twain was) often are called upon to say a few words. Follow their example and have your thoughts in order on possible topics so you are not caught entirely unprepared.
2. Don't panic. Call on everything you know about speaking in public. Go through all the steps of speech preparation and organization we've discussed so far, but do it *quickly!*
3. If you have even a few minutes, jot down some notes before you speak.
4. Quickly identify a main thesis and one or two relevant supporting ideas.
5. Write a brief outline and prepare an attention getting introduction and a conclusion.

6. Mentally go over the outline until it is time to speak.
7. Stick to the subject. Don't ramble, but try for fluency.
8. Be brief. You cannot possibly cover all aspects, so pick a couple of the most important ones, then present your conclusion.

Memorized

The memorized speech is first written out, then memorized word for word. This style of delivery was used exclusively by Greek orators, by preachers, and speakers/performers on the Chautauqua circuit in the early 1900s in America. Today the mode is seldom used; more often the speaker will memorize only the outline and perhaps a line or two at the beginning and at the end of the speech.

Advantages

We list here some of the advantages of using the memorized speech.

1. Just as with the manuscript speech, the memorized speech benefits from your careful choice of language and polishing of style.
2. You can move about more readily and can have total eye contact.

Disadvantages

Some of the disadvantages of memorizing a speech are:

1. The beginning speaker may seize on this technique as an answer to his or her worry about stumbling and forgetting what comes next. But the truth is that only a *very* skillful and experienced speaker can pull it off and make it sound natural. If you are concentrating on remembering, you are not concentrating on communicating ideas. Reciting a canned speech may cause you to speak in a choppy, mechanical way.
2. Preparation requires a great deal of time (you do have other classes to prepare for also), and even then, you can draw a blank on one word and be stuck completely.
3. You have no flexibility to be able to adapt to changing conditions. If you deviate at all, the whole speech could collapse.

Special Uses

There are, however, some occasions when a memorized speech will do very well. In certain kinds of short ceremonial speeches and occasional addresses, such as speeches of presentation and acceptance of awards and honors, eulogies and commendations, speeches of welcome and farewell, the speaker wants to sound sincere and spontaneous, yet give careful attention to choice of language.

> Public speaking is an audience participation event; if it weren't, it would be private speaking.
>
> *Anonymous*

Advice about Preparing for Memorized Delivery

1. Write out your speech as you would a manuscript speech.
2. Allow additional time to memorize the speech.
3. Practice giving the speech aloud until it is as familiar as a favorite song. Learn it well enough that one idea naturally suggests the next one in your mind.

Using Feedback

During the rehearsal phase of your speech, your best approach to feedback is better described as "feedforward." Anticipate and plan for contingencies, so you are not stunned by them when they occur. Decide what you consider to be a minimum acceptance ratio. This means that you cannot expect to win total acceptance of everything you say, so you must decide what points are absolutely necessary for the audience to understand and accept if your speech is to be successful. Then plan ahead for extra proofs or illustrations to bolster those points if you observe that your audience is not accepting them.

Look for general reactions in your audience, not just those of one or two listeners. Nonverbal cues that indicate a favorable response from the audience include smiles, nodding of heads, eye contact, comfortably erect posture, and note-taking. Unfavorable cues from the audience include frowns, shaking of heads, looking around at others, blank stares, slouching posture, restless shifting movement, playing with objects or perhaps rubbing the chin or hair, and doodling.[5]

If the feedback cues you receive are positive, keep up the good work, but if you observe negative feedback cues, you can conclude that some of the following are true:

1. Your audience is not interested, does not understand, or is opposed to a point or a subpoint you are presenting. You might add anecdotes to spark interest, examples and comparisons to clarify, or additional arguments or evidence to convince.
2. Audience responses can arise from factors outside the speaker or the speech, such as the time or the temperature. As we mentioned earlier, Murphy's Law says that, "If anything can go wrong, it will." A number of things can go wrong when you are a public speaker. The meeting might be running late, perhaps because the preceding speakers exceeded their allotted time. A previous speaker could have covered all or part of what you planned to say. If you are outside, it

may start to rain, or if you are inside, the air conditioning may cease to function. Or you may instantly lose your listeners' concentration when it is announced that lunch is now being served.

If something like any of these occurs, you must be ready to delete a whole section or several small parts of your speech, being careful not to weaken your thesis. You might say, "Because the hour is late, I'll just summarize this point." Your ability to deal with such contingencies will increase with experience, but planning ahead will help you to maintain fluency while you are coping.[6]

If, on the other hand, you observe too little feedback from the audience, you can invite it by asking a rhetorical question such as, "Don't you agree that this situation is one that demands action?"

By observing and responding to audience feedback, the speaker demonstrates continual concern for message transmission and an awareness of the circular (transactional) nature of speech communication. The ability to project ourselves into the reactions of others is called empathy, a sensitivity to other people's emotions and a vicarious living of other people's experiences. How do your mouth and throat feel when someone describes how it feels to suck on a lemon, or how does your skin feel when there is mention of basking in the hot sun on a Hawaiian beach? These reactions are largely involuntary. You as a speaker must first empathize with the ideas and images in your speech, thus suggesting the sensations you invite your audience to share with you. You can transmit ideas and suggest emotional reactions to the audience by your voice and by nonverbal means of communication.

Vocal Aspects of Delivery

Breath support is performed mainly by the diaphragm, a muscular membrane that forms a partition between the lungs and the abdomen, aided by the chest muscles. Control of the diaphragm is essential to speech, because it is by gradual, controlled relaxation of this muscle that a steady stream of air is directed over the vocal folds, producing the voice.

Four variable aspects of the voice are of importance to the speaker: pitch, quality, force, and rate. Add to these the necessity of proper pronunciation and of articulation—the function performed by the articulators, the lips, teeth, tongue, and hard and soft palates.

There is no index of character so sure as the voice.

Benjamin Disraeli

Practicing with a tape recorder can help a speaker improve voice quality, force, pitch, or rate.

Pitch

The pitch of a sound is how high or low it is on the musical scale. The natural pitch of a person's voice is largely determined by the length and thickness of the vocal folds; men generally have lower-pitched voices than women because men's vocal folds are longer and thicker.

Tense vocal folds can affect pitch by forcing it higher. An audience usually perceives raised pitch as tension on the part of the speaker and interprets it as lack of poise and confidence. Yawning or swallowing can help relax your vocal cords.

You should use a wide range of pitch when you speak and not speak only in a monotone. Glides between pitches, called inflection, produce melody and cadence; these changes in pitch indicate your emotional involvement with the words you speak and your interest in your subject and in your listeners.

Quality

To the basic pitch of the voice are added overtones, which are produced in the resonating cavities. Different sizes and shapes of resonating chambers cause differences in the quality of the sound. For example, a note played on a violin differs in quality from the same note played on a cello; the size and shape of the instrument are important factors in determining how the note will sound. The distinctive characteristics of a voice, which cause it to be identifiable among all other voices, are produced by the size and shape of the pharynx, the mouth, the nose, and the sinuses. A voice has good vocal quality when it is *not* harsh, husky, hoarse, breathy, shrill, strident, thin, nasal, or denasal (lacking in nasal resonance—as when you have a cold). A rich, resonant voice is a great asset to a public speaker; this is best achieved by maintaining adequate breath support and speaking with a relaxed throat. Normally when we speak, we hear the sounds that others hear, those that pass through the air as sound waves and strike our eardrums; we also hear the vibrations conducted through the bones of the head. And the combination of the two gives us an erroneous impression of how our voices sound to others. Listening to yourself on tape for the first time can be a startling experience!

Volume and Intensity

The loudness or softness of a speaker's voice and the energy with which it is projected is determined by the amount of air supporting the tone and the force with which it is exhaled.

Volume

Many beginning speakers do not support the tone sufficiently and thus do not provide enough volume. If you do not speak loudly enough to be heard, communication with the audience is impossible from the outset. Listeners soon tire of straining to hear, and they tune out. Speaking too loudly for the room or place can also interfere with the listeners' concentration; they feel that they are being intruded on psychologically. Be alert to competing sounds and stimuli, and adjust to be sure that you speak above competing noise.

If you need amplification to be heard—as in a large auditorium—place the microphone at about the same height as your mouth, adjusting it before you begin to speak. Stand about ten to eighteen inches away from the microphone, and do not lean forward.

Intensity

Intensity refers to the amount of energy the speaker expends in projecting sounds, apart from the volume being used. Try speaking in a whisper and projecting it to someone across the room. You will find that you expend just as much energy as if you were shouting.

Emphasis

The public speaker uses the principle of emphasis to stress words or phrases, vocally highlighting or underscoring important ideas. Discover how useful this technique can be by reading the following sentence four times, emphasizing a different word each time, and noting the difference in meaning that results: "This pizza is quite good."

It is important to use a variety of intensity, with major emphasis reserved for major ideas. If everything is treated equally, then nothing stands out as being important. You should never risk losing attention by failing to highlight and signpost with vocal emphasis.

Rate

Rate—how fast or how slowly the speaker speaks—consists of the number of words per minute, and the number and length of pauses used. The best rate to use will vary between speakers and is dependent on how simple or how complex the material is, but generally speaking, you should not go so fast that your audience gets lost, nor so slowly that everyone in the audience becomes bored.

If your speech is to have any lasting effect you must help your listeners to remember what you say. Complex ideas when presented slowly are easier to retain than when presented rapidly.[7] However, "rapidly" is a relative term; the speaker whose rate is *very* slow will be perceived as less competent. Listeners have been found to respond fairly well to rates between 150 and 225 words per minute, preferring about 175 words per minute.[8] Speaking to a large audience tends to require a slower rate, as does any situation in which there is interference with hearing. Varying your rate is important to maintain audience interest, and a change of pace on a given point will make that point stand out. Billy Sunday, a turn-of-the-century revivalist, was particularly good at this, and a present-day evangelist, Billy Graham, is equally as effective in changing speaking rates to emphasize points.

Pause

An important factor in speech rate is the use of pauses to separate the introduction, body, and conclusion of a speech, and to set off main points. Avoid filling these pauses with "er . . . . , ah . . . . , um . . . ." or other examples of hesitancy and lack of fluency; such fillers are awkward and distracting to the listener. Appropriate phrasing (grouping of the words) makes your speech more listenable. If a speech contains too few or too many pauses, the speaker sounds hurried or uncertain.

Pauses will vary the rate. They also draw attention to and emphasize the ideas given before and after the pause. In this way you can verbalize the form of your outline so it stands out for your audience. Particularly effective is a pause before you begin and after you conclude the speech; such pauses emphasize the very important opening and closing points you wish to make.

Two final aspects of vocal delivery—articulation (or enunciation) and pronunciation—take on importance primarily if they are badly done.

First among the evidences of an education I name correctness and precision in the use of the mother tongue.

Nicholas Murray Butler

> Higgins: Remember that you are a human being with a soul and the divine gift of articulate speech: that your native language is the language of Shakespeare and Milton and the Bible; and don't sit there crooning like a bilious pigeon.
>
> *George Bernard Shaw*, Pygmalion

Articulation

Articulation is the distinct and accurate formation of consonant and vowel sounds, using the lips, teeth, tongue, and hard and soft palates. Poor articulation leaves out sounds ("goin'," "libary"), distorts them (most often by slurring them together), substitutes one sound for another ("git," "jist," "fer," "nucular"), and occasionally adds sounds ("athaletic"). Poor articulation makes a speaker more difficult to understand, affecting both attention and comprehension, and conveys an impression of incompetence and lack of education. Overprecise articulation calls attention to itself and is equally inappropriate, but it is far more common for beginning speakers to be "lip lazy." If you want to improve your articulation, you can do so by noticing good and bad examples in others and listening to your own daily speech, not just when you are speaking in public. Then concentrate on breaking your bad habits and establishing new ones.

The famous Greek orator Demosthenes (384–322 B.C.) is said to have overcome a speech defect by long hours of practice by the seashore. He filled his mouth with pebbles, then delivered his speech so it could be heard and understood over the roar of the ocean's waves. He considered this effort at improvement to be absolutely essential to his success as a public speaker. "When asked what was the most important element in oratory, he replied 'Delivery.' And what the second? 'Delivery,' and the third? 'Delivery.' "[9]

Pronunciation

Articulation refers to the speaker's skill in forming sounds accurately, but pronunciation is a matter of knowing how the sounds and stresses should be combined to say the word correctly.

Correct pronunciation is determined by the accepted standard of the educated people of that area. If the speaker deviates from that standard, his or her credibility might be affected in two ways: (1) The audience may not grasp the meaning of a mispronounced word; and (2) research shows that listeners perceive a speaker who uses the "general American" dialect to be more intelligent than one who speaks with an accent, even by listeners who themselves speak in a regional dialect.[10]

Other research indicates that listeners react more favorably to a message that is delivered in the same dialect as that spoken by the listeners.[11] Southerners enjoyed saying in 1976 that Jimmy Carter was the first president in a long time who didn't speak with an accent. Dialects can divide people, so if you speak with an accent, try to avoid the most extreme aspects of that dialect when speaking to people who do not share your regional background.

Names of persons should be pronounced as they are pronounced by the possessors of that name, and names of places as they are pronounced by its inhabitants.

Nonverbal Aspects of Delivery

We have been discussing the vocal elements of delivery: pitch, quality, volume, intensity, rate, articulation, and pronunciation. Studies show that under some circumstances listeners place more than five times as much (65 to 90 percent) credence on nonverbal cues (including these vocal characteristics) as on the content of the verbal message itself.[12] The speaker who seeks to communicate ideas defeats his or her purpose if the vocal presentation of the speech is marred by speaking too fast or not loud enough, or by using unpleasant voice quality, sloppy articulation, or mispronounced words.

Nonverbal behavior is used to make judgments about another person every second you are with that person, but verbal behavior is judged only when the person is actually talking. This principle operates especially in the formation of a first impression, and a positive first impression is particularly important in the speech setting because this specific speech occasion is often the only time you and these particular listeners may interact. A high percentage of this process goes on below the level of conscious awareness, with nonverbal and verbal patterns blending in complex patterns of message exchanges. The excitement created by Michael Jackson's video performance "Black and White" is a dramatic example of the dynamic interaction of verbal and nonverbal elements to create a total impression.

To become a better public speaker, you must make an effort to become aware of your nonverbal processing, in order to be alert to feedback from listeners and to be in better control of the cues you display to others.

Our words express the content level of communication; thoughts, ideas, and reasoning. The nonverbal elements of communication express our feelings and attitudes toward ourselves, the subject, the listeners, and what we hope to accomplish by the presentation. Remember that your audience will tend to mirror you. If you show that you have confidence in yourself, the listeners will recognize you as being credible, and if you show enthusiasm, they will react with interest toward you and your subject. You should expect to feel some nervousness and excitement, feelings that are natural and even desirable. Your goal should be to channel and control this nervous energy so that your nonverbal cues are consistent with and enhance the effectiveness of your verbal message. Delivery is not just the frosting on the cake, but a major factor in whether your message is accepted or not. Your delivery strategies should work to establish you as competent, powerful, dynamic, and trustworthy.

> Suit the action to the word, the word to the action.
>
> William Shakespeare, *Hamlet*

Your audience wants to feel comfortable and assured that your speech will be a success; they don't want to have to worry about you. An overt display of anxiety is counterproductive to your personal force, or credibility. This personal force is very important to you as a speaker. Without it you might as well distribute copies of your speech and sit down. A speaker must both know and give the appearance of knowing. Powerful people speak confidently, not fearfully. Dynamic people speak with enthusiasm and force, not dully and haltingly; they gesture freely and move the rest of the body naturally and effectively. People do not trust someone who doesn't look them in the eye. If we set out to give a speech but show no interest in communicating, the audience tends to reject the message and to believe the nonverbal cues. Research has established a strong connection between these aspects of delivery, credibility, and persuasiveness.[13]

We have discussed the elements of the voice in the preceding section: resonance, pitch, rate, volume, and the effects of pauses and vocalized pauses such as "um. . . ." and "er. . . ." Research shows that how you say and emphasize each word can affect both the meaning of the words and the interpersonal perception of the speaker by the audience.[14] As was pointed out previously, each answer in an interview constitutes a short public speech. A survey of a number of different employers revealed a high degree of agreement about the intelligence, competence, self-assurance, and agreeableness of potential employees based on audiotaped job interviews.

Still other research points out that posture and gesture are critical in communicating information about emotional states and relationships.[15] Body language complements the verbal meaning and reveals the degree to which the speaker is interested or indifferent toward the audience, the topic, and the communication situation.

Posture

When you speak you should stand up straight, not rigidly, with the weight equally distributed on both feet. Don't shift weight from one foot to the other, cross and uncross legs, or lean on a desk or podium. You should take time to assume a comfortable position before you start speaking and maintain this alert and interested stance while you pause after your speech. Don't at any time drape yourself over the lectern or attempt to hide behind it. Your posture should indicate stability and assurance. You should be poised but not stiff, relaxed but not sloppy.

Facial Expression

The Mehrabian research cited earlier pointed out that 55 percent of the impact of a face-to-face spoken message results from facial expression.[16] There has been a great deal of recent interest in this field of bodily action, called variously "action communication," "action language," "body language," and "nonverbal communication." Ray L. Birdwhistell, for instance, reports that the human face may be capable of as many as 250,000 different expressions.[17] Further research has established that some of these facial expressions are universally recognized as representing particular emotions. New Guinea natives were able to match narrative stories with pictures of Caucasian faces portraying anger, disgust, contempt, surprise, happiness, determination, and fear; and American college students were highly accurate in judging these emotions shown in pictures of New Guinea natives.[18]

Eye Contact

Eye contact is especially important to the public speaker. Direct and intense eye contact (1) reveals how the speaker feels about himself or herself and the audience; (2) supplements the verbal content to make the meaning clearer and more readily accepted; and (3) commands the audience's attention by establishing a visual bonding.

A speaker who fails to maintain good eye contact appears aloof and untrustworthy, and also sacrifices the opportunity to observe and profit from feedback.[19] It is important that eye contact be made with first one and then another section of the audience so that listeners in all areas of the room feel personally addressed. The speaker must also remember not to overuse notes or fail to maintain strong eye contact while reading from a manuscript.

Bodily Action

Good bodily action is characterized by three qualities: (1) it does not call attention to itself; (2) it fits the mood and content of the message so that it reinforces the speaker's ideas; and (3) it appears natural and spontaneous.

It's often difficult to convince a beginning speaker of this. You may say, "I never know what to do with my hands. How can I use natural gestures when I feel unnatural?" This is a good question. Your gestures and bodily movements should be those you would use naturally when expressing emotions and thoughts—*if you weren't holding back*. You may have to make a conscious effort to bring them back in at first. Then when you are more experienced, gestures and movement will come more easily.

Gestures

Gestures consist of purposeful movements of the head, shoulders, arms, hands, or some other part of the body. Gestures should be vigorous and definite, to show conviction and enthusiasm; they should be full and varied, rather than partial and repetitious; and generally, they should be made larger for larger audiences. The hands and arms should be about waist-to-chest high when used in gesturing.

Walking

Walking is a very effective way to stress an important idea. It's essential that your walk appear to be purposeful and intentional, not just a random shift of position. Walking about three steps usually works best, moving at a shallow angle toward your audience. You should start far enough back on the platform to allow yourself space to make several of these walks without finding yourself in the laps of listeners in the front row. Too much movement can work against you, and continuous pacing back and forth will be distracting. As with any other form of emphasis, walking should be saved for major points because if everything is stressed, then everything appears to be of the same importance. The walk from your seat to the speaker's stand will be among your most important; you should appear confident and eager to speak, not reluctant and as if you were about to be executed. Pause before you begin, then move out from behind the lectern. Use the lectern as a point of departure, not as a barrier to hide behind. When you have concluded the speech, maintain your poise and control as you walk calmly to your seat.

Timing is very important when walking or gesturing, the movement should be on or slightly before the point it reinforces. In some process descriptions, the movement *is* the message, such as a demonstration of judo or a speech explaining a new dance step. The definition of gestures as "purposeful movements" points up the importance of avoiding nervous, random movement that does not reinforce the speaker's ideas, but rather distracts the listeners from paying attention to those ideas.

There is ample research evidence attesting to how useful bodily action is to the speaker. For instance, John E. Baird, Jr. found that the speaker who gestures is perceived as more dynamic and as a leader.[20] Ray Ehrensberger demonstrated that a statement accompanied by a gesture is better remembered than the same statement without the gesture.[21]

Use of Space

The physical space between the speaker and the audience results in both a physical distance and a psychological distance between them. If the speaker is too far away, the audience remains unengaged, and if the speaker is too close, listeners feel uncomfortable. Be aware of such factors as the seating arrangement of the room in which you are speaking and any physical barriers between you and your audience, such as a lectern or an orchestra pit between the stage and the seats. The distance between members of the audience affects the cohesiveness of their reactions also; if a small number of people are scattered in a large room, take time before you begin to have them gather together at the front of the room.

Clothing and Personal Appearance

Clothing, furniture, or architectural elements in the surroundings may be used, intentionally or unintentionally, to communicate feelings and ideas. The way in which we decorate our physical territories—our houses, cars, and offices—signals things about ourselves, and the speaker should try to make the speech stage enhance him or her.[22]

Clothing and grooming, in particular, send nonverbal signals. In the business setting they are often viewed as a yardstick of attitudes toward work. A conservatively dressed woman is more likely to be taken seriously as a professional colleague, and people who dress well are perceived to be more interested in advancing up the corporate ladder.[23]

Your attention to clothing and appearance for a performance occasion not only sends a signal to your listeners, but it affects your own attitude as well. Joe Paterno has been head football coach at Penn State for more than twenty years, and his won-lost record there is truly impressive. While it should be clear that his teams have not relied on appearance alone, he does insist that his players adhere to strict standards of appearance and behavior. Coach Paterno tells this story:

> When I was a kid growing up in Brooklyn, my high school baseball coach took me to a World Series game between the Yankees and the St. Louis Cardinals, and he said, 'I want to show you a couple of things. Take a look at the Cardinals. Take a look at their shoes.' I didn't quite know what he was driving at. Then he said, 'Now take a look at the Yankees.' Every one of their shoes was polished. He said, 'Now, it's a little thing, but the Yankees know their shoes are polished, and they know the Cardinals' aren't. I don't know whether that helps or not, but it can't hurt.' That's why things like neatness matter to me.[24]

The speaker should dress appropriately for the audience and the occasion, avoiding extreme, flashy clothes. Even in these liberal times, you would look out of place wearing sneakers and jeans when giving a speech if everyone else is in formal attire. Apparel should reinforce the speech, not distract from it. Every moment spent either in admiring or disapproving the speaker's appearance is a moment when the listener is not giving full attention to what is being said.

Delivery for Radio and TV

The electronic media, radio and television, have become an accepted part of our daily life. Today's high school graduates have spent more hours watching television than they have spent in school, and Americans in general own more television sets than they do refrigerators, automobiles, telephones, or bathtubs. All we have said, to this point, about the preparation and delivery of messages is applicable in the mediated speech setting as well as in the face-to-face setting. There are, however, some additional factors to be considered. Alistair Cooke has called television "the language of the twentieth century," and we would be remiss if we did not offer some suggestions on how you can speak that language effectively.

Because of your position or special knowledge on a subject, you have been invited to appear on radio or television. What should you know, and what do you do to get ready for the experience?

Preparation

Prepare and mark your script as discussed in the section on manuscript reading, or if the presentation is to be not from script but, rather, ad-lib, plan and organize your ideas just as you would any other extemporaneous presentation.

Find out as much as you can about the physical setting and the planned procedure. Visit the studio if possible, but if not, at least get there early on the day of your appearance. You will feel more at ease if you have had a chance to acquaint yourself with the surroundings and with the other participants.

Even an experienced public speaker can feel a little nervous the first time he or she faces a microphone or a television camera. If this happens to you, try these simple relaxation exercises while the technical crew is getting ready: yawn, stretch, and rotate your head and shoulders to release any tight muscles. If you feel you have a tense throat, a hot drink such as coffee, tea, or even hot water may help relax the vocal folds.

Prepare yourself mentally with the realization that you are here to communicate ideas and feelings to *people,* and that the microphone and the camera are simply the means for you to reach those listeners who are just on the other side of the microphone or that lens. Talk to *them* as naturally and directly as you can.

Audience Analysis

Electronically broadcast speeches may be delivered before an audience or simply over the air. If no live audience is present, then your audience will be large; but it will be small in the sense that your viewers or listeners will be individuals or very small groups. The tactics you might use if these people were all gathered together would be inappropriate here. You need to approach this audience as if you were talking to a good friend. In fact, you might ask someone to join you in the studio (out of sight of the camera, of course) and talk to him or her. Remember also that it is very easy for your audience members to change stations. These audience members may be involved in other activities (like washing dishes, reading the paper, driving) and you are competing for their attention. Take advantage of all the factors of attention, use variety in delivery, and include relatively more stories, jokes, anecdotes, than you might otherwise.

If, on the other hand, you are delivering a speech to an immediate audience and the speech also happens to be being broadcast, you should direct your speech to the immediate group. The broadcast audience will understand the situation and make allowances for differences in delivery.

Using a Microphone

The following tips may help you to use a microphone effectively:

1. Microphones are delicate and expensive, handle them carefully. Do not blow into the microphone or tap it to test if it is "live."
2. If you are using a lavaliere mike (a small microphone that is clipped to your clothing or hung around your neck on a lightweight cord), don't forget to put it on. Attach it so it isn't muffled by or rubbing against your clothing.
3. Remember to remove the microphone before you move out of the scene. Don't tear it out by the roots.
4. If the microphone is in a fixed position, like on a stand or lectern or hung from a boom, be sure to stay within its range when you are speaking. If the microphone is too high or too low for you, don't bend or stretch to it. Ask that it be adjusted.
5. Adjust your distance from the microphone to get good resonance without distortion. Speak across the microphone, not directly into it, to avoid popping "p's" and sizzling "s's."
6. When you are asked to "take a level," read from the script you will use and speak *exactly* as you will later on, in the same position and with the same volume and energy. Continue speaking until the audio engineer signals that he or she has finished adjusting the volume control of your microphone.
7. Do not make sudden, extreme changes of volume during your presentation, unless this has been planned with the sound engineer.
8. Avoid any extraneous noises—tapping a pencil, rustling papers, squeaking of a chair. Such sounds are exaggerated by the microphone and will be annoying to your listeners. Pages of your script should be quietly slid to one side.
9. You may be surprised to learn that *physical* action, such as facial expression and head and shoulder gestures, are very important even when you are speaking on radio. Your voice will mirror the muscle tone and degree of physical involvement, projecting interest and enthusiasm or the lack of it.

Television-Camera Consciousness

Here are some tips that may help you when you appear before a television camera:

1. Look *through* the camera at your imagined audience, not at other people in the room, and do not watch yourself in the monitor. The National Association of Broadcasters advises, "Remember that although you are talking to a large audience, you should pretend you are speaking to a few friends who are in their homes."[25]

2. Avoid inappropriate movements, such as swinging in your chair, large hand gestures, or bobbing your head. These movements will appear exaggerated in the small frame of the television and will distract from what you are saying.
3. Sit on the front edge of the chair, with your shoulders square and facing directly into the camera.
4. If you are standing, assume a comfortable position, and do stand still without shifting your weight.
5. If you are talking with another person on camera, do not face each other directly. Instead, you should "cheat" toward the camera by positioning yourselves close together and at about a 25-degree angle from one another. You might have noticed this use of positioning in the political debates during the 1992 elections.
6. Do not turn your head or your eyes to see the floor director who may be giving you signals. Try to pick up these directions with your peripheral vision.

Poise and Control

Present your material with the same consideration for content and organization and the same efforts for arousing and keeping the attention of your audience that you would use in any speech situation. You may find it difficult at first to do without the opportunity to respond to feedback, which is possible with a visible audience, but you will soon adjust as you gain more experience in this medium.

As we said earlier, public speech should be like enlarged conversation. This is particularly true in radio and television because the audience members are in an intimate setting in their own homes. Keep your conversational tone and fluency, while paying attention to good enunciation and to correct pronunciation. If you should make an error or a misstatement, correct it unobtrusively. Do not call attention to the error verbally or by making a face. The chances are that it will not be obvious or important unless you make it so. Keep going unless you are told to stop.

Your Appearance on Camera

What you say is always most important, but your appearance matters also, and the television camera requires some special adaptations on the part of the speaker.

Clothing

When appearing on television, choose your clothing carefully. The camera tends to add pounds to your appearance, so simple, slim lines are best, not loose or baggy. Wear something comfortable and in which you feel at ease—no too-tight collars. Avoid busy patterns, small checks, and very narrow stripes. Such fine, high contrast patterns will cause a wavy, shimmering effect when seen through the camera.

When speaking on television, visualize two or three people in their living room and speak directly *through* the camera to them.

Both women and men look attractive and professional wearing a suit, and a tie for men. (A man may find it helpful to pull the jacket down in back and sit on it, to avoid a bunching at the neck.) Women may also wear a dress or an attractive blouse outfit, but never anything fussy or overstated. Variety can often be achieved with scarves or other accessories. Jewelry should be unobtrusive, never shiny, and women should avoid dangling earrings. Lean forward to check that your necklace (or your hair) will not brush against the microphone when you change positions.

Black, white, and especially black-and-white are not good choices. They cause problems for engineers and they also tend to make you look washed out. Do not wear clothing the same shade and color as your skin or hair, or a color that will merge into the background color of the set.

Hair Style

Hair styles for both men and women should be neat and attractive, not trendy, and should be sufficiently off the face and forehead so as not to cast shadows, especially over the eyes.

> The search for effective delivery starts from a realization that vocal and physical manner are the outward form for one's beliefs, attitudes, and emotions.
>
> *Donald K. Smith*

Makeup

In some studios there may be someone to help you with makeup, but most often you are on your own. The television lights are very hot; they will wash the color out of your face and cause you to perspire, so everyone looks better with makeup. Yes, men too need at least powder and probably base. If blemish cover or beard cover are required, they should be applied first, then the foundation, or base.

Most people find that the cake style makeup, which is applied with a moist sponge, works better for the close medium of television than the heavier oil-based makeup used on stage. Base should be a shade darker than your skin for television. Spread the base evenly and smoothly, including your ears if they are exposed, your neck down into the collar line, and your forehead up into the hair line.

Women will usually add eye makeup, blush, and lipstick. Makeup should enhance your overall appearance, not call attention to itself, but most women will find that their street makeup is not enough and that evening style makeup will look better under the intense lights. The camera keys on red, green, and blue, so green and blue eyeshadow and pink shades of blush tend to be too obvious. Brown or coral shades are better.

Because the camera keys on red, even tiny skin blemishes show up, so blemish cover used under the base is often advisable for both women and men. The last item you apply is powder, to set the makeup and give a matte finish. If you have to wait around long, powder again at the last minute.

Tips for Handling Miscues

Whether your speech is being broadcast or is being delivered to an immediate audience, miscues sometimes occur. Naturally what is required depends on the miscue, but we will suggest some tactics that ought to cover most situations:

1. Be prepared. If you know what you wanted to say, you will recognize when you have said something that is in error.
2. When you have misstated something and it is important to the point being made, apologize for the error and restate the point. "Oops, that's not quite what I meant to say. What I meant to say was. . . ."
3. If the misstated point is not important, then just proceed as if nothing was in error.

4. If you completely lose your train of thought, refer to your note cards to help you recover. It's always a good idea to have some prepared remark to cover this situation. "I'll come back to that point in a minute. I did want to mention the importance of. . . ." then go to a point you know well.
5. Oftentimes no matter how much we practice a demonstration, it simply does not work as planned. Be prepared to describe what should have happened. "Well, this worked just a minute ago, but I don't have time to fix it now. Let me tell you what. . . ."

Tips for Coping with Nervousness

We present, in some detail, ways to cope with speech anxiety in chapter 2. Those tips were developed by professionals. What we present here, in their own words, are tactics students report using to cope with nervousness during the delivery of a speech.

During the Introduction

"Thought to myself—I can do it."
"I decided to look directly at people."
"Forged ahead, even though I did not feel in control."
"Imagined the people in the audience were my friends to make me feel more comfortable."
"Spoke slowly so I could stay calm."

During the Body of the Speech

"I pictured everyone being interested in what I was saying. Taking deep breaths. Thinking slow and easy."
"I forced myself to think about what came next."
"I kept looking at people knowing they would think I was scared if I didn't."
"Thought to myself, I really don't care what these people think of me. What matters is what I'm saying."

These tactics are similar to those suggested in chapter 10. However, they are somewhat unique to these students and did help these students cope with their nervousness during the delivery of their speeches.

Summary

Delivery is vital in establishing the speaker as a credible source. Audiences expect a conversational tone from speakers, and using a conversational tone often helps the audience identify with your speech purpose. Such a tone can be developed by showing you want to relate to the audience (communicative thrust), by showing directness, focusing on ideas, using yourself as a visual aid, and by conveying a sense of spontaneity. The speaker must choose an appropriate mode of delivery: extemporaneous, manuscript reading, impromptu, or memorized.

Speakers can use and elicit feedback as a very important aspect of delivery. In order to relate more effectively to an audience, you, as a speaker, should adjust your delivery to changes in the audience.

The rate, pitch, force, and quality of one's voice can be manipulated to enhance the impact of the message being delivered. You can use pauses to convey your meaning to an audience. Clear articulation and correct pronunciation are necessary attributes of the good speaker. Facial expressions, eye contact, bodily action, gestures, walking, and the use of space are important aspects of speech communication.

Radio and television are so much a part of everyday life that the likelihood is great that you will convey your ideas by way of microphone or television camera. You should develop skill in adapting to the microphone and the camera, and a knowledge of how to look good on camera, to add to the delivery techniques presented earlier in the chapter.

Sometimes things go wrong even when they are well-prepared and well-planned. We offer tips on how to handle some common problems. We also present tactics students use to cope with nervousness during a speech.

Exercises

1. Speak to someone across the room, using only a whisper and projecting so that you can be heard and understood.
2. Get together with three or four members of your class and read the list of sentences that follows. Each person should read his or her sentence with an emphasis different from that used by the preceding person so that the meaning of the sentence is changed each time it is read. (Or have each person write on a slip of paper the words *happy, angry, sad, indignant, sarcastic*; or a description of the attitude or point of view of the speaker. Then have the other members of the group guess what was being expressed.) After the readings, discuss the differences in volume, pitch, and rate used to achieve the differences.
   a. Who do you think I saw in class today?
   b. Oh, yes I'd love to go.
   c. You aren't really sure of that, are you?
   d. I've never seen such food.
   e. There are always a lot of men at the movies on Saturday night.
   f. There was the book just where I'd left it, rain-soaked and falling apart.
   g. No, I simply can't believe that's so.
   h. Who ever heard of a person doing such a thing?
   i. Oh, my dear, what have you done?
3. Identify two contingency plans for a speech you are preparing. That is, look over your speech structure and identify two points where an addition or deletion can be made if necessary, keeping in mind your minimum acceptance ratio.

4. Audiotape or videotape a presentation (perhaps a few lines out of a novel or some material written by you). Have the class comment on delivery characteristics. Repeat the reading, taking the class comments into account. Have the class comment on the effectiveness of the changes. If class time is not available, you can record and critique the reading yourself.

Assignments

1. Use gestures, movement, and facial expressions when describing a process (how to make a dress, how to give a haircut, how to repair a flat tire, how to put on makeup, how to string a tennis racket, how to swing a golf club, etc.).
2. Read aloud a passage from a novel in which there is more than one character. Differentiate between the characters by varying the rate, pitch, volume, and quality of your voice.
3. Obtain permission to visit a local TV station and observe a show being taped.

Suggested Reading

Blythin, Evan and Samovar, Larry A. *Communicating Effectively on Television.* Belmont, Calif.: Wadsworth Publishing Co., 1985.

Hyde, Stuart W. *Television and Radio Announcing.* 4th ed., Boston: Houghton Mifflin Co., 1983.

Mayer, Lyle V. *Fundamentals of Voice and Diction.* 8th ed., Dubuque, Ia.: Wm. C. Brown Co. Publishers, 1988.

Zettl, Herbert. *Television Production Handbook.* 4th ed., Belmont, Calif.: Wadsworth Publishing Co., 1984.

Notes

1. Anthony Mulac and A. Robert Sherman, "Behavior Assessment of Speech Anxiety," *Quarterly Journal of Speech* 60 (1974): 134–43; and Albert Mehrabian and Martin Williams, "Nonverbal Concomitants of Perceived and Intended Persuasiveness," *Journal of Personality and Social Psychology* 13 (1969): 37–58.
2. W. Barnet Pearce and Bernard J. Brommel, "Vocalic Communication in Persuasion," *Quarterly Journal of Speech* 58 (1972): 298–306.
3. Thomas Henry Huxley, *On the Origin of the Species: or, The Causes of the Phenomena of Organic Nature* (New York: D. Appleton & Co., 1895).
4. Jack Valenti, *Speak Up With Confidence* (New York: William Morrow & Co., 1982): 129.
5. Joe Ayres, "Observers' Judgements of Audience Members' Attitudes," *Western Speech* 39 (1975): 40–50.

6. Steven C. Rhodes and Kenneth D. Frandsen, "Some Effects of Instruction in Feedback Utilization on the Fluency of College Students' Speech," *Speech Monographs* 42 (1975): 83–89.

7. Robert N. Bostrom and Carol L. Bryant, "Factors in the Retention of Information Presented Orally: The Role of Short-Term Listening," *Western Journal of Speech Communication* 44 (1980): 137–45.

8. Norman J. Lass and C. Elaine Prater, "A Comparative Study of Listening Rate Preferences for Oral Reading and Impromptu Speaking Tasks," *Journal of Communication* 23 (1973): 95–102.

9. Plutarch, *Lives of the Ten Orators,* trans. Harold N. Fowler, Loeb Classical Library (Boston: Harvard University Press): 845b.

10. Anthony Mulac and Mary Jo Rudd, "Effects of Selected American Regional Dialects Upon Regional Audience Members," *Communication Monographs* 44 (1977): 185–95.

11. Howard Giles, "Communication Effectiveness as a Function of Accented Speech," *Speech Monographs* 40 (1973): 330–31; and Dale T. Miller, "The Effect of Dialect and Ethnicity on Communication Effectiveness," *Speech Monographs* 42 (1975): 69–74.

12. A. Mehrabian, *Silent Messages* (Belmont, Calif.: Wadsworth Publishing Co., 1971).

13. Judee Burgoon, Thomas Birk, and Michael Pfau, "Nonverbal Behaviors, Persuasion, and Credibility," *Human Communication Research* 17 (1990): 140–169.

14. Robert Hopper and Frederick Williams, "Speech Characteristics and Employability," *Speech Monographs* 40 (1973): 296–302.

15. Mark L. Knapp, *Nonverbal Communication in Human Interaction* (New York: Holt, Rinehart & Winston, 1972): 97–107.

16. Albert Mehrabian, "Communication Without Words," *Psychology Today* 11 (September 1968): 53; also Albert Mehrabian, "Significance of Posture and Position in the Communication of Attitude and Status Relationships," *Psychological Bulletin* 71 (1969): 359–72.

17. Ray L. Birdwhistell, *Kinesics and Context* (Philadelphia: University of Pennsylvania Press, 1970): 8.

18. Paul Ekman, "The Universal Smile—Face Muscles Talk Every Language," *Psychology Today* (September 1975): 35–39.

19. Steven A. Beebe, "Eye Contact: A Nonverbal Determinant of Speaker Credibility," *Speech Teacher* 23 (1974): 21–25.

20. John E. Baird, Jr., "Some Nonverbal Elements of Leadership Emergence," *Southern Speech Communication Journal* 42 (1977): 352–61.

21. Ray Ehrensberger, "An Experimental Study of the Relative Effectiveness of Certain Forms of Emphasis in Public Speaking," *Speech Monographs* 12 (1945): 94–111.

22. Jurgen Ruesch and Weldon Kees, *Nonverbal Communication* (Berkeley: University of California Press, 1956).

23. John T. Molloy, *The Woman's Dress-for-Success Book* (Chicago: Follett Publishing Co., 1978): 16.

24. William McCoy, "Neatness Counts: Joe Paterno," *Vis à Vis,* November 1987: 92.

25. National Association of Broadcasters, *So You're Going on TV* (Washington, D.C.: 1978).

12 The Speech to Inform

Chapter Outline

Memory is a net; one finds it full of fish when he takes it from the brook; but a dozen miles of water have run through it without sticking.

Oliver Wendell Holmes

No one has ever seen a personality. If you could see one, what do you suppose it would look like? Would it look different for every person? Say like a cat for an independent person or like a bull for an aggressive one. Psychologists, who are in the business of trying to identify a useful working model of personality, have suggested that personality looks like an onion. That sounds pretty strange but comparing personality to an onion turns out to be a very productive way of approaching some important problems. I'll spend the rest of my time pointing out how it may be useful for you to think of yourself as an onion when considering your relationships with other people.[1]

An intriguing introduction like the one we have quoted can get an informative speech off to a good start. The speaker must then (1) present new facts or ideas or (2) provide new interpretations or insights about something the audience already knows. In either case, the speaker must accomplish two goals: getting the audience members to *understand* the information and getting them to *remember* it. So all the strategies used in a speech to inform are aimed toward clarity of expression and ease of retention. In order to accomplish these twin goals, it is very important that the informative speaker make a special effort to use techniques for arousing the audience's interest in the topic. It's a little like the proverbial story about the farmer who hit the mule over the head with a two-by-four, then told him what to do, because "first he had to get his attention." Some possible ways to gain and maintain your audience's attention are: attention to audience needs and motivations, usefulness, novelty, familiarity, immediacy, oral style, effective delivery, suspense and conflict, humor and wit, and organization. These "factors of attention," fully discussed in chapter 4, are useful to the speaker any time, but they are especially necessary in a speech to inform. In this chapter we will discuss some elements that are common to all speaking situations, then add those that are specific to the persuasive speech in chapters 13 and 14.

The Setting for the Informative Speech

We are all familiar with the informative process as it goes on in the educational setting; the chief task of the teacher is to inform and to prepare others to learn further, and for them to inform others of their discoveries. The ability to transmit information is valuable in other settings as well: you may be called upon to give directions to a stranger, report to a committee, instruct an employee, or demonstrate a procedure to a fellow worker; or perhaps when you get home at night, you'll be asked to describe how your day went.

> A good speech is like a pencil; it has to have a point.
>
> *Anonymous*

In every setting, the stimulus for the informative speech is the fact that you have some information that your audience lacks. If this is not the case, if, in fact, you are not telling your listeners anything they don't already know, then your speech is not informative. The speaker must analyze the listeners in the audience to find out their level of knowledge about the subject and their attitudes toward it. How can the speaker get from where the audience is to the material he or she wants to present? "A little knowledge is a dangerous thing," and speakers may find it more difficult to inform an audience on a subject about which they have formed a prejudgment than on one about which they are more open to new information. It is equally dangerous for the speaker to abandon his or her own objectivity. In the speech to inform, the purpose is to expand knowledge, not to persuade.

The Structure of the Informative Speech

As we pointed out in chapter 6, the most common patterns of overall organization—whether your speech purpose is to inform, persuade or move to action, or to entertain—are the following:

1. Chronological sequence. (Discuss the development of computers from the turn of the century to the present.)
2. Topical sequence. (Discuss the attributes needed to be a politician.)
3. Spatial sequence. (Discuss the aerodynamic features of an automobile starting with the front of the car.)

When composing an informative speech, you should consider your purpose for speaking, how you will introduce the topic, what you are going to do in the body of the speech, and how you are going to end the speech. Research suggests that highly structured messages are more readily recalled than those with less structure.[2] So, try to blend all of the elements of your speech into a cohesive whole.

Specific Purpose

The specific purpose, which may be phrased as a subject sentence in the introduction, can provide the audience with an accurate preview of what the speech will cover. (As you will learn in chapter 14, when you are attempting to persuade a hostile audience, it may be strategically desirable to withhold revealing your purpose until you have established a rapport with your audience.) It is often helpful to repeat this subject sentence, in one form or another, during the main body of the speech and again in the conclusion. This repetition helps the audience to remember it. Naturally, all the information you present in the introduction, body, and conclusion should be relevant to your specific purpose. Introducing material that is interesting but irrelevant to your specific purpose only blurs the point you wish to make and makes it difficult for the audience to comprehend what you are trying to accomplish.

Felice Schwartz used the following specific purpose statement to preview her speech on corporate women:

> I'd like to share with you my thoughts on how the workplace is changing as it assimilates women, how it will continue to change, what are some of the problems faced by business and individuals and what I see as their logical solutions.[3]

Introduction

Now that you have chosen the specific purpose for your speech you are ready to introduce your speech topic.

1. Arouse attention and interest in the subject, beginning with a general treatment of your subject.
2. Limit the scope of the topic, how much of the possible subject you plan to cover.
3. Formulate your statement of purpose.

Body of the Speech

There are a number of guidelines you may follow in developing the body of your speech.

1. It is best to cover no more than two to four main points.
2. Provide at least one piece of supporting material for each main point. Try to vary the type of supporting material you use (e.g., don't always use statistics or quotations).
3. A common error that speakers make is to provide support for a point without first stating the point to be amplified.
   a. Make the statement.
   b. Enlarge upon the statement by restating it in more familiar language, giving an example, quoting an expert, making a comparison, showing a visual, or by using any of the other means of support we have discussed before.
   c. Restate the point you have made and amplified. For instance:

> Sometimes design principles are more significant than the material used. For example, canoes can be made of concrete and still float. If the basic principles of buoyancy and flotation are followed, a material that we commonly think of as heavy and solid becomes capable of floating—a triumph of design.

> A speaker who exhausts the whole philosophy of a question, who displays every grace of style, yet produces no effect on his audience, may be a great essayist, a great statesman, a great master of composition, but he is not an orator.
>
> *Thomas Babington Macaulay*

4. Supporting materials must clearly pertain to the point being amplified. If the example does not really fit, invent a hypothetical example.
5. Supporting materials must be placed where they belong, not added later.
6. The number of supporting materials should be enough, but just enough, to avoid overkill on any one point, making that one point so important that you destroy the balance of your speech. The most vivid examples, statistics, and so forth, should be attached to major points. You should use only short examples or less weighty materials on minor points.

Summaries and Transitions

You can help your listeners follow your speech more easily if you use summaries and transitions throughout your speech.

1. Include frequent previews, enumeration of points, and summaries to keep your listeners aware of the structure of your speech.
2. "A chain is only as strong as its weakest link," and you as speaker must provide links from thought to thought, forming associations for your listeners so they can remember what you say.[4]

James Simon used the following summary to drive home his main thesis that the Supreme Court of the United States is influenced by the values of the broader society:

> I am not suggesting that those decisions were necessarily correct or that they perfectly reflect the dominant constitutional values in the country. I am suggesting, however, that the pattern is unmistakable and noteworthy: the court majority has affirmed an expectation that has dominated Supreme Court jurisprudence for almost fifty years—that our Constitution and our people place individual rights and liberties very high in the hierarchy of constitutional values.[5]

Conclusion

You have introduced the topic of your speech and have developed its specific purpose in the body of your speech. Now you are ready to bring it to a conclusion.

1. Your primary purpose is to draw together all the elements of the speech—the main ideas and the supporting materials—so that the audience takes away a unified, coherent understanding of your subject, an understanding that is as nearly like your own as possible. Pierre Dobbelmann uses this technique in the conclusion of his speech on protectionism:

   > If I leave you with only one thought today, I hope it is this: Although it some-times gets lost in the swirling debate, there really are considerable friendship and common interest between the U.S. and its trading partners.
   > And, in the final analysis, that friendship and common interest—not protec-tionism—will be the answer to the economic and trade-related problems af-fecting us today.[6]

2. Begin the introduction with a general thesis, proceed to the specific points you wish to make in the body of your speech, then conclude with a general overview of the topic as you have discussed it.
3. All of the material on conclusions in chapter 8 applies here, but one technique is especially valuable in the speech to inform (perhaps along with another, more vivid appeal). Restate your main points in the same order in which you presented them in the body of your speech. The last position you present is a strong one; listeners pay close attention when you signal them that the speech is drawing to a close. An effective summary can help the audience remember the points you believe to be most important.

As we said earlier, the purpose of the informative speech is to convey a clear understanding of the ideas and to have these ideas remembered, both of which depend heavily on the ability to arouse and to maintain au-dience interest in the subject. Whatever you may think you have said, it is what the audience heard, understood, and remembered that determines the success of your informative speech.

Types of Informative Speeches

Every informative speech sets out to provide information and to have that information remembered. The subject addressed is sometimes concrete and sometimes abstract. To illustrate the difference between these two cate-gories, we'll use first an example of a concrete topic for an informative speech, this one being a demonstration of a process. Let's assume you know how to perform the trick of making a coin disappear, and you perform that trick for the audience while explaining the process. When you make the coin disappear, it's not apparent to the audience how you did it. In your speech of demonstration, you take us through the steps of making the coin disappear. When you finish, we may not be able to perform the trick, but we should know how it is done and the steps by which it is accomplished.

You can find other concrete topics from within your own experience: how the shape and material used affect a guitar's tone quality, differences between rough and finished lumber, making stained glass, 101 ways to serve hamburger, making a campfire, differences between bait and fly-fishing, what to look for in a running shoe, or specific details to observe when choosing an apartment to rent.

When the speaker's purpose is to provide information on an abstract subject, he or she deals in general principles, rather than in specifics. The speaker might discuss Andy Warhol's famous "pop" art painting that consists of a multiple reproduction of a Campbell's soup can, using it to illustrate the social significance of "pop" art. In this instance, you would not tell us how Warhol went about creating this work, but you would try to show us that "pop" artists were making the statement that Western culture in the 1960s was unimaginative and sterile. Other subjects in this abstract category might include the theory of relativity, the nature of Zen, the law of gravity, or the power of positive thinking.

We have presented the explanation of concrete and abstract subjects as separate and distinct, but in reality, these lines are not so clear-cut. If your subject is abstract, like the nature of gravity, you might very well include a demonstration in which you drop an apple and an iron ball to point out the relative speed of their fall. And if your subject is concrete—a demonstration of how to build a soap box racer—you may find it useful to explain the principles of streamlining the body of the vehicle to cut down wind resistance.

The setting and the purpose of the informative speech may vary. Some basic types of informative speeches are: (1) a description of a person, place, object, or event; (2) a lecture explaining an idea, theory, concept, issue, or event; (3) a report—committee report, or report on a book or an article; (4) instructions or directions on performing a specific act or task; and (5) a demonstration of a process.

Description

In the descriptive type of informative speech, the goal is to give a vivid, accurate picture of a person, place, event, or object. To accomplish this, a spatial sequence works well. The choice of language is an essential factor in description. Specific, concrete words, not vague, abstract ones, will help to evoke sharp and accurate images in the minds of the listeners. Contrast the image evoked by, "a black-and-white-spotted pony with a long, slick tail and short mane," with "a small horse."

An item may be described by defining the class into which it falls—for example, "a mammal" or "a woodwind instrument." Then, by comparison and contrast, note the ways in which this particular item is different from the others in its class. For example, "Unlike most mammals, the whale is a marine creature . . ." or "Unlike most woodwind instruments, the modern flute is made of metal."

The intrinsic features of that which is being described provide a basis for description. Among these features are size, shape, weight, color, the material of which it is made, age, condition of repair, and relationship of the component parts of the item. Don't forget that visual aids can help you to communicate these features as well.

Trina Griggs describes a place that is special to her:

One lazy afternoon I lay curled up on our couch with my hand-knit afghan, taking a snooze. I awoke for some unknown reason and peered sleepily around the room. I started to doze off again when a familiar scent brought me to my feet.

Barefooted, my steps were cushioned by the soft plush carpet, as the smell drew me to the stairs. Five, six, seven stairs I counted until I reached the landing. The scent intensified and I knew I had almost reached my destination, the kitchen.

That's when I saw "them." Uniform in color, size and shape, they stood parallel to each other, lined up like seven British soldiers going off to war. Just as I had thought . . . "they" were my mom's homemade wheat bread, fresh from the oven.

My groggy nature disappeared as I gripped the firm loaf and positioned the knife on the freshly buttered crust. My 1 1/2-inch slice was light and airy; the steam warmed my face as I took my first bite. I felt my whole body melt.

While savoring my last bite I glanced at the wall next to me. "Home, Sweet Home," the picture read. And all I could think was, "True, how true."[7]

Lecture

A familiar example of this type of informative presentation is the classroom lecture; another is the lecture on public affairs, presented in person or on radio or TV. The speaker presents an objective explanation of an idea, theory, concept, issue, or event, with the intent of increasing the audience's understanding or appreciation for a particular branch of knowledge. Chronological or topical sequence are the most likely organizational patterns for a lecture. Visual aids such as charts and diagrams may help to make the information clear, and it may be desirable to present handouts to the listeners, for use during the speech or for follow-up study.

The following speech is from a series of lectures delivered by Sir James Jeans, a nineteenth century English scientist. His purpose in this series of lectures was to help common people, who were largely illiterate, understand the science of his day.

Why the Sky Looks Blue
by
Sir James Jeans

Commentary

Jeans does some excellent things in this lecture. He recognizes immediately that he will need to explain light waves by reference to an easily understood experience. So he uses a figurative analogy to link the audience's understanding of ocean waves to light waves. Clearly, ocean waves and light waves are different and such a comparison would be rejected by scientists, but the inexact parallel is acceptable to this audience and allows it to achieve a level of understanding it would never reach with a purely scientific description. Jeans also keeps the speech short, to the point, and uses simple language. Notice how he allows the title of the speech to alert the audience to his purpose and reminds it of the purpose in the conclusion. The speech is structured largely on a time order (light enters the atmosphere, then strikes particles, etc.). All in all, Jeans does an admirable job of presenting a difficult subject to an audience whose background is limited, and of doing it in an informative, interesting manner.

Speech

Imagine that we stand on any ordinary seaside pier, and watch the waves rolling in and striking against the iron columns of the pier. Large waves pay little attention to the columns—they divide right and left and reunite after passing each column, much as a regiment of soldiers would if a tree stood in their road; it is almost as though the columns had not been there. But the short waves and ripples find the columns of a pier a much more formidable obstacle. When the short waves impinge on the columns, they are reflected back and spread as new ripples in all directions. To use the technical term, they are "scattered." The obstacle provided by the iron columns hardly affects the long waves at all, but scatters the short ripples.

We have been watching a sort of working model of the way in which sunlight struggles through the earth's atmosphere. Between us on earth and outer space the atmosphere interposes innumerable obstacles in the form of molecules of air, tiny droplets of water, and small particles of dust. These are represented by the columns of the pier.

The waves of the sea represent the sunlight. We know that sunlight is a blend of lights of many colors—as we can prove for ourselves by passing it through a prism, or even through a jug of water, or as Nature demonstrates to us when she passes it through the raindrops of a summer shower and produces a rainbow. We also know that light consists of waves, and that the waves are different lengths; for example, red light has long waves and blue light has short waves. The mixture of waves which constitutes sunlight has to struggle through the obstacles it meets in the atmosphere, just as the mixture of waves at the seaside has to struggle past the columns of the pier. And these obstacles treat the light-waves much as the columns of the pier treat the sea-waves. The long waves which constitute red light are hardly affected, but the short waves which constitute blue light are scattered in all directions.

Thus, the different constituents of sunlight are treated in different ways as they struggle through the earth's atmosphere. A wave of blue light may be scattered by a dust particle, and turned out of its course. After a time a second dust particle again turns it out of its course, and so on, until finally it enters our eyes by a path as zigzag as that of a flash of lightning. Consequently, the blue waves of the sunlight enter our eyes from all directions. And that is why the sky looks blue.[8]

Reports

Reports are also common in the academic setting. As a student you are often called upon to prepare and deliver an oral report for a class, perhaps on a book, an article, or on some other element of the course. Topical order is most promising in this instance, but either all or part of the report will fall into chronological order as well.

Careful research of your subject is especially important; you are expected to become the expert on this segment of the class content. You should be sure you understand what you are asked to contribute so you can select from the material you find only that information that is exactly relevant to your assigned task, and then organize it carefully. Reports most often must be presented within a limited period of time; visual aids can often help you communicate more information in less time.

Reports also play an important part in the functioning of clubs and business organizations. These may be in the form of reports or facts, or reports made by an individual or committee charged with writing a recommendation for action. In either case, you should be sure you know what you are asked to do, and then limit your presentation to that purpose.

When presenting a report that makes recommendations to the group, be sure to include a complete rationale for the course you advise, based on the facts you have found.

Instructions

Directions on how to perform a specific act or task may be required in the classroom, at home, or on the job. Telling everyone in your family how to play a card game falls into this category. Your task is to give exact information on steps, procedures, or a plan of action. Instructions must be given clearly, accurately, and precisely so they will be understood and remembered, and physical action is a must.

Chronological order is the most likely choice for giving instructions, but in some sections you may use topical order. You should make good use of such clarifying devices as definitions, comparison and contrast, and examples. Techniques for providing emphasis, such as repetition and restatement, forecasts and enumeration, transitions, and internal summaries are also important. When explaining how to do something, you may have found it essential to go back over the material. By anticipating that need, you can make the task of sharing instructions much easier.

All this may sound like the burden of transmitting instructions is entirely on the speaker, but this is not really true. In most situations the listener needs to understand the directions being given in order to carry out a task, so she or he is motivated to grasp their content even if the directions are poorly delivered. (Any student knows that this same point could be made regarding the classroom lecture as well.)

Description of a Process

In the informative speech that explains a process, the speaker will demonstrate and explain ("show and tell") how to do something. A critical element in this type of speech is whether the steps in the process are identified and presented systematically by the speaker, leaving out none of the essential steps in the process. In this way the discussion and its accompanying demonstration are made clear and easy for the listener to understand. The

Showing, as well as telling, is a useful informative technique.

chronological or time sequence is most often used for such demonstrations, although using a topical order or showing spatial relationships between parts might also be used for some topics.

Don't let the visual aspect take over completely; this is a *speech*, illustrated by a demonstration.

Choosing a Process
Speech Topic

Because it combines both verbal and visual stimuli to a high degree, the process speech is easy to make interesting to your audience, provided that you ask yourself a few basic questions about your proposed topic.

1. Is the topic something you know (or can find out) enough about?
2. Is this topic interesting (or can it be made interesting) to this audience? (See the section "Factors of Attention" in chapter 4.)
3. Can this topic be covered in the time allotted?
4. Are the objects or materials available for performing the demonstration? (Chapter 9 describes the use of visual aids.)
5. Will this speech provide the audience with new information or new insights?
6. Do you know the subject well enough to demonstrate it successfully?

You shouldn't demonstrate a process that is too simple or one that your audience already knows how to do, but neither should the topic be so broad or so complex that you cannot communicate the essence of the process to this audience in the time allotted. If the process is complex, it still might be possible to present it if you can figure a way to simplify the procedure, perhaps by grouping some steps under a single heading, or by using what is called a *skip-ahead* technique. A student who was describing how to make homemade pizza not only described how to make the dough, but brought with him some dough that already had been mixed and allowed to rise. He showed how to put the sauce together, but the sauce he spread on the pizza rounds had already been mixed and simmered. Then he added pre-sliced pepperoni, grated cheeses, and the other ingredients. By this *skip-ahead* technique, a process that required many steps over a period of hours was completed in a seven-minute demonstration speech—complete with hot, baked pizza for samples!

Outline of a Process Speech

The following outline for a process speech uses a chronological pattern to show how one goes about giving mouth-to-mouth resuscitation. The various devices for gaining and maintaining attention are noted beside each section.

Artificial Respiration
by Laura Kaser
Washington State University

Commentary

Outline

Laura used rhetorical questions to arouse interest here. The slight restatement of the specific purpose statement directs attention toward the goal of this presentation.

Specific Purpose: To teach the audience the steps involved in artificial respiration.

Introduction
I. What would you do if suddenly you found yourself in a situation in which your actions could mean life or death for another person?
  A. Would you know how to respond?
  B. Would you know the proper techniques that could save this person's life?
II. The most efficient and practical way to save a life is with mouth-to-mouth resuscitation.
III. We will consider three steps in learning mouth-to-mouth artificial respiration.

Notice that the first main point here alerts listeners that there are going to be several subpoints. As we proceed from subpoint A to subpoint C, phrases like first, next, and last keep us oriented as to our progress.

Body
I. There are several precautionary steps that should be taken before giving mouth-to-mouth resuscitation.
  A. The first thing you want to do is shake the victim and shout to him or her.

1. There have been incidents in which a person has been harmed when someone needlessly tried to resuscitate him or her.
   2. Shout something like, "Hey, are you ok?" and shake the victim to make sure that person is not sleeping.
B. The next three steps you want to remember are to look, listen, and feel.
   1. Look at the victim's chest to see if it is rising and falling.
   2. Put your ear against the victim's mouth to see if you can feel breath against your cheek.
   3. Feel for a pulse either at the wrist, jugular vein, or at the temples.
C. Lastly, if the victim still appears not to be breathing, turn his or her head to the side and remove all debris.
   1. When there is an obstruction visible in the victim's mouth, it should be wiped out immediately.
   2. If the obstruction is located in the back of the throat, the victim should be leaned forward and be struck firmly on the back between the shoulder blades.

II. When you are positive the victim cannot breathe on his or her own, begin mouth-to-mouth techniques.
A. Tilt the victim's head back so that the chin points upward.
   1. The jaw should be pulled so that it is in a jutting-out position.
   2. By tilting the head back, you are moving the position of the tongue and freeing the passageways.
B. Pinch the victim's nose while resting your palm on the forehead.
C. Take a deep breath and cover the victim's mouth, creating a firm seal.
D. Blow air into the victim's mouth.
   1. Start with three quick breaths.
      a. If you are not getting an air exchange, recheck head and jaw positions.
      b. Make sure mouth and throat are clear.
   2. Continue to blow one breath into the victim's mouth.
      a. This should be done every five seconds for an average of twelve breaths a minute for an adult.
      b. For a child, give one breath every three seconds for an average of twenty per minute.
   3. Mouth-to-mouth resuscitation should be continued until a doctor arrives or until the victim is breathing alone.

III. As soon as a natural breathing rhythm is established, the victim should be turned into the recovery position.
   A. He or she should be lying on the stomach with the head slightly tipped back to maintain a clear airway.
   B. The upper knee should be raised at a right angle.
   C. The lower arm should be placed behind his or her back.

Conclusion

I. Mouth-to-mouth resuscitation is so simple that even a child could save the life of an adult.
   A. Four steps need to be remembered.
      1. Tilt the victim's head back to free the passageways.
      2. Pinch the nose.
      3. Breathe into the victim's mouth on the average of one breath every few seconds.
      4. Check to see that you are getting an air exchange by using the look, listen, and feel method.
   B. Remember to continue mouth-to-mouth resuscitation until a doctor arrives or the victim is breathing on his or her own.
II. Mouth-to-mouth resuscitation saves lives.
   A. It is the most efficient and practical form of artificial respiration.
   B. Just think how many lives could be saved every year if everyone knew this form of artificial respiration.

Bibliography for Laura Kaser's Speech

American National Red Cross. *Basic First Aid.* Book 1. New York: Doubleday & Company, 1979, 69–72.
Better Homes and Gardens. *Family Medical Guide.* New York: Meredith Press, 1964, 472–76.
Garland, Thomas. *Artificial Respiration.* London: Faber and Faber, 1965, 70–79.
Miller, Benjamin. *The Family Book of Preventive Medicine.* New York: Simon and Schuster, 1971, 338–42.[9]

Materials and Equipment

Nothing could be worse than a demonstration speech in which the demonstration doesn't work! Be sure you have everything you need, and that all equipment operates properly; that you have the materials organized step-by-step; and that you have rehearsed the speech and the demonstration together many times. The old joke about "not being able to talk and chew gum at the same time" won't seem so funny if you have trouble coordinating the "show" with the "tell" while you're in front of a group.

REAL LIFE ADVENTURES by Gary Wise and Lance Aldrich

The business presentation: unintentional stand-up comedy.

Importance of the Informative Function

The ability first to understand and assimilate, then to communicate information to others has always been a valuable asset in human society. At one time, a talented and diligent scholar could learn all that was known in the sciences and arts. Today, even the most learned person cannot grasp more than a tiny fraction of the explosion of knowledge, much of it scientific and technological in nature, that has taken place in recent times. The concept of *student* has changed from one in which she or he is to be a storage place for knowledge to one in which she or he is expected to know where to find information, to know how to retrieve it, and to be able to transmit that information to others. Libraries and computer banks enable each of us to use not only our own brain and nervous system, but to hook into a vast depository of knowledge from the past and present. But it still remains for us to develop our abilities to transmit this information to others.

Example of an Informative Speech

The following speech was delivered by a student at a national forensic tournament. Our comments inserted at various points draw your attention to certain strengths and weaknesses in the speech.

Informative Speech
by Mark Nelson
University of Alabama, Birmingham

Commentary

The opening portion of this introduction piques interest because we are wondering what is going to happen. Mark calls this a quiz, so we wonder if we are going to have to produce answers. He quickly lets us off the hook but just as quickly shifts our interest to a consideration of eye movements. The introduction ends with a concise preview of what is to come.

This portion of the speech contains a lot of information. Mark couples the presentation of statistical information with concrete, easy to grasp examples which allow us to remember the reason the statistic was presented. He uses a variety of evidence, ranging from a personal example to testimony, which helps keep us interested.

Speech

Let's start with a simple quiz. Now, don't call out the answers; just think of them in your mind. Ready? (1) What color was your first bike? (2) How many rooms were there in the house in which you grew up? (3) How many letters in the word anthropology? and finally, describe how Lee Harvey Oswald was shot.

Now, whether or not you could answer these questions is irrelevant, but the way in which you tried to achieve the answers is very relevant. The questions I asked you were the same ones asked to volunteers in a study at Yale University, conducted by Bonnie Meskin and Jerome Singer. In the study they noticed that depending on the type of information demanded, that is, whether the request was for verbal concepts, visual memories, or auditory memories, the eyes naturally and subtly softened in particular directions, as though this eye movement aided in the accessibility of the data. According to old folk psychology, the eye is the gateway to the mind and now it seems modern science is confirming this age-old belief. Through studies, like the one conducted at Yale, scientists are learning more and more about the connection between eyeshifts and information, a field known as neurolinguistics. It is a fascinating field, one worth more than just a passing glance. So for the next few minutes, let's focus on neurolinguistics. Let's first take a look at some basic information about the brain and eye; second, we will consider the research that has been done concerning eyeshifts; and, finally, we will take a look at the individual eyeshifts and how they work. At that point I'm sure you will agree that the eyes have it.

Eighty years ago, the novelist Joseph Conrad wrote, "the mind of man is capable of doing anything, because everything is in it; all the past as well as all the future," and he may not have been wrong. Neurophysiologist Charles Herrick estimates that there are at least 102,789,000 possible connections in the brain for receiving, storing and correlating data. That's the number 1 followed by 3 million zeros, at a rate of one digit per second, just writing that number down would take an entire month. The brain therefore is much more complex than any computer ever developed. So it's not surprising that the brain needs help in dealing with all of this information. And that's where the eye comes in— in early human embryonic development, the brain and eye are actually one. Eventually, the eye grows away from the brain but remains linked to it by the optic nerve. However, the real focus of interest by researchers is a small bundle of densely packed nerve cells roughly the size of the little finger. Known as the reticular formation and located in the central core of the brain stem, this area of tightly packed nerve cells runs from the top of the spinal cord into the center of the brain. The reticular formation contains nearly 70 percent of the brain's estimated 200 billion nerve cells. It is this part of the brain that governs consciousness and acts as a sensory filter; that is, it filters out everything but the relevant information at any particular moment.

According to Steven DeVoe, an educational psychologist and author of *The Neuropsychology of Success,* the nerves that control eye movement, known as the ocular motor nerves, originate and derive in the reticular formation area. Therefore, with the proper eye movement we can open up specific channels to access information stored within the brain. So, as well as being the organ for vision, the eye has non-visual functions as well.

Now, everyone is familiar with the story about the student who, when asked a question by his teacher, looks upward. Whereupon the teacher advises him, you are not going to find the answer on the ceiling. Well, undoubtedly he won't, but we are now aware that his instinctive eye movements were allowing him to access the particular information he needed from the memory stored within his brain. And I always thought I was just stalling because I didn't know the answer.

Well, in addition to the study conducted at Yale, a similar study conducted at the Langly Porter Neuropsychiatric Institute at the University of California asked volunteers similar types of questions. And once again, depending on the type of information demanded, specific patterns of predictable eyeshifts were noted. Numerous other studies by university researchers such as Dr. Karl Prilman, surgeon and neuroscientist at Stanford University, have confirmed the relationship between eye movement and sensory memory recall.

OK, we've assimilated some complicated new information—with the help of our eyes, of course. So let's recall that we have learned about the eye/brain connection and research which indicates the association between eye shifts and sensory memory recall. Next let's take a look at the actual process of eyeshifts.

The book *Neurolinguistic Programming* by Richard Bandler outlines nine specific eyeshift movements and the senses with which they are associated. The first pattern of eyeshifts is the eye movement that activates visual memory. When you draw from visual memory—say the face of an old friend—your eyes will naturally move to an upper left position. The harder the memory is to recall, the higher to the left your eyes will go. By the way, it is important to note that if you're left-handed or ambidextrous your eyeshifts may differ. The second eyeshift is for the construction of visual images. When you imagine something, like how you would spend a million dollars. The third pattern of eye movement is the eyeshift that activates auditory memory. This is your storehouse of remembered sounds. Here your eyes are in a lateral left position, and for the constructions of sounds the fourth eye shift movement is lateral right. The eye movement, used a good deal by writers and composers, comes into play when you are blending or creating words or sounds. The fifth eye shift position is for the recall of emotional sensation and feelings. When you draw emotions and feelings from the past, your eyes may first move to a lower left position to signal the brain for a memory search. Then you may activate a visual memory, upper left, to see the person or event involved. Followed by a move to the lower left, to focus into the motion for the recall of body sensations and motion, the sixth eyeshift position is lower right and to recall the sense of taste from memory you would activate the eighth eyeshift position which is an approximate ten degrees lower central position. And the ninth and last eyeshift position is known as the sensory synthesis position. Now, the position, which is the central focus position is where your eyes are when any memory is in sharp focus, or when you can recall it without any conscious effort.

While all of these eyeshifts are distinct movements in the direction indicated, they are fleeting, almost imperceptible movements, and in most people they can be seen only by close observation. But do the eyeshifts really work? Well, the best way to demonstrate the principle behind memory activation through movements in the eye is to show you how difficult it is to recall sensory information with your eyes in conflicting patterns. For example, if you will close your eyes please. Now, move your eyes to the lower left position—this opens up the channel for the memory of emotion. Now try to solve the following math problem while your eyes are in this position, what is the solution to 198 divided by 6? Do you feel any internal resistance? Do your eyes want to move upward? Now, with your eyes still closed move them to an upper right position if you're right-handed or to the upper left if you're a pure left-hander. Is it easier to concentrate on finding the solution to 198 divided by 6, while your eyes are in this position? OK, you can open your eyes now. Well, this example should clearly demonstrate the relationship between eye movement and clear access to information stored within the brain. Oh, by the way, the answer to the problem is 33.

In today's hurried world, it is imperative that we learn to recall precise information rapidly. By learning about neurolinguistic movements, we can make this task a little easier and more efficient. Remember, the human brain is the model for computers—not the other way around. And who knows, perhaps we really can study for that calculus test or memorize a poem, in the blink of an eye.[10]

Overall, this is a very solid speech. The topic is interesting and presented in an authoritative, involving manner using a variety of evidence and helpful transitional devices. The introduction and conclusion are particularly strong features in this speech.

Summary

In the speech to inform, the speaker's purpose is to give listeners some new information on a subject, with particular emphasis on their understanding and remembering what is said. Informative speeches can take several forms, including descriptive speeches that provide a vivid picture of something; lectures that stress the objective features of ideas or theories; reports that develop a limited aspect of a subject; instructive speeches that focus on how to perform a specific task; or process-oriented speeches that explain and demonstrate how to do something. All of these types of speeches should have introductions that gain attention, precise specific purposes, bodies that present essential content, and conclusions that summarize the primary features of the speech.

Exercises

1. Identify which of the following things you like to talk about:
   Horseback riding
   Golfing
   Educational systems
   Unemployment
   The welfare system
   Traveling
   Spectator sports

   Discuss why you would like to talk about those things you selected and why you wouldn't like to discuss the others. How would you present these topics? What organizational patterns would you use? What forms of development? How would these things change if your audience was much younger or older than yourself?

2. Have each student describe an object without naming the object. Have class members identify the object after each presentation. Discuss what factors contributed to the identification of objects.

Assignments

1. Prepare a five- to seven-minute informative speech. This speech may be a descriptive speech, a lecture, a report, an instructive speech, or a demonstrative speech. The speech should be outlined and should strive for attention, clarity, and retention.
2. Write a two-page analysis of an informative speech. Discuss factors that worked to help or hinder its informative function. Discuss organization, development, transitions, etc.

Suggested Reading

Charles R. Petrie, Jr. "Informative Speaking: A Summary and Bibliography of Related Research. *Speech Monographs,* 30, 1963: 79–91.

Notes

1. The material quoted is the introductory portion of a lecture delivered by Joe Ayres entitled "Personality and Interpersonal Relations," October 1981. Those interested in finding out more about this way of viewing personality are encouraged to read Irwin Altman and Dalmas Taylor, *Social Penetration: The Development of Interpersonal Relationships* (New York: Holt, Rinehart & Winston, 1973).
2. Tom D. Daniels and Richard F. Whitman, "The Effects of Message Introduction, Message Structure, and Verbal Organizing Ability Upon Learning of Message Information," *Human Communication Research* 7 (1981): 156.
3. Felice M. Schwartz, "Corporate Women: A Critical Business Resource," *Vital Speeches* (January 1, 1988): 173.
4. John E. Baird, Jr., "The Effects of Speech Summaries Upon Audience Comprehension of Expository Speeches of Varying Quality and Complexity," *Central States Speech Journal* 25 (1974): 124.
5. James F. Simon, "Conflict and Leadership: The U.S. Supreme Court from Marshall to Rehnquist," *Vital Speeches* (November 1, 1986): 48.
6. Pierre F. Dobbelmann, "The Perils of Protectionism: A Dutch and European Perspective," *Vital Speeches* (July 15, 1987): 594.
7. Trina Griggs, "Descriptive Speech." Speech presented in a basic public speaking class at Washington State University, October, 1986.
8. Sir James Jeans, *The Mysterious Universe.* (London: Penguin Books, 1937).
9. Laura Kaser, outline of a speech delivered to a public speaking class in September 1981.
10. Mark Nelson, Informative Speaking Final Round Winner, *1986 Championship Debates and Speeches,* (Normal, Ill.: Printing Services, Illinois State University, 1986): 125–27.

13 Bases of Persuasion

Chapter Outline

If all my talents and powers were to be taken from me by some inscrutable Providence, and I had my choice of keeping but one, I would unhesitatingly ask to be allowed to keep the Power of Speaking, for through it, I would quickly recover all the rest.

Daniel Webster

The function of this chapter is to help you understand the essential ingredients of persuasion. Every person in a democratic society needs to understand these ingredients because persuasion is the antithesis of violence; in a democracy, persuasion is the only acceptable means of effecting social change. Without absolute power, as would be the case in a totalitarian state, a leader cannot command any kind of clout other than by being persuasive. The essence of living in a democracy is the freedom to make choices; the purpose of the persuasive speech is to demonstrate the greater desirability of making the choice favored by the speaker, as compared with all the other possible choices. For example, in spite of the statistics presented by the Surgeon General's office about the harmful effects of smoking, many people still smoke. Some may not believe the data, but of those who continue to smoke anyway, most do so, not because good health is not desirable but because, to them, something else is more desirable. The persuasive speaker tries to find arguments that will help the listener decide to accept his or her proposition. The following material presents some of the factors to be considered as you search for arguments to influence others' choices when you speak.

Persuasive Speech Defined

In a persuasive speech, the speaker's primary purpose is to influence the thinking or the behavior of the listeners. She or he presents a combination of logical and extra-logical arguments to convince them that they should believe or act as the speaker urges. The most distinctive aspect of the persuasive speech is the conscious intent of the speaker to effect a *change* in the listener, and every decision about the speech is made with that end in view: the choice of subject for a given audience; approach to the subject, whether head-on or more gradual; the choice of arguments and proofs; selection of language; organization; and style of delivery. The general organizational pattern of the persuasive speech (introduction, body, and conclusion) is the same as the speech to inform, and so are the building blocks from which the speech is constructed: facts and opinions presented in the form of examples, illustrations, statistics, and quotations.

The general purpose of the persuasive speech, however, differs from that of the informative speech. The informative speech seeks to explain, clarify, and promote understanding; the persuasive speech attempts to motivate, to change beliefs, to reinforce existing beliefs, and may seek to bring

In a sermon, the speaker seeks to reinforce ideas or beliefs the audience already holds.

others to action. The specific purpose of the persuasive speech is to convince the audience to accept the speaker's *proposition*—what you want your audience to do or to believe.

Specific Purpose

As a persuasive speaker you may set out to convince an audience of the truth of a proposition (such as: Drafting women is morally wrong) or to try to get listeners in the audience to take an action (such as: You should register to vote). Just as electricity cannot be seen but can be measured only by its effects, so it is difficult to measure the degree of conviction that exists in the mind of a listener. Thus, persuasive results are most reliably demonstrated when they culminate in action. However, it is not always desirable or possible for you to aim for or to expect overt action to result from a persuasive speech. Perhaps more than ever, you need to pay careful attention to drafting a specific purpose. Is it your purpose to *convince* your listeners, to secure their agreement on an issue? Do you want them to take some *action*—sign a petition, write to a legislator, or see a movie? Is it your intention to *reinforce* ideas or beliefs your audience already has, such as is done in a sermon, a pep rally, a commencement address, or a political convention? As a persuasive speaker, you must feel some need for a change, take a position as to what that change should be, and then set about getting others involved.

In determining your specific purpose, or proposition, not only must the subject be limited by the background of the audience and the time available, but you must assess where the audience is now, the attitude of its members in relation to the chosen subject, and how far you can realistically expect to move them by this speech. A single speech can seldom change listeners' beliefs or incite them to take action, but it may be one factor among many that, over a period of time, inspires the desired effect. Few of us will ever have the experience of seeing an audience turned completely around by the force of our eloquence, but we can hope our listeners will feel more receptive toward the proposition we advance.

The persuasive speaker is always aiming for an effect, either a specific and meaningful change, or a recommitment to an existing attitude or belief. It stands to reason that if the audience already believes as you do, or if the nature and extent of the change desired is minor, you will have a better chance of achieving your goal than you will if you try to get them to make a major change. You as an individual may want to effect some significant change; a political party wants to elect more public officials, or a company attempts to build its reputation and goodwill. Some goals will require a lengthy campaign and will not be accomplished by a single speech. Still, you should not withdraw from making an effort to influence. "The journey of a thousand miles begins with but a single step." Or to cite another metaphor, "Toss a pebble in the water, and the ripples will extend far beyond the immediate effect."

Audience Analysis

The persuasive speaker should analyze his or her audience. We discussed audience analysis thoroughly in chapter 3, and here we summarize the major points made in that chapter.

1. Find out the general makeup of the audience (age, gender, and so forth) and make broad assumptions about the motivations of its members based on this information.

Does everyone just believe what he wants to? As long as possible, sometimes longer.

Isaac Asimov

2. Be aware of your listeners' basic human needs: self-preservation, sexual attraction, property, self-esteem, personal enjoyment, constructiveness, destructiveness, curiosity, imitation, altruism. (Remember Maslow's hierarchy of needs.) Speak to the unfulfilled needs of the members of your audience, to provide them with reasons for accepting your proposition by showing how it serves their short-term and long-term self-interests. Self-interests are not necessarily selfish or bad—many of the goals we seek are good for ourselves and for others—good health, a desire for fun and adventure, achieving a comfortable standard of living for ourselves and our families, gaining the respect and goodwill of others, achieving success and social esteem, enjoying personal freedoms. We have feelings of duty, such as obligations to family, state, nation, and religion. We also have a desire to be truthful and to keep promises, and to see ourselves as kind, fair, courageous, and sincere. The persuasive speaker can appeal to these worthwhile motives to elicit the attitude changes that can lead to the desired belief or action.
3. Determine how your listeners feel about your topic. That is, what attitudes do they currently hold? Do they have favorable, unfavorable, or neutral attitudes?
4. Assess the audience's attitude toward you as a spokesperson on this topic.
5. Learn what you can about your listeners' group standards of decision-making. Do they consistently accept or reject certain kinds of ideas or arguments? Members of the National Rifle Association, for example, tend to reject arguments favoring gun control.
6. Are individuals in the group known to hold specific biases or prejudices? Do they pay especial attention to the attitudes of opinion leaders in the group?

Opinions, Attitudes, and Beliefs

We mentioned attitudes several times in the list of factors to consider when analyzing an audience for a persuasive speech. This section distinguishes between beliefs, attitudes, and opinions.

A *belief* is the acceptance of the truth or falsity of a proposition, based on evidence, opinion, or experience—"Dogs are loyal."

An *attitude* is a tendency to feel positively or negatively toward people, ideas, or objects—"I prefer dogs to cats, because dogs are loyal, while cats are fickle and selfish."

An *opinion* is usually the verbal expression of an attitude or belief. Opinions are similar to beliefs, but they tend to be more factual and less emotional. Because an opinion is held at the intellectual level only, it is more subject to change than is a belief, which is more deeply rooted in our emotions. New and better information may change an opinion, but beliefs die hard. "I've already made up my mind—don't confuse me with the facts." Beliefs that are really central to our value systems are seldom modified except over a long period of time or as a result of severe shock or a traumatic experience.

In addition to whatever attitudes we hold regarding a given subject, we humans have a general attitude of resistance to change. Even if the stimulus to change comes from within ourselves, we feel some risk when we think of altering present behaviors or beliefs.

It is vital to learn as much as you can about your audience's position on the proposition you intend to present. If you understand your listeners' opinions, attitudes and beliefs, you can then attempt to modify any attitudes that are inconsistent with your proposal.[1]

Of equal importance is learning whether an existing position is newly formed, is specific, and is lightly held, or whether it has been held for a long time, is generalized over a wide variety of situations, and is strongly held. In general, positions that have been adopted recently and that are lightly held are easier to change than are more established beliefs. In constructing arguments to change lightly held beliefs you can usually be direct. Using a direct approach to change a long-standing belief may cause your audience to simply stop listening.

Summary of Audience Analysis

To summarize what we have said about audience analysis:

1. Find out the general makeup of the audience and its attitudes (favorable, neutral, or unfavorable) toward the topic and you, the speaker.
2. Provide the listeners with a motivation for accepting the proposition by showing how it serves their basic needs, their short- and long-term self-interests.
3. Inspire your listeners to want to believe and to act as you would like them to by (1) establishing a common ground of shared attitudes and beliefs between you and the audience; and (2) identifying the proposition as one that is of immediate interest to the listeners or to someone near to them. The values that underlie a speech must appear familiar and important to the *listener*.

Newspaper writers Lou Cannon and Lee Lescaze of the *Washington Post* studied the decision-making process of President Ronald Reagan in 1982. From their interviews with presidential aides they reported the following:

> On policy issues Reagan makes strong ideological arguments that sometimes with difficulty can be countered by factual rebuttals. Aides know that their chances of changing Reagan's mind usually depend on whether they can fit their arguments into the president's philosophical framework.[2]

4. Maximize the possibility that the attitude/behavior change will be a lasting one by making use of repetition.

Whatever persuasive arguments you use to attempt to win the audience to your point of view will have to meet the listeners' tests for what will convince them. They think they already have the rational view, so the burden of proof that they should change that view lies with you. Dale Carnegie, in his famous *How to Win Friends and Influence People,* advised, "There is only one way under high Heaven to get anybody to do anything . . . and that is by making the other person *want* to do it." Even if the communication appears to be successful, the change of opinion or behavior will not last unless the audience participates willingly in making the change.

Even when a listener changes his or her position on an issue, there is a strong tendency to return to the attitude previously held, perhaps as a result of hearing contrary information that reaffirms the position previously held by the listener. The likelihood that this reversion will occur is strongly dependent on the credibility of the source and supporting material, and on how often the listener is reminded of the reason for a change. Communications via the mass media are more likely to reinforce existing opinion than to lead it; enduring change is more likely to result from a continuing series of personal interchanges among people who are closely associated.

Proofs

To convince an audience to accept a proposition, the persuasive speaker will have to offer proof that the point of view (or action) is worthy of adoption. The speaker can use emotional proofs, logical proofs, and personal credibility (in rhetorical theory called "ethical proofs"). After having analyzed the listeners to learn how best to influence them, the speaker should then marshal the proofs that seem most likely to be persuasive. All of us like to think that we make decisions based primarily on facts, and we appreciate being furnished a logical basis for making the change requested by the proposition. However, the most successful persuasive communication consists of a balance among emotional proofs, logical proofs, and personal credibility.

The elements of logical proof are the evidence presented to support the proposition and the reasoning process used to arrive at the speaker's interpretation of the evidence on the issue—the belief or action he or she wants the audience to adopt. ("Why should I accept this analysis of the situation? Why is the action you suggest the best one to choose?")

Emotional aspects seek to arouse the feelings of the audience to cause changes in their behavior. ("Why should I care about this? Why is this relevant to me now?")

A speaker's personal credibility is based on the audience's attitude toward the speaker, which in turn influences the listener to react favorably or unfavorably toward the proposition. ("Why should I listen to you on this matter?")

In combination then, the persuasive speaker uses logical proofs to demonstrate relationships between ideas, and psychological or extra-logical proofs to convince the audience to accept his or her version about what conclusions to draw from the evidence presented.

In order to accomplish this specific purpose the speaker presents the audience with proofs for the proposition. The three kinds of proofs—emotional, logical, and personal credibility—are described in the next section of this chapter.

Emotional Proofs

Far from being inferior, emotional proofs are at least an equal partner to their logical counterparts. Effective emotional proofs consist of good, solid reasons for a change, phrased in a way that appeals to basic human emotions, such as love, hate, happiness, sadness, anxiety, fear, anger, guilt, or pity. These feelings already exist in your listeners; your goal as a persuasive speaker is to arouse and reinforce them, and to relate them to your proposition. The language in the following ad, entitled "Idaho: The Great Getaway," would be particularly effective with a listener who already enjoyed winter sports, arousing sensory images of remembered good times: "In Idaho, you'll find a four-season vacationland—not the least of which is our magnificent winters. Imagine a soft white blanket of fresh, newly fallen snow; silvery dusted ponderosa pines offset by rocky, jagged peaks; a soft, serene blue sky, and a warm, blazing fireside. In Idaho that's just the start." When added to some rational reasons for choosing to vacation in Idaho (specifics about facilities and terrain for skiing and snowmobiling, and availability and cost of accommodations) this appeal to emotions could contribute a lot toward clinching the proposition, "Take your winter vacation in Idaho."

The sincere speaker must be certain that emotional appeals are "extra-logical," not "illogical," means of motivation. If the listener's experience points to the falsity of the proposition, an emotional appeal is not helpful, but instead is seen as crassly manipulative. Even very young children soon learn to mistrust advertisements that promise wild trucking adventures with unbreakable toys made of "high impact polyethylene styrene plastic."

If your proposition is, "Take safety precautions around a home swimming pool," you might recount an illustrative incident that would arouse discomfort and fear in your audience: "I know of a two-and-one-half-year-old boy who could really have benefited from a program of safety inspection for home swimming pools. This little boy didn't understand that water is dangerous, so one hot California day he stepped into eight feet of water and couldn't get out. His mother heard his cries, but by the time she got there he was lying on the bottom of the pool. His mother was a nonswimmer, but she jumped in to try to pull him out. She couldn't reach him but did manage to crawl out, get to a phone, and call a rescue squad. The rescue squad used CPR, then transported the boy to the hospital. He had gone without breathing for at least ten minutes, but miraculously he survived, and without any physical or mental damage. I suppose you think he'd learned his lesson? Guess again—he doesn't remember his ordeal and isn't the least bit afraid of water. A simple fence or pool cover could have averted this near tragedy. . . ."

Research spanning a period of years reveals that appeals to emotions, such as fear, are effective, but that a speaker should mesh the intensity of the appeal with the nature of the audience and relevant facts.[3] Threats or intensely emotional messages may backfire and provoke resistance in listeners (such as the notorious driver-training films showing grisly scenes of mangled bodies). Audience members may (1) quit listening or looking; (2) react negatively to the communicator; or (3) ignore or minimize the danger being described.

However, it has been shown that if the speaker takes care to supply a way to avoid the undesirable consequences of the feared action or circumstances, the use of fear messages will generate the desired persuasive result.[4]

Personal Credibility

The speaker uses personal credibility to persuade by adding the weight of his or her intelligence, goodwill, personality, character, sincerity, and reputation for past accomplishments to help support the proposition.[5] Quintilian, a renowned Roman orator and teacher of rhetoric, refers to this persuasive appeal as "the good man speaking well."

You can use personal credibility to persuade an audience by attention to (1) identification, (2) yes-response, (3) delivery, and (4) suggestion.

When the conduct of men is designed to be influenced, *persuasion,* kind, unassuming persuasion should ever be adopted. It is an old and true maxim, that a "drop of honey catches more flies than a gallon of gall." So with men. If you would win a man over to your cause, first convince him that you are his sincere friend. Therein is a drop of honey that catches his heart, which, say what he will, is the great high road to his reason.

Abraham Lincoln

Identification

Speaker credibility rests on identification between speaker and audience. If the listeners in the audience perceive the speaker to be "one of them," they will accept a wider range of ideas as being plausible, whereas they will have a strong tendency to reject even slightly differing ideas from someone with whom they do not identify.

An important first step for the speaker is to establish a common ground with the audience, to reduce the psychological distance between them. You will remember that this is one of the three main purposes served by the introduction to a speech, along with arousing interest and leading into the speech that follows. As a persuasive speaker, you must move quickly to establish confidence and respect for yourself as a speaker or run the risk that hostility toward the ideas presented will turn into hostility toward you. The *New Yorker* tells of an incident in which Margaret Thatcher, while serving as the Conservative Prime Minister of England, showed an insensitivity to the differences between her own and her listeners' experiences, and thereby alienated her audience. Mrs. Thatcher, whose own degree is from Oxford in chemistry, was touring the schools in a run-down North London borough. She tried to explain oxidation to the boys in a chemistry class by asking them to recall what happens when they eat an egg with a sterling-silver spoon. The boys had never eaten with a sterling-silver spoon so they would not have seen how the sulphur in an egg turns a silver spoon black.[6] Mrs. Thatcher failed to find a common ground on which she and her audience could meet.

You should establish a unifying connection between your ideas and the listeners' currently held beliefs, and show how your purposes mesh with theirs. Choose those aspects that do coincide and accentuate them, while minimizing the points of difference. Kelly Zmak, a student at San Jose State University in California, established common ground with other college students in the following manner:

. . . you know, as college people we all have something in common. We want to be successful. The levels of our success vary, but to be successful is something we all strive for. Having an advantage in today's world is something none of us would mind. But having a disadvantage is something that none of us can afford. . . .[7]

Without civic morality, communities perish; without personal morality their survival has no value.

Bertrand Russell

After pointing out this common concern, Kelly goes on to suggest students should purchase a personal computer. If Kelly had started by stating students should buy computers, the speech would be much less effective.

Yes-Response

Generally speaking, if you open your speech on common ground, on things you and the audience can agree on, you enhance the chances the audience will continue to agree with you as you move on to things you may disagree about. Sales representatives certainly appreciate the value of the "yes-response." For example, life insurance agents have learned to ask a number of questions that call for a yes-response. They ask you if security is important, if x number of dollars would provide a decent retirement income, if saving a portion of your income each month is a good idea, and so on. Experience has taught these agents that getting you to answer yes to such questions makes it easier to say yes to an insurance policy. John F. Kennedy used this agreement to disagreement pattern with great effect in his inaugural address. Even though there are numerous possible points for disagreement, there is always something listeners can agree with in every line of this address, which is in the following excerpt:

> We observe today not a victory of party but a celebration of freedom, symbolizing an end as well as a beginning, signifying renewal as well as change. For I have sworn before you and Almighty God the same solemn oath our forebears prescribed nearly a century and three-quarters ago.
> The world is very different now. For man holds in his mortal hands the power to abolish all forms of human poverty and all forms of human life. And yet the same revolutionary belief for which our forebears fought is still at issue around the globe, the belief that the rights of man come not from the generosity of the state but from the hand of God.
> We dare not forget today that we are the heirs of that first revolution. Let the word go forth from this time and place, to friend and foe alike, that the torch has been passed to a new generation of Americans, born in this century, tempered by war, disciplined by a hard and bitter peace, proud of our ancient heritage, and unwilling to witness or permit the slow undoing of these human rights to which this nation has always been committed, and to which we are committed today at home and around the world.
> Let every nation know, whether it wishes us well or ill, that we shall pay any price, bear any burden, meet any hardship, support any friend, oppose any foe to assure the survival and the success of liberty.

Delivery

If you are lively, self-assured, and enthusiastic when you speak, you project a positive image that is likely to influence the audience favorably toward your message. Whether your personal style is animated or quietly intense, you must show conviction yourself if you would hope to convince others.

Good bodily action is especially vital to the success of the persuasive speaker. Read again the information in chapter 11 and redouble your efforts to *show* your interest and involvement in the topic.

Suggestion

Suggestion, one of the most subtle forms of exerting control through communication, is the process of stating a message in such a way as to plant an idea in the mind of the listener, although no reasons for it or evidence to support it are offered by the speaker. Suggestion then shapes a listener's response without rational deliberation and sometimes without conscious awareness. To illustrate how suggestion might influence your thinking, try counting to ten *without* thinking of a rabbit. Suggestion is most successful if the persuader does the following:

1. Uses his or her own prestige to establish personal credibility.
2. Aligns the speech proposition with the motives and beliefs of the listeners, seeking to have the suggestion seem to originate with the listener.
3. Uses vivid, positive language. Throughout the speech, suggestion will be enhanced if the persuader states ideas positively, not negatively, in favor of his or her own ideas and not against the opposing view. Word choices are critical, and such phrases as "I think we can all agree," or "As we all know," can lead the audience toward the acceptance of your ideas.
4. Delivers the message forcefully.
5. Repeats the message.

Techniques of suggestion are widely used in politics and advertising. Politicians are using suggestion when they claim to have voted favorably on an issue. They leave it up to the listener to decide if favorably meant being for or against!

Ethics of Persuasion

The ability to persuade others is important and useful to us personally, professionally, and in society. It is important that these techniques be used responsibly and ethically, and nowhere is this more important than in the matter of persuasion by suggestion. If suggestion may cause a listener to accept uncritically an idea we have proposed, we bear a heavy responsibility to be sure that we do not violate that trust.

We all know of instances in which persuasive techniques have been used for personal gain. One of the most chilling examples is that of Adolf Hitler. Detestable though he was, Hitler was a master of using both verbal and nonverbal suggestive techniques to achieve his goals. Analysis of the content of his speeches shows them to be shallow and unimaginative. Today we are horrified by his demagogic appeals to race pride and his doctrine of hatred and persecution of the Jews as a scapegoat for national problems, but he was able to influence audiences. He spoke in the town squares of Germany, and whenever possible he delivered the speech from an elevated location, like a second-story balcony. Knowing that music can create a receptive mood, Hitler arranged for drums to play a particular rhythm to rouse the crowd before his appearance. His speech then echoed the same rhythm the drums had been playing, and the resultant delivery pattern had such a hypnotic effect that weaknesses in logic and content went unnoticed.

Credibility can be a powerful factor in persuasion; if you are seen as trustworthy, competent, and dynamic, you will be a more effective persuader than one who is not. Richard Nixon is a good example of a powerful figure who was rendered virtually powerless by loss of his credibility. During the course of the two-year investigation following the Watergate break-in, Nixon issued many statements that he later had to retract or that proved to be untrue. In 1972 he won an overwhelming reelection victory, but by 1974 he was forced to resign from office. Although Nixon was never actually convicted of a crime, he was so widely thought to be untrustworthy that he could no longer function as president.

A great deal of attention has been paid in recent years to image building, both by individuals and by corporations. Many advertising dollars are spent, not to sell a specific product but to promote the image of a particular oil company or public utility as "good guys."

In political campaigns, too, we see a blending of substantive issues and image, with more and more emphasis being placed on a candidate's image. The most successful strategy seems to be to make vague statements that do not commit the candidate to any stand on controversial issues, but that allow the listener to "fill in the blanks" with his or her own conclusions.

(The following is condensed from an article by Lloyd Shearer, "Stamp Out 'Doublespeak'," *Parade Magazine,* January 10, 1988, p. 16.[8])

'In this world nothing is certain but death and taxes.' Benjamin Franklin penned those immortal words to a friend in France on Nov. 13, 1789.

"If he were writing that letter today," says William Lutz, "Franklin's update might easily read: 'In this world nothing is certain except negative patient care outcome and revenue enhancement.' "

> Because there has been implanted in us the power to persuade each other . . .
> not only have we escaped the life of the wild beasts but we have come together
> and founded cities and made laws and invented arts. . . .
>
> *Isocrates*

Professor William Lutz chairs the Committee on Public Doublespeak. (Doublespeak is a word which combines "doublethink" and "newspeak" from George Orwell's novel *1984,* and which now stands for double-talk and all forms of deceptive language, including gobbledygook and officialese.)

Lutz maintains that doublespeak has become increasingly prevalent in government, where officials use words to conceal rather than communicate, to obscure rather than clarify. He has collected the following examples:

Military officers have referred to a pencil as a "portable hand-held communications inscriber." A bullet hole has been defined as a "ballistically induced aperture in the subcutaneous environment." A tent is a "frame-supported tension structure." To kill is to "terminate with extreme prejudice." A parachute is an "aerodynamic personnel decelerator," and a toothpick is a "wood interdental stimulator."

Doublespeak is infectious. In the field of medicine, malpractice is described delicately as a "therapeutic misadventure." Death frequently is referred to as a "terminal episode," and amphetamine pills are classified as "activity boosters."

To define what is ethical is not easy, but some basic points can be agreed upon: a communicator is unethical if (1) his or her purpose or goal is to manipulate the listener with the intent to harm someone else; (2) if the content of the message is known to be untrue; or (3) if, however good the end may be, the means of achieving it are questionable. Deliberately suppressing information that would help the listener to make a balanced judgment is unethical behavior on the part of the speaker.

At a broad level, we can all agree that people should act in an ethical manner, but just what is ethical in a specific instance might be difficult to discern. For instance, is it wrong to tell a lie to avoid hurting someone's feelings? Some people would feel you should not lie even in this instance, but others believe it could be justifiable. Thomas Nilsen offered the following suggestion: "Whatever develops, enlarges, enhances human personalities is good; whatever restricts, degrades, or injures human personalities is bad."[9] This approach to ethics is situational: that is, what is ethical or unethical ought to be determined by the circumstances surrounding the event. Others hold that there are overarching guidelines that apply to human conduct in any circumstance. Standards of fairness and decency are reflected in our constitutional safeguards of speech, press, and assembly, and we as individual speakers should seek to uphold those standards.

"Who is the fairest one of all, and state your sources!"

Drawing by Ed Fisher; © 1984. The New Yorker Magazine, Inc.

Credibility in the Classroom

You can enhance your own credibility as a communication source in the classroom if throughout the course you show yourself to be a conscientious person who prepares assignments well and delivers them on time; you look for subjects that will be of interest and benefit to the others in the class; you are friendly, enthusiastic, attractive to be around; and if you seem to be genuinely interested in improving your own speaking ability and helping others to improve theirs by offering positive encouragement and thoughtful evaluations of their strengths and weaknesses.

During a speech you can build your own credibility by citing the sources you are using to back up your arguments. Thus you show respect for your listeners by recognizing that strong proofs are necessary to convince them, and you indicate the effort you have extended to get accurate information.

Logical Proofs

Logical proof consists of evidence and reasoning.

Evidence

Evidence consists of sources outside the speaker's own opinion and knowledge, which may be used to provide proof or lend support to a conclusion. Evidence may take many forms: oral or written statements by authoritative

> Speech is power: Speech is to persuade, to convert, to compel.
>
> *Ralph Waldo Emerson*

sources, graphs, charts, visual aids, or documents. It should be current, from a credible source, specifically relevant to the issue, and should provide real and important support for the point being made.[10]

Evidence is of three kinds: (1) authority, (2) examples, and (3) statistics:

1. Authority means quoted testimony from another person whose opinion supports the speaker's. You should quote a recent statement by an expert appropriate to the topic, whose opinion will be respected by the audience. Source credibility should be established by citing the background of experience, training, or special knowledge that qualifies this person as an expert on the topic. Sources of evidence may be classified as being (a) unbiased, which is a competent source who has nothing to gain from the statement; (b) reluctant, which is a source who has a strong interest in this issue, but who provides information that does not support or is actually contrary to that person's own best interests (this kind of evidence is *very* strong); (c) biased, which is a source who has something to gain and who provides information that supports his or her interest (this doesn't mean the information from this source *must* be distorted, but an intelligent audience would think twice before accepting it without other supporting evidence). Quotation from an authority is a relatively weak form of evidence, because you can almost always find an "expert" who supports the opposing view, so testimony should be used in combination with other forms of proof.
2. Examples are specific illustrations of the point you are making. You must provide examples that are sufficient in number and representative in kind, and that support the conclusions drawn from the examples.
3. Statistics are numerical examples of quantitative information that support your point. You should get figures that are clear, accurate, and sufficient in number to support the major points, especially, and to be certain that the source and the method of gathering the data are credible.

> We may take Fancy for a companion, but must follow Reason as our guide.
>
> *Samuel Johnson*

Test for Evidence Both speaker and listeners should carefully test the validity of all evidence by answering the following questions:

1. Does enough evidence exist to support the conclusion?
2. Is the evidence clear to the members of the audience or appropriate to their information and interest levels?
3. Is the evidence consistent? Does other evidence agree with the evidence in question?
4. Is the evidence correctly quoted? Can this be verified?
5. Is the source of the evidence clearly identified?
   a. If a publication—list author, publisher, sponsor.
   b. If an authority—name specifically and give credentials, not "Nine out of ten doctors. . . ."
6. Is the source one that will be recognized by this audience as being authoritative on this subject?
7. Is the source of the evidence reliable, competent, truthful, or unbiased?
8. Is the evidence relevant? Does it lead logically and directly to the conclusion?
9. Is the evidence statistically sound? Accurate? Based on valid sampling procedures? Reported in context? Supported by fair visual representations?
10. Is the evidence recent, not out-of-date?

Reasoning

Reasoning is the ability to recognize or create patterns of relationship between ideas, objects or events. By using reasoning, the speaker arrives at logical conclusions and the process is one of making inferences based on the available information. Such reasoning may proceed from (1) inductive proofs, (2) deductive proofs, (3) cause and effect relationships, (4) an analogy, or (5) from sign.

Inductive Inductive reasoning draws a general conclusion based on what was observed to be true in specific cases. "Every apple I've ever cut into contained seeds. I conclude (inductively) that apples have seeds."

Induction is widely used in science, political polling, and television ratings. In rating television shows, for example, a relatively small but carefully selected sample of viewing patterns is collected, and an inference is made that everyone else follows the same viewing pattern. Inductive reasoning always involves an inferential leap from known instances to the conclusion that the same thing will be true in other unknown instances. A speaker cannot prove anything "beyond a shadow of a doubt" unless every single case has been checked, and the speaker should recognize such doubts by using such terms as *can, might, probably,* and *more than likely.*

The quality of an inference or conclusion depends to a large degree on the quality of the evidence on which it is based. The probability that inductive reasoning will be valid can be improved if the speaker asks himself or herself these questions:

1. Are there a sufficient number of cases? The strongest generalization is one based on a large group of cases.
2. Are the cases fair and typical examples? If the number is not large, then the cases must be representative.
3. If there are exceptions, can they be accounted for? That is, do these exceptions make a difference?
4. Is the conclusion supported by other facts and reasoning?

Several of these questions can be applied to the following excerpt from a speech by David Bickford, a student at Brown University:

First, we need to look at how South Korea is now stronger against its international rivals, . . .

Now, when looking at the situation in South Korea as it exists right now, it is certainly easy to say, without equivocation, that the South Korean economic miracle has made it a stronger contender against traditional rivals Japan and North Korea. Kim Jung Young, a prominent South Korean journalist, noted in an interview with the *World Press Review* of October of last year, that already the South Korean position vis-à-vis Japan had improved significantly because of the economic growth. It noted normally that South Korea felt subordinate to Tokyo, but because of the vigor being felt within Seoul, the relationship was more on an even footing. And there were even bilateral trade agreements between the two nations that allowed for the sharing of technology improving vastly the image of the government of Chun Du Won of South Korea by making it appear to bring peace and prosperity to its people.

But an even more important rivalry for South Korea is the rivalry which exists with the Communist North. And that, too, has been improved somewhat as a result of this economic miracle. On November 30, 1986, *The New York Times* spoke about reunification talks between the North and the South at Panmunjom in the demilitarized zone. And said, because of the economic improvement in South Korea, South Korea was in a stronger position. *The Times* said that formerly, North Korea was more industrialized and more prosperous. But because of the reversal in the economies that had taken place, the South was now in a better position to resist the Communist infiltration and aggression from the North. So, from an international perspective, it certainly seems that South Korea is better-off. The economic miracle is driving political reform.[11]

To support his claim that "South Korea is now stronger against its international rivals," David cites changes in relationships with Japan and North Korea. Should he cite more instances? Are these typical relationships? Do the facts cited in these cases support David's conclusion?

Deductive   Deductive reasoning applies an accepted general principle to a specific instance. "All apples have seeds, so when I cut open this apple, I will expect to find seeds." The speaker should test deductive reasoning by asking these questions:

1. Is the general principle true or probably true?
2. Does this specific instance clearly comply with the general principle?

Two persuasion models are used to explain the process of logical reasoning by deduction; the traditional one was constructed centuries ago by Aristotle, and a modified version was developed by the twentieth-century theorist Stephen Toulmin.[12]

The Aristotelian system of logic is based on the syllogism or on its shortened form, the enthymeme. Aristotle's classic example of the syllogism is:

All men are mortal. (major premise)
Socrates is a man. (minor premise)
Therefore, Socrates is mortal. (conclusion)

This pattern is easily applied to many topics. If you wanted to convince your classmates that they should contribute to the local United Way campaign, you might construct the following pattern.

Charities deserve our support.
The United Way is a deserving charity.
The United Way should be supported.

This could be the basic structure of your speech. You must provide supporting data and appeals at each of these steps. Some things you can assume your audience will accept and fill in for themselves. In this instance, you can probably assume your audience already believes that charities deserve support and you can spend most of your time pointing out why this specific charity, the United Way, should be supported.

Figure 13.1 Toulmin's model of logic.

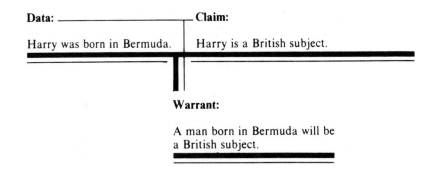

Data: ————————— Claim:

Harry was born in Bermuda. | Harry is a British subject.

Warrant:

A man born in Bermuda will be
a British subject.

Toulmin has constructed a slightly different logical model, which is illustrated in figure 13.1. You will notice that Toulmin used different terms, but both Aristotle and Toulmin have designed their models to answer three basic questions:

1. What are the facts?
2. What is your conclusion?
3. How did you arrive at that conclusion?

Mike Stolts, a student at the University of Wisconsin-Eau Claire, applies reasoning that can profitably be analyzed from Toulmin's perspective:

"Obesity is rapidly becoming a serious problem. . . . John C. McCabe, chairman of Blue Cross and Blue Shield, says, 'We are the fattest nation in the world. . . .' Children who are obese face tremendous obstacles. . . ."[13]

Figure 13.2 shows how the Toulmin model can be applied to this argument. Once an argument is analyzed from this perspective, you can determine how sound the position is. For instance, in the above argument we would like to know what obstacles are faced by obese children, whether there is any hard evidence we are the fattest nation, etc.

Figure 13.2 Application of Toulmin model.

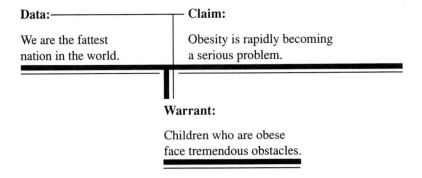

Data:————————— Claim:

We are the fattest
nation in the world. | Obesity is rapidly becoming
a serious problem.

Warrant:

Children who are obese
face tremendous obstacles.

And a further example:

It doesn't take a football expert to spot a probable kick play, but how do you do it? By what process of reasoning do you arrive at the "certainty" that a kick is about to happen? If we apply these two models to a fourth down situation, they might look like this.

Aristotle:

> A team that sends in its kicking specialist on the fourth down will punt. (major)
> It is fourth down and the kicking specialist just came in. (minor)
> This team will punt. (conclusion)

Now, Toulmin in for Aristotle:

Data: _____ Claim:
It is fourth down and the kicking   This team will punt.
specialist just came in.

Warrant:
A team that sends in a kicking
specialist on the fourth down will punt.

Notice that the major premise in the Aristotelian syllogism and the warrant in the Toulmin model are generalizations that come from having watched many football games, and if those general "truths" are not accurate the conclusion will not be correct, no matter how logical the reasoning process.

Even now you may be saying, "Wait just a minute! Maybe it's late in the game and the team is behind, and they've decided to fake a kick and take a chance on running or passing." It was just to allow for these surprise exceptions that Toulmin constructed an expanded model which further develops the warrant (figure 13.3). Try fitting our football example into this reasoning model.

The data or backing that supports the warrant is listed to indicate more fully the basis for judgment in arriving at the claim; any stated or unstated qualifiers or exclusions to the stated claim are also noted. The Toulmin model then has six major components:

1. Data: evidence.
2. Warrant: connecting premise that shows the justifiable connection between the evidence (data) and the conclusion drawn from it (claim).
3. Claim: conclusion.
4. Backing: support for the warrant.
5. Rebuttal or reservation: possible exceptions to the warrant; situations in which the warrant would not necessarily apply.

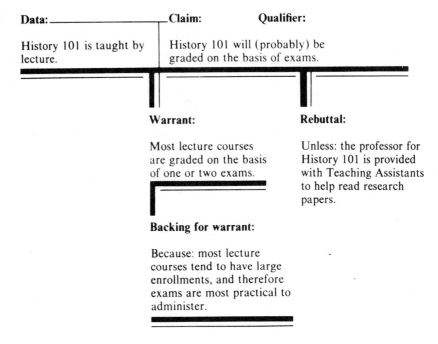

Figure 13.3 Expanded Toulmin model of logic showing its six major components.

Data: History 101 is taught by lecture.

Claim: History 101 will (probably) be graded on the basis of exams.

Qualifier:

Warrant: Most lecture courses are graded on the basis of one or two exams.

Rebuttal: Unless: the professor for History 101 is provided with Teaching Assistants to help read research papers.

Backing for warrant: Because: most lecture courses tend to have large enrollments, and therefore exams are most practical to administer.

6. Qualifier: word or phrase indicating the degree of certainty or the extent of probability.

An example of this expanded Toulmin model, with each of its six components labeled, is illustrated in figure 13.3. Either Aristotle's Toulmin's model, if conscientiously used, can result in a carefully reasoned persuasive argument.

Cause and Effect   Cause and effect relationships deal with probabilities, based on past experience with the cause and effect relationships between observable signs.

1. In reasoning from *cause* to *effect,* you see a known cause operating and assume that the accustomed effect will follow. If it is raining outside, you assume that, in all probability, the streets will be wet.
2. Reasoning from *effect* to *cause* proceeds in the opposite direction. You see wet streets and conclude that it has probably been raining. A medical diagnosis relies partially on observing the effects felt by the patient, and then attempting to reason back to discover the problem.
3. *Effect* to *effect* reasoning links two events, both of which are attributable to the same cause, and tend to appear together: if you see wet streets, you may expect to see people carrying umbrellas. The wet streets do not *cause* umbrella carrying, but they have the same cause and tend to appear together.

In testing cause and effect reasoning, the speaker attempts to discover whether a causal relationship actually exists by asking these questions:

1. Does one event result from another or, by coincidence, does it just happen to occur after it? A 10 o'clock class occurs after a 9 o'clock class, but it is not caused by it.
2. Has the cause been confused with the effect—which caused which? The longer you stay in the hospital after surgery, the more likely you are to get an infection. Did you get the infection *because* you stayed in the hospital, or did you stay in the hospital *because* you got an infection?
3. Could some other factor prevent the expected result? Based on population trends and food supplies in 1800, Thomas Malthus predicted that a worldwide famine was imminent, but improved methods of growing food have thus far prevented such a famine.
4. Could some other cause be responsible for producing this effect? Consumer advocates and car companies often are at odds over the cause of accidents. For instance, consumer activist Ralph Nader, in *Unsafe at Any Speed,*[14] argued that a primary cause of automobile accidents is the way that cars are designed. Following the publication of Nader's book, General Motors produced a film on auto safety, which stressed the individual driver and faulty road construction as the major causes of accidents.
5. Is the "effect" ever seen to be present when the "cause" has not been operating?
6. Has the causal relationship been oversimplified, attributing the result to one cause when actually several causes are operating?
7. Is this cause necessary but perhaps not sufficient to create the predicted effect? It is true that getting up in the morning is necessary to succeeding in school or keeping a job, but it is not sufficient; success will not inevitably follow unless other causes are also present.

In the following speech excerpt, Kim K. Fageroos, a student at San Diego State University, uses cause and effect reasoning to point out that withdrawing our investments in South Africa would harm rather than help black people in South Africa.

Common Cause magazine, in their May/June 1985 issue stated that critics, including the Reagan administration, say that sanctions would gain little but moral superiority for the United States. And they might even backfire—resulting in a significant loss of jobs for South African blacks. According to *Time* magazine, at present, approximately 80 percent of the workers in American firms in South Africa are black.[15]

"We must be in the Italian Alps."
Drawing by Woodman; © 1988. The New Yorker Magazine, Inc.

Analogy If two objects or events are alike in certain known respects it can be predicted that they will be found to be alike in some other respect about which the speaker wants to draw a conclusion. Cause and effect reasoning makes broad generalizations; reasoning from analogy compares two specific objects or events. An example of argument from analogy is, "I have worked for five years as a part-time bookkeeper for Murphy and Sons, and I am confident that I can handle the work in your office."

1. Do the two instances have a great many similarities? (Is the work in this office similar to that at Murphy and Sons?)
2. Are the similarities significant to the point being made? (If you are to do public relations work in the new office, your bookkeeping experience is not very significant.)
3. If there are points of difference, can they be shown to be insignificant to the comparison? (Perhaps the office you have been working in has a much smaller staff, but you may be able to point out that this is not important if the work is similar.)

Reasoning from Sign Reasoning from sign is based on the association between one event and another event. If you go outside in the summer and the ground is wet, you take that to be a sign that it has recently rained. In the past, speakers argued that the United States should not open diplomatic relations with mainland China because doing so was a sign that we approved of their policies.

Several tests can be applied to arguments based on reasoning from sign. First, is there an inherent relationship between the two events? In the case of recognizing China you could argue that no inherent relationship exists because we maintain diplomatic relationships with many countries whose policies we find unacceptable. Second, are there mitigating circumstances that suggest the item being taken as a sign of one thing might be better understood as a sign of something else? For instance, you might argue that a tariff on computer chips from Japan is a sign of a deteriorating relationship between the countries. However, freer trade policies on beef, cars, and other goods between these countries would suggest an improving relationship.

Faulty reasoning from sign, in everyday terms, is called "jumping to conclusions."

Example

Let's examine the following quotation:

"It seems to me the metaphor of saving the wild salmon may be the metaphor for saving ourselves," suggested anthropologist Courtland Smith.

Smith said efforts to save the salmon runs may also have a more important result.

"Any great institution that will maintain the wild salmon will also maintain habitat for humans as well.

"And isn't also saving the wild salmon saving something of ourselves as well?"[16]

Smith's statement is primarily an example of reasoning from analogy: Human beings are like salmon. Both are life forms. Both depend on a healthy environment. Thus we save ourselves when we protect the environment.

But also, as is the case with so many arguments from real life, the reasoning from analogy also exists side-by-side with cause-effect reasoning: A poor environment will cause both humans and salmon to die.

And with reasoning from sign: The salmon may be the best gauge of the region's environment.

Summary

The persuasive speaker seeks to present listeners with impelling proofs that cause them to believe or act in a particular way. Your persuasion is successful when your arguments appear to be so sound, so reasonable that, given its own beliefs, attitudes, and values, the audience sees that the only sensible course is to agree with your proposition. To achieve this effect, it is necessary to engage emotions as well as intellect. Information might be accepted on logical bases alone, but to inspire action, the listener must be involved emotionally as well. Further, when you persuade you take it upon yourself to lead and to advise, and we don't make a habit of accepting advice from people who know less about the matter than we do. Therefore, as a persuasive speaker you should use logical and emotional proofs and personal credibility to demonstrate that you know the subject, are reasoning well, and that the action you urge is in the listener's best interests.

| Exercises | 1. Read the following passages, decide the type of reasoning used, and determine how the reasoning could be improved. |

Exercises

1. Read the following passages, decide the type of reasoning used, and determine how the reasoning could be improved.
   a. Students of the eighties are more involved than the students of the seventies. Students ten years ago "dropped out" rather than "helped out" as do students today. The seventies student studied irrelevant material about how to improve humanity rather than working in constructive roles the way students do today.
   b. The NATO forces are unprepared for war. There are many more Warsaw Pact troops than NATO troops. The NATO forces' tanks are out of date. The NATO troops are not properly placed to engage the enemy promptly.
   c. Harvard is a fine university. Yale is also excellent. All Ivy League schools are superior.
2. Find one example of each of the types of reasoning discussed in this chapter. Be prepared to present and discuss your examples in class.
3. To gain insight into emotional appeal, examine a newspaper or magazine ad for its emotional appeals. What are the motivations the ad plays on (love, belonging, beauty, etc.)? What is the primary appeal the ad is making?
4. You might like to test your aptitude for recognizing doublespeak by trying your hand at the Doublespeak Quiz (on p. 267), which consists of matching letters on the right with the numbers on the left. The correct answers appear below.

Assignments

1. Prepare an analysis of a historically important persuasive speech. You should consider (1) what the logical and emotional proofs and appeals based on personal credibility were; and (2) what proofs were offered. You should organize this material into a two- or three-page paper to be presented to your instructor.
2. Write a two-page paper in which you advance an argument about some social issue (e.g., crime could be eliminated through social reform). Analyze the argument from Toulmin's and from Aristotle's perspectives. Which seems to be more useful?

Suggested Reading

Clark, Ruth A. *Persuasive Messages*. New York: Harper & Row, 1984. Chapters 2, 5, and 8.

Petty, Richard and Cacioppo, John. *Communication and Persuasion: Central and Peripheral Routes to Attitude Change*. New York: Springer-Verlag, 1986.

Reinard, John. "The Empirical Study of the Persuasive Effects of Evidence: The Status After Fifty Years of Research," *Human Communication Research* 15 (1988): 3–59.

```
┌─────────────────────────────────────────────────────────────┐
│                    DOUBLESPEAK QUIZ                          │
│  1. __ safety-related occurrence    A. to smell something    │
│  2. __ incomplete success           B. used car              │
│  3. __ fiscal underachievers        C. pig pens and chicken coops │
│  4. __ service technician           D. thermometer           │
│  5. __ non-goal oriented member     E. repairman             │
│        of society                   F. newspaper delivery person │
│  6. __ single-purpose               G. accident              │
│        agricultural structures      H. failure               │
│  7. __ downsizing personnel         I. the poor              │
│  8. __ advanced downward            J. bum, street person    │
│        adjustments                  K. firing employees      │
│  9. __ collateral damage            L. budget cuts           │
│ 10. __ experienced automobile       M. bank robbery          │
│ 11. __ media courier                N. civilian casualties during │
│ 12. __ unauthorized withdrawal         war                   │
│ 13. __ digital fever computer       O. grocery-store checkout │
│ 14. __ organoleptic analysis           clerk                 │
│ 15. __ nail technician              P. anti-satellite weapon │
│ 16. __ philosophically              Q. scared                │
│        disillusioned                R. greeting cards        │
│ 17. __ kinetic kill vehicle         S. manicurist            │
│ 18. __ ultimate high-intensity      T. nuclear war           │
│        warfare                                               │
│ 19. __ social-expression                                     │
│        products                                              │
│ 20. __ career associate                                      │
│        scanning professional                                 │
├─────────────────────────────────────────────────────────────┤
│ ANSWERS:              14-A, 15-S, 16-Q, 17-P, 18-T, 19-R, 20-O. │
│ 1-G, 2-H, 3-I, 4-E, 5-J, 6-C, 7-K, 8-L, 9-N, 10-B, 11-F, 12-M, 13-D, │
└─────────────────────────────────────────────────────────────┘
```

Lloyd Shearer in PARADE

Sanders, Robert E. *Cognitive Foundations of Calculated Speech: Controlling Understandings in Conversation and Persuasion.* Albany, N.Y.: State University of New York Press, 1987. Chapter 10.

Smith, Mary J. *Persuasion and Human Action.* Belmont, Calif.: Wadsworth, 1982. Chapters 5, 6, 7, and 8.

Notes

1. Bernard Berelson and Gary A. Steiner, *Human Behavior: An Inventory of Scientific Findings* (New York: Harcourt, Brace, & World, 1964): 558.
2. *Lewiston Morning Tribune,* March 28, 1982.
3. Mary John Smith, *Persuasion and Human Action* (Belmont, Calif.: Wadsworth, 1982): 230–32.
4. Mike Allen and Raymond W. Preiss, "Using Meta-Analyses to Evaluate Curriculum: An Examination of Selected College Textbooks," *Communication Education* 38, April 1990: 103–116.
5. Ruth Anne Clark, *Persuasive Messages* (New York: Harper & Row, 1984): 189–215.

6. Jane Kramer, "A Reporter in Europe: London," *New Yorker* (May 11, 1981): 104.

7. Kelly Zmak, "Sales Speech," *Championship Debates and Speeches,* eds. J. K. Boaz and J. R. Brey (Normal, Ill.: American Forensic Association, 1987): 127.

8. Lloyd Shearer, "Stamp Out 'Doublespeak'," *Parade Magazine,* January 10, 1988: 16.

9. Thomas R. Nilsen, *Ethics of Speech Communication* (New York: Bobbs-Merrill, 1966): 9.

10. John Reinard, "The Empirical Study of the Persuasive Effects of Evidence: The Status After Fifty Years of Research," *Human Communication Research* 15 (1988): 3–59.

11. David Bickford, "Extemporaneous Speech," 1987 *Championship Debates and Speeches,* eds. J. K. Boaz and J. R. Brey (Normal, Ill.: American Forensic Association, 1987): 137.

12. James C. McCroskey, "Toulmin and the Basic Course," *Speech Teacher* 14 (March 1965): 91–100.

13. Mike Stolts, "Persuasive Speech," 1987 *Championship Debates and Speeches,* eds. J. K. Boaz and J. R. Brey (Normal, Ill.: American Forensic Association, 1987): 122.

14. Ralph Nader, *Unsafe At Any Speed* (New York: Pocket Books, 1965, rev. ed. 1971).

15. Kim Fageroos, "Persuasive Speech," 1986 *Championship Debates and Speeches,* eds. J. K. Boaz and J. R. Brey (Normal, Ill.: American Forensic Association, 1987): 129–30.

16. Bill Loftus, "Prof Takes Fresh Look at Salmon," *Lewiston Morning Tribune,* September 1, 1988.

14 Constructing the Persuasive Speech

Chapter Outline

The fool tells me his reasons, the wise man persuades me with my own.

Aristotle

As Aristotle points out, attaining congruence between your motives and those of your audience should be a prime consideration as you approach the task of putting a persuasive speech together. This chapter is designed to help you with the practical aspects of constructing your persuasive speech.

Patterns of Organization

The structure of a persuasive speech should (1) provide familiarity of form for the listener, and thus arouse attention, and (2) constitute a framework to show the proofs of your arguments to their best advantage. They are not scattered around, but are organized. The structural form of a persuasive speech should follow that of our customary thought patterns. This structure consists of the proposition you want the audience to accept and the arguments that support the truth of the proposition. Arguments justify your position by giving your listeners reasons to believe that what you say is true, not absolute proof that they are, but rational grounds for believing them to be true. The listeners decide what issues need to be resolved before they will accept the proposition, and they decide what and how many proofs will constitute satisfactory answers to their questions. As a persuasive speaker you seek to have the audience accept the individual supporting arguments and go from there to accept the proposition that the arguments support. The number, weight, and quality of these arguments, and the degree to which they are clear, relevant, and consistently supportive of the proposition will determine how persuasive your speech is. In addition, the logical relationship between these arguments themselves (inductive, deductive, and causal relationships) is both pleasing and persuasive, since these follow the natural order of our own thought patterns.

Among these generally accepted thought patterns are the following:

1. Present the need before the solution to the need. For example, if you present a plan for an escort service to protect female students walking on campus at night and then cite statistics on the incidence of rape, your audience may tune you out before they see the relevance of the solution to any concern of theirs.
2. Present the cause before the effect. If your subject is automobile maintenance, "Keeping your car tuned up increases its efficiency and saves you money" is stronger than "To increase efficiency and save money, keep your car tuned up!"
3. Present the known before the unknown. Especially if you are introducing complex material, attempting to dispel erroneous information, or trying to modify attitudes based on a failure to

understand the elements of the case, you should begin with the most familiar elements and proceed to the new, unfamiliar elements of the case. Jan Moreland uses this principle to introduce her topic in the persuasive speech that is presented at the end of the chapter. She draws a scene reflecting a familiar television commercial and uses that as the springboard for her discussion of the dangers of using a particular pesticide.

4. Place your most important points first and last. The principle of primacy-recency holds that material placed first is in a prominent position, and that material placed last has a very good chance of sticking in the minds of the audience. So, for instance, if you are arguing in favor of gun control and you plan to discuss constitutional protection, needless deaths, and the ability to enforce gun control laws, you might choose to discuss needless deaths first and enforcement ability last. Those would most likely be your strongest arguments, since opponents of gun control argue that the Constitution provides citizens with the right to bear arms.

Organizational Patterns for Persuasive Speeches

Some overall organizational strategies that you may use for persuading an audience to accept a proposition include the following:

1. **Criterial approach.** Set up criteria for a good solution and show how this solution fulfills the criteria best. In facing the problem of crowding in classrooms and no capital funds to build additional rooms, an acceptable solution has to meet the criteria of reducing crowding and not spending additional money. You might argue that holding split sessions of classes meets these criteria.

2. **Comparative advantage approach.** As compared to making no change, or making any other change, the solution you propose offers the most advantages and the fewest disadvantages. In this structure, you outline the problem, identify the possible solutions, and then compare their respective advantages and disadvantages. Let's assume you live in a state where there is general agreement that taxes need to be raised to improve highways and to better finance the school system. The question is not whether taxes should be increased but what kind of taxes should be levied. The suggested choices are property taxes, income taxes, and sales taxes, and you want to point out the advantages and disadvantages of each. You might point out who would be taxed the most under which system (some argue that sales taxes harm the poor more than the rich), which approach would generate the needed revenue, and which would be least likely to harm the economy. The concluding portion of the speech would be devoted to highlighting the approach that has the most advantages and the fewest disadvantages, and urging its adoption.

If the past is irrelevant to the present, the present is irrelevant to the future.

Alfred North Whitehead

3. **Residual reasoning.** Consider each potential solution, eliminating each one because of some fatal flaw. Yours is the one that is left with no major disadvantages. Those Canadians who believe that Quebec should become a separate nation argue that this is the most reasonable course of action since everything else has been tried.

4. **Proposition-to-proof.** A straightforward statement of the proposition, followed by the proofs that support it. For example, the proposition, "You should donate blood," could be followed by information about the number of lives that depend on such donations, the ease and painlessness of giving, and the fact that the listener's own life may depend on it someday.

5. **Monroe's Motivated Sequence.** This sequence contains five elements:
   a. **Attention.** Causes the listener to focus on the speech topic—"Do you realize that most of you will be prevented from purchasing a home when you want to?"
   b. **Need.** Identifies the problem that needs to be solved—"Interest rates need to be lowered."
   c. **Satisfaction.** Provides a solution to meet that need— "The Federal Reserve Board should be directed to reduce interest rates."
   d. **Visualization.** Creates a mental image of how things will be if the solution is put into effect—"People once again will be able to finance a home."
   e. **Action.** Directs listeners to what they can do to put the plan into effect—"Write to your representatives."

6. **Problem-solution order.** This organizational pattern is based on John Dewey's five steps of reflective thinking:
   a. What problem exists at the present time? What is the nature? Extent? Cause?
   b. What policy or course of action would solve this problem?
      (1) Does this policy or course of action specifically address the evils described in (*a*) and solve at least some of them?
      (2) Is this solution better than any of the other possible solutions?
      (3) Does the solution have any drawbacks that could create other problems? Do the benefits outweigh the disadvantages?

(4) Are there any significant obstacles to implementing the solution? Impractical? Legal obstacles? Cost? Powerful opposition?

(5) What are its chances of succeeding? Has it worked anywhere else?

(6) Describe the expected effects, noting how they differ from the present situation as described in (*a*).

c. How can we put the solution into effect?

(1) What should speaker and audience do to accomplish it?

(2) How can they go about it?

(3) Is it necessary to act immediately?

You might use this approach in discussing our foreign trade deficit.

A. What historical pattern exists in U.S. deficit spending? Is the current deficit spending pattern similar or different from the past? **Answer:** The current pattern is quite different; until recently the United States has recorded surpluses, not deficits. The cause seems to be complex: high domestic wages, low trade restrictions, favored nation status for certain developing countries, protectionism on the part of some of our trading partners, and government regulations, to name but a few factors.

B. A course of action to deal with the situation might be to reconsider favored nation status for those countries that can produce goods cheaper and more efficiently than can our domestic industries, to construct reciprocal protective barriers (i.e., their cars should have to pass the same list of inspections as ours), reduce government regulations, lower wages for our workers to make our goods more competitive. Trade unions may be expected to oppose any efforts to lower our workers' wages. It can be argued that lowering wages could have an effect at least as adverse on our domestic economy as continuing with the present trade deficit. Parallels can be drawn with the experience of other countries, for example Great Britain. If we take these steps we risk retaliation from other countries and the possibility that industry will be irresponsible.

C. Legislation would be required to put these solutions into effect. Individual audience members might be urged to write or call their senator or representative or to vote on pending legislation.

Step (*c*), the call for action, commonly takes the form of a challenge or appeal, an inducement, or a statement of personal intention on the part of the speaker.

One fact stands out in bold relief in the history of man's attempt for betterment. That is that when compulsion is used, only resentment is aroused, and the end is not gained. Only through moral suasion and appeal to man's reason can a movement succeed.

Samuel Gompers

With the friendly audience, the speaker's main objective is to intensify these positive feelings and to ensure action.

Persuading the Friendly, Neutral, or Hostile Audience

In chapter 11 we discussed the importance of analyzing the audience in order to determine listeners' attitudes regarding the speaker's proposition. Listener attitudes are classified in terms of direction (friendly, neutral, or hostile); the strength of the attitude (the degree to which it is held); and how important this attitude is to listeners (whether it occupies a central place in their value system). Let's look at each of these types of audiences—friendly, neutral, and hostile—to determine how best to approach them.

The Friendly Audience

If the audience is already interested in your subject and favorably inclined toward the course favored by you the speaker, then your main objective is to intensify these positive feelings and to ensure action. A proposition-to-proof order will be acceptable to this audience. However, you could lose

> Public speaking is an audience participation event; if it weren't, it would be private speaking.
>
> *Anonymous*

your listeners' interest and support if you simply restate what they already know. Discuss a few major issues to reinforce their beliefs and erase any doubts; then take them further by presenting a specific plan to move them to meaningful action.

The Neutral Audience

"Persuasion is the art of moving apathy in your direction." Apathy is the common state of the majority of listeners, often referred to in recent years as "the silent majority." Political campaigns concentrate on the uncommitted voter on the premise that the friendly voter is already in their camp and the hostile voter offers little hope of conversion.

Since one never knows what might appeal to a neutral audience, try to include as many sources of persuasion as you can. If the audience is at least open-minded on the issue you may be able to swing a few listeners who are moderates over to your point of view. For listeners who are interested but undecided, you will have to use your strongest arguments. If they are not really interested in the subject, try to motivate them by linking your proposition to some aspect of their self-interest. If they lack information, inform them. And establish yourself as a credible speaker through your logic, sincerity, and reference to your accomplishments in the subject under consideration.

Methods of organization to use with neutral audiences include proposition-to-proof, problem-solution, or comparative advantages. If your listeners do not disagree that something needs to be done, but have no opinion as to what the action should be, use the comparative advantages method of organization to show that the solution you propose is comparatively more advantageous. You can't answer every possible objection, so select the primary one that you think has prevented them from making a decision thus far. This block may well be caused by practical considerations. If so, show how the procedure you suggest has worked elsewhere, and the audience may be inclined to accept your proposal.

The Hostile Audience

First, keep in mind that it is almost impossible to change behavior if the audience is truly hostile and that in any case you can't take it very far in just one speech, so set your sights accordingly. If audience attitudes are hard and fixed, you may need to settle for a chance to speak your piece and hope that your listeners will give you a fair hearing. If given sufficient information and time to think over the ideas and talk to others regarding them, the audience may at least become more open to your message.

PEANUTS reprinted by permission of UFS, Inc.

Avoid any appearance of aggressiveness in the introduction. Start with areas of agreement. If you present the proposition at all at this point, it might be better to phrase it as a question. Attempt to do the following:

1. Establish a common ground. Introduce facts and ideas acceptable to the audience, to lay a foundation for agreement and to lead toward the conclusion favored by the speaker. Try to avoid running headlong into any hard-core beliefs or prejudices that are counter to your goal. Make use of any audience attitudes that are favorable to your purpose, if you can honestly identify with them.
2. Sometimes excluding factors that are irrelevant can serve to set aside points of disagreement.
3. Make any concessions you can to your listeners' point of view, without weakening the logic of your case.

If your audience holds an opposing attitude to your proposition, here are some strategies for dealing with the problem:

1. Acknowledge the worth of the attitude. Admit that it has been justified in the past. Then point out that changes have created a situation that demands a different attitude.
2. Show that this different attitude is desirable and give the rewards that will come from adopting it.
3. Show that this change in attitude is a minor one, not drastic; it does not destroy other beliefs, but is actually more consistent with values currently held by the audience.
4. If listeners have previously gone on record in support of a differing policy, they might also have gone on record in favor of progress, efficiency, and so forth. Link your proposal to one of those attitudes, allowing them to retreat gracefully from the position you want them to alter.

> A serious man ought not to waste his time stating a majority opinion—there are plenty of others to do that.
>
> *G. H. Hardy*

Methods of organization that may be used with a hostile audience are (1) criteria satisfaction method—first get agreement on the criteria that a good solution should meet, then show that your solution fits the criteria; and (2) residual method—show why each of the other solutions won't work, leaving only your solution. It is best to present both sides of the issue when speaking to people who oppose your position.

Refutation or Counterattack

Refutation or counterattack against an opponent's arguments consists of two steps: (1) point out the weaknesses in the opposing position; and (2) establish your own case. This is true whether you are anticipating possible objections in the minds of your audience or whether you are in fact answering objections voiced by an opposing speaker.

To be prepared to refute the opposition, thorough research for your speech should include close attention to counterarguments as well. If your speech is a rebuttal to a preceding speech, take careful notes on your opponent's speech.

There are a number of ways to effectively refute challenges to your position.

Evidence

You can uncover weaknesses in your opponent's material by asking the following questions. Is there enough evidence to warrant the counterclaim? Is the evidence he or she presented consistent with other known evidence? Is the evidence internally consistent (e.g., does it claim one thing in one case and the opposite in another)? Is the evidence verifiable? Is the evidence recent? Is the source credible? Once you have carefully examined your opponent's evidence, your counterattack can often use the weaknesses you unearth.

Let's assume we will respond to the claims made in the persuasive speech by Jan Moreland presented at the end of this chapter. She argues that chlordane should be banned because it is dangerous to humans. In support of this claim she states that the Environmental Protection Agency (EPA) received 7,500 calls concerning chlordane last year. She does not tell us the source of that information. She does not place that into the context of how many calls the EPA receives totally on all subjects. In fact, she does not even claim the calls were complaints about chlordane, merely that they concerned chlordane. Even if 7,500 turns out to be a large number of calls, a listener can raise the issue that the EPA would have acted if those calls had produced a body of evidence warranting the banning of the chemical. This counterargument would be even stronger if evidence were presented that the EPA has acted in cases with similar complaint levels when investigators found significant damage.

Each piece of evidence in Jan's speech could be examined in this fashion. A knowledgeable opponent would not only be able to raise these questions but would also have learned the answer to these questions.

Reasoning

Rebuttals/counterattacks may question whether the reasoning presented is valid. To do so you apply standard tests of reasoning. If a person has presented examples and drawn a general conclusion (inductive reasoning), consider the following. Are the examples relevant to the issue at hand? Are there enough examples? Are the examples typical? If a speaker argues that unions should be regulated because they are corrupt, you might counter by claiming that corruption in unions is not typical by presenting a large number of examples of honest, noncorrupt unions. In essence, you would be claiming the reasoning was in error because the examples cited were not typical.

Similarly, if presented with a case based on an analogy, you can determine whether the cases being compared are similar in all important respects. When he was running for president, Ronald Reagan claimed that he was qualified because being governor of California was the best preparation one could have, since California has a large, diverse population, a budget larger than most countries, etc. Opponents claimed that this comparison was invalid because it ignored such crucial elements as the fact that California did not have to deal with foreign policy or maintain an army.

If cause-effect reasoning is used, one of the questions you should ask is, "Is this the only cause?" If the speaker contends that obesity is produced by overeating and lack of exercise, you could point out that this is one cause but it certainly is not the only cause. In at least a small number of cases, people who do not overeat and do exercise are overweight due to inherited characteristics or glandular abnormalities.

Other tests of evidence and tests of reasoning are presented in chapter 13. Use these to develop a rebuttal or counterattack to your opponent's arguments.

Fallacies

Fallacies—errors in the opponent's reasoning—are a chief source of ammunition for counterattack. Inaccurate conclusions may be drawn, either innocently or purposefully, if the reasoning is fallacious. The speaker tries to avoid such errors in his or her own arguments, and the listener seeks to detect such errors to avoid being influenced falsely. The following are some of the most common types of fallacies to watch for in your own and in your opponent's reasoning. As you will see, some fallacies result from the use of faulty language and some result from faulty form.

A cat can have kittens in an oven, but that doesn't make them muffins.

Mark Twain

1. Does the speaker use glittering generalities? Speakers may say things like, "Every great American has believed in the ultimate importance of the individual human spirit." Such a statement is hard to disagree with. The critical listener, however, will seriously question the worth of such statements, because while they include everything, they say almost nothing. Using terms that are abstract and general, rather than concrete and specific, may mislead the audience about the speaker's meaning.

2. Quoting experts on the subject is an excellent way to support ideas. However, some critical questions should be asked? Which "experts" are being cited? Is the source of the testimony someone who is knowledgeable on the subject? Does the source represent some specific position or interest group that should be noted in order to understand his or her possible bias on the subject? Does the quotation accurately represent the quoted authority's viewpoint? Statements taken out of context can misrepresent or may totally falsify an expert's position.

3. Another questionable practice is card-stacking, or slanting information in such a way as to make it appear that everything available supports the speaker's viewpoint. Look for alternatives to the viewpoint expressed, then become suspicious when there are such exceptions and the speaker has made no effort to suggest that there *is* another side to the question. Some politicians are guilty of using the available data to justify false or self-seeking conclusions. You listen to one and everything points to his or her conclusion; then you listen to the opponent and the opposite seems to be true. Each is drawing different conclusions from the same evidence.

4. Non sequitur—the conclusion does not follow from the premises stated; the reason cited is irrelevant. "I know we're headed the wrong way, but I don't want to turn around because we're making such good time!" or "No one in my family likes bananas, but at ten cents a pound you can afford to buy them and throw them away!" or "Food prices are so high in the supermarket that it's cheaper to eat in a restaurant."

5. Faulty analogy—even though two instances are alike in some respects, they may still not be alike in the aspect being compared. "If they're old enough to vote, they're old enough to drink." Whatever may be the desirable age at which to allow either of these activities, there is no demonstrated relationship between them.

WIZARD OF ID   BY BRANT PARKER & JOHNNY HART

By permission of Johnny Hart and Creators Syndicate, Inc.

6. Composition and division—the properties of individual parts are not necessarily those of the whole. "Look at the body on this car, not a dent or a scratch. It's a real buy." Of course, the engine may be terrible. We have to know more than one part to judge the whole car.

7. False cause—because one event occurs after another does not prove that there is a causal relationship between them. "We won the game because I wore my lucky hat." This is called "post hoc, ergo propter hoc" reasoning—which means, "after the fact, therefore because of the fact."

   A faulty conclusion may be reached if you fail to note a third factor which in fact has caused both "cause" and "effect." For example, if there is a close correlation between a rise in the salaries paid to Presbyterian ministers and the price of rum in Havana, do you conclude that the ministers are benefiting from the rum trade, or that they are supporting it? This one is so obvious as to be easy: both figures are growing because of a third factor, the historic and world-wide rise in the price level of practically everything due to inflation.

8. Hasty generalization—jumping to a conclusion based on too little evidence. High school students visiting the campus of WYZ University observe that Robert Redford is the featured speaker at a convocation. Prospective mass media students might conclude that this university must place a great deal of emphasis on its cinema program; others in the visiting group might elect to attend WYZ because they infer that Redford's topic, "A Balanced Approach to the Environment," indicates a strong program in environmental science. Either or neither might be the case, and a judgment based solely on the fact that a well-known actor whose pro-environmentalist views are also well known, spoke on the campus of WYZ on one specific occasion is on shaky grounds.

9. Faulty extension—applying an argument further than is logical so it is carried to the point of absurdity: "If the Equal Rights Amendment is ratified, men and women will be forced to use the same bathrooms."

10. Two wrongs make a right— "So what if I did dip into the campaign funds; my opponent was doing it too." This fallacy consists of accusing the opponent of having a similar problem, rather than proving the truth or the falsehood of the original charge. Does shoplifting beer become acceptable if others are observed doing it, too?

11. Another common technique is "bandwagoning," citing the popularity of a course of action as being sufficient reason to adopt it. For instance, if a speaker supported an argument by saying, "Everyone is voting the Independent ticket this year," you should check to see if the speaker gives some examples of who "everyone" is and why they are voting that way. Many of you experienced this when you were younger and a friend suggested you do something like smoke or drink because "everyone else does." A satirical bumper sticker in Montana sheep country makes a point, using the bandwagoning technique: "Eat American Lamb—ten million coyotes can't be wrong."

12. False dilemma or black-and-white fallacy—allows for no gray areas as middle ground—"Either love America or leave it." Such polarities tend to close off rational debate. However, even such previously accepted certainties as "alive or dead" and "pregnant or not pregnant" are now recognized as being open to differing interpretations.

13. Does the speaker resort to ad hominem—name-calling—attacking the speaker intead of the argument: "That's the kind of proposal you'd expect from a pinko environmentalist." Is the speaker presenting a value judgment about another person, but not saying why this is true? Senator Joseph McCarthy used name-calling to build his own reputation after World War II, during a time when Americans were especially frightened of Communism. McCarthy accused defendant after defendant before the House Un-American Activities Committee of being a Communist, with no backing for his claim. He ruined many careers when the public accepted the label and didn't demand that he present any proof to back his accusations. The term *McCarthyism* is used to describe the practice of calling people names without providing evidence that the names apply.

14. Watch for the use of the "plain folks" appeal, an exaggerated and often insincere way to establish common ground with an audience. The suggestion that "we" are all alike (outsiders to politics and government, for instance) and "they" (the opposition) are responsible for everything wrong in the country, sets up a simplistic either/or dichotomy.

> The test of a first-rate intelligence is the ability to hold two opposing ideas in the mind at the same time, and still retain the ability to function.
>
> *F. Scott Fitzgerald*

Planning Your Response to Disagreement

Faced with a strong opposing argument, with which you disagree and that is central to the audience's acceptance of your proposition, follow this procedure:

1. Organize your response. If you need to answer three objections, answer one at a time or group them under a larger heading.
2. State clearly and concisely the opponent's claim that you intend to refute.
3. State your objection, pointing out what you will prove.
4. Offer proofs for your position, complete with documentation. Make use of strong evidence, and strong proofs of credibility, not an emotional plea.

      If the opponent's argument rests on
   a. inadequate information and facts, then you supply more and better information and facts.
   b. unacceptable authority and testimony, you cite stronger authority on the other side.
   c. unsound inference, then you show how the reasoning is fallacious, and why your conclusion proceeds more logically from the facts as presented.
5. State your conclusion. Show how answering this argument is significant to establishing your proposition.

   Do not be defensive. Keep the interchange courteous and impersonal; avoid name-calling (ad hominem). If you are calm and controlled, you will be listened to with more respect, and a reasoned discussion will be the likely result.

Organizing the Persuasive Speech: General Principles
Types of Arguments

The persuasive speech should be composed partly of constructive arguments (those that support the speaker's proposition) and partly of destructive arguments (those that refute opposing arguments) with the majority of the arguments being constructive in nature.[1]

Number of Arguments

You should limit the number of arguments to suit the time limits for your speech and to avoid overloading the audience's capacities to assimilate the information. Relatively few of the statements you use will require proof, so look for information on those points that are controversial and that are crucial to establishing your case. Analyze your speech to determine the hinge of the issue, that point on which the case turns. (It helps if this can be one you know you can prove!) "Size" is also an important factor in attracting the attention of the audience. Those arguments that are strongest should be developed most and given the most time and space.

Order of Arguments

Place your most convincing arguments in the most important positions, at the beginning and ending of the speech.[2] Arguments that present your own case should be placed in these positions of strength, with opposing arguments and the answers to them placed somewhere in the middle. If your audience is strongly in agreement with opposing arguments, you may have to defuse those arguments before you can proceed, but otherwise it is unwise to give counterarguments the prominence of first or last position.

Present Both Sides

Persuasion properly consists of encouraging rational decision-making. This implies covering all the possible alternatives and allowing your listeners to make choices. The speaker who presents a two-sided message appears more informed and logical, which makes the persuasive communication seem less polarized and radical.

In addition to an ethical concern for treating issues fully and fairly, presenting both sides helps you to understand possible counterarguments. You have to research both sides to understand the total picture. And as a result, you should be able to counter these arguments before they can have an adverse effect. Not only is presenting both sides the fair thing to do, but your purpose (to persuade) is more effectively achieved.

Two-Sided Presentation in Relation to Audience Attitude

For the hostile audience, presenting both sides of an argument is like inoculating it against opposing arguments. If you don't mention the arguments against your viewpoint, the audience members will often be thinking, "Oh, yeah, what about. . . ." By acknowledging and answering these opposing arguments, you forestall such reactions and help the audience to perceive you as well-informed and objective.[3]

The neutral listener, if genuinely unpersuaded by either side, needs information from you to allow him or her to weigh the arguments on both sides and to become persuaded that your point of view is comparatively more acceptable.

For the friendly audience, it might not seem necessary to present opposing views; in fact, a one-sided presentation can be effective with a friendly audience.[4] For example, a partisan political speech delivered to fellow members of your own party will be well received even if it is frankly one-sided.

> Men are never so likely to settle a question rightly as when they discuss it freely.
>
> *Lord McCauley*

Pointing out areas of agreement is often an effective way to cope with a hostile audience.

If you are interested in short-term effects (immediate response), then a one-sided presentation (providing only arguments which support your position) is acceptable with an audience that is totally friendly. However, if you want to effect a long-term change, you should show yourself to be objective by presenting both sides, even with an audience that is friendly to you and to your message.[5]

If your listeners hear opposing arguments later, they might lose confidence in your views. Research indicates that groups persuaded with both sides of the issue were more resistant to counterpropaganda than were those persuaded with only one side of the argument. Only 2 percent of the group who had heard only one side maintained the desired attitude when exposed to counterpropaganda, while 61 percent of those hearing both sides maintained the desired opinion.[6]

Good "both-sides" persuasion is characterized by objectivity (fair, based on evidence) and accuracy (does not overstate the speaker's evidence or position, is careful not to overgeneralize).

> He who speaks well on any single subject holds a kind of arbitrary power over all who hear him.
>
> *St. Bernard of Chartres*

Outlining the Persuasive Speech

Specific Purpose: State clearly in a complete, simple sentence your persuasive intent (i.e., to convince, to reinforce, or to actuate the audience about something).

I. Introduction
   A. Arouse and focus attention, in a favorable way, upon the subject.
   B. Provide a motivation for change by appealing to short-term and long-term self-interests.
      1. Visualize current audience needs that are not satisfied.
      2. Show the undesirability of the current situation.
   C. Identify common interests, ideas, values. Although you should hold the proposition clearly in mind at all times, it may be unwise to state in specific terms at this early point just what beliefs or actions you want the audience to adopt, unless they are already very favorable toward the idea. Government sources often leak information to a newspaper, rather than make an announcement, so the information might seem to have been "accidentally overheard." This softens the disclosure by downplaying the official's intent to persuade.

   Begin with points of agreement, then proceed through linkages to your proposition. Relate the new attitude to currently held audience values. It is usually best to minimize differences, but sometimes they must be met head on. An exception to this rule, for instance, occurs in a bargaining situation, in which you want to maximize demands and then gradually compromise on points of difference to reach the most favorable agreement.

II. Body

   Develop an attitude leading to the change you propose; use a balance of emotional and logical proofs, and personal credibility to support your arguments. Structure your arguments in the following manner:
   A. Clearly and concisely identify the crucial issues to be addressed.
   B. Show how each issue is related to the major issue at hand.
   C. Establish a definite claim about each issue.

D. Support each claim with convincing evidence—relevant, substantive, consistent, credible, and sufficient to meet the requirements of the audience. Document your sources. If the credibility of the source is very high, state it first. If not, present the quotation first and then cite the source.

E. Demonstrate logical connections between each piece of evidence and the claim it supports.

F. Organize your message so that the arguments presented build on one another to form a logically coherent whole.

G. Make ethical use of suggestion, by using the following:
1. **Appeal to authority.** Make use of your own status and cite others who support the proposition.
2. **Imagery.** Make use of concrete and specific language.
3. **Directives.** Used best if stated obliquely, such as, "I believe we can all agree that. . . ." or, "This point is the one that most clearly demonstrates the need for this action."
4. **Group participation.** Use rhetorical questions such as, "Who knows better than we the importance of this issue?"

H. Show how the suggested behavior satisfies current audience needs.

I. Overcome barriers to doing the behavior by anticipating and answering questions and objections.

J. Provide a concrete plan for accomplishing the action you propose.

K. Help the audience resist counterpersuasion by previewing and refuting opposing arguments it may hear.

III. Conclusion
A. To bring the line of reasoning to a culmination you should:
1. Summarize and restate the major points of the speech.
2. Reinforce your thesis, that is, the desired belief or action.
3. State your conclusion clearly and specifically. It is unwise to rely on the hope that, after hearing the evidence, the audience will arrive at the same conclusion you favor.

B. End with strength and vigor, perhaps a relevant quotation, or a carefully constructed sentence of your own. Some memorable last lines delivered by speakers include Lincoln's "Government of the people, by the people, and for the people shall not perish from the earth"; Webster's "Liberty and Union, now and forever, one and inseparable"; Patrick Henry's "Give me liberty, or give me death"; and Kennedy's "Ask not what your country can do for you—ask what you can do for your country."

Conclude your speech with a strong statement, such as the memorable line from John F. Kennedy's inaugural address "Ask not what your country can do for you—ask what you can do for your country."

Language and Delivery

Two elements we have discussed previously must be stressed as vital to achieving persuasion: clear, accurate, and vivid language; and active, forceful delivery. Their importance cannot be overemphasized in moving audiences to belief and action.

The following is an outline of a speech that was used during a speaking contest in January of 1984. We present the outline to point out how it relates to the issues raised previously about outlining.

The Case for Handguns
by Amy Blalock
Duncanville, TX

Commentary

Outline

Specific Purpose: To convince the audience that passing laws banning handguns would be unwise.

Introduction

This introduction uses a figurative analogy to catch our attention and highlight the speaker's feeling that banning handguns is the wrong solution to reducing crime. The alert respondent would also note that this analogy will not stand close scrutiny (e.g., diagnosing illnesses, which have

There was once a man who suffered from frequent, terrible headaches. He went to his doctor, who prescribed aspirin to combat the pain. However, the pain persisted until the man died two months later of a brain tumor. The physician made a deadly mistake in assessing the patient. He attempted to cure the symptoms of the man's disease, not the disease itself. He overlooked the fundamental problem of the man. The doctor neglected the reason for the pain and his remedy proved to be not only inappropriate but also deadly.

relatively concrete causes, is not at all like determining social influences that have less clear-cut causes). Of course, Amy did not intend this to be taken literally but rather as a way to draw attention to what she considers to be the basic problem with gun control. Notice how tactfully the introduction lets us know she's aware that the proponents of gun control are well-intentioned.

Notice how Amy leads with a very strong argument here that is well documented. The tactic of quoting a "businessman" is of interest as well. This quote reminds people of a generally accepted belief. It might be more effective if this were a prominent local businessperson.

America is ravaged by a number of diseases, if you will. Poverty, racial prejudice, sexism, and educational inequity are just a few examples. They manifest themselves in a variety of ways. Perhaps the most noticeable is crime. Most attempts to stop crime aim only at the symptom and not at the underlying reasons for crime. One such "Band-aid" is the ban of guns. Though many people argue that guns foster violence and ought to be banned, it becomes obvious after careful analysis of the issue that guns should not be banned. One reason why guns must not be banned is mostly pragmatic. Such laws would be totally unenforceable. Also, a ban on guns would have many adverse effects. Finally, a ban on handguns would be futile because it neglects the underlying problem of crime.

Body

I. Laws banning guns are unenforceable.
   A. Despite such laws, guns will not magically disappear.
      1. Over 55 million guns already exist, according to *Time*.
      2. The black market will supply additional guns to those who want them.
   B. Halting those people who wish to carry guns would be impossible.
      1. There is no real pragmatic or constitutional way for police to check everyone for guns.
      2. People would continue to carry guns despite fear of arrest. As one businessman said, "Everybody I know keeps a gun close. We'd rather take our chances with the law than with criminals."

The authorities cited in this section do much to make the case. However, as we noted earlier, citing authorities is not the strongest form of evidence and Amy was wise to place this material near the middle of her speech.

II. Banning handguns is sure to produce adverse effects.
   A. A ban on handguns would result in an increase of crime.
      1. There is no relationship between the rate of homicide and gun ownership, according to Dr. Gary Kleck of Florida State University.
      2. Lack of availability of handguns would prompt criminals to use other weapons (i.e., shotguns or knives), resulting in just as many violent deaths.
         a. Since the possibility of concealment is not important in most indoor murders (i.e., murders in the home), and that is where most handgun murders occur, shotguns and knives could easily substitute.
         b. According to *Commonwealth,* if long guns were to be substituted in only 30 percent of the assaults currently conducted with handguns, the rate of homicides would *double.*
   B. People need handguns for self-protection.
      1. Violence is rampant.
      2. Guns are the only means of protection some people have. A good example of this is my elderly grandmother who lived alone.

C. Banning handguns would pose a constitutional dilemma.
   1. The "right to bear arms" is guaranteed in the Second Amendment.
   2. The framers' intent was to ensure that the militia was well-armed. However, men were expected to provide their own weapons. Also, a general lawlessness pervaded the land then.

III. A handgun ban would neglect the source of the problem of crime.
   A. People will still want handguns and get them.
      1. Failure of registration and bans attests to this truth.
      2. Most murders are committed by aberrant, sociopathic persons with long records of violence. If these individuals still want to commit crimes, a ban on guns will not stop them.
   B. Society must attack the source of crime.
      1. To eliminate crime, one must eliminate the social ills which initially cause crime.
      2. The history of England proves this premise. The nation was steeped in violence, far worse than our nation, until progressive reforms were made to ease the social problems.

This is an effective common-sense argument. "Everyone knows that guns don't commit crimes, people do—so don't treat the guns, treat the people." However, Amy provides no detail or documentation for the "profound improvements" that make people stop "wanting to commit crimes and using guns."

Conclusion

In reference to my story at the beginning of the speech, my sympathies lie with the misdiagnosed man. The doctor's prescription only neglected the real problem. It is a cheap solution, or really no solution at all, to attempt to cure only the surface symptoms of a problem. Yet that is the course that many people choose, perhaps because it is easier or less expensive or looks better. However, in the end, most "cheap solutions" turn out to be exactly that.

Banning handguns will no more stop crime than aspirin will cure a brain tumor. Unfortunately, the popularity of this "cheap solution" persists. I suppose that on the surface it may "look good." However, the tumor did not go away and neither will crime. Banning handguns is not pragmatic; people will still want guns and get them. A ban is undesirable because it will inevitably increase violence while leaving ordinary citizens defenseless. Despite the illusionary attraction of a cosmetic shortcut such as banning handguns, the only real way to stop crime is by social, economic, and political reform. That will reduce the number of people who *want* to use guns. But until that time arrives, perhaps we should heed the lesson of the doctor: aspirin just won't heal a brain tumor. And when you use cheap solutions, you get what you pay for.

Amy uses her introductory story and logic to tie the speech together quite nicely. Note how she forcefully makes the point that gun control treats only the symptom, not the problem. You need not accept her conclusions to agree that, overall, the speech captures attention and presents a set of convincing arguments against gun control. She employs a statement-of-reasons approach, placing the strongest reasons for opposing gun control in first and last positions. Amy uses a variety of emotional proofs and finishes with a strong conclusion, which ties the speech together and leaves the audience with the clear message that gun control will not deal with the basic cause of crime.

References for Amy Blalock's Outline

1. Ted Gest, "The Battle Heats Up Over Gun Control," *USNWR* (May 31, 1982):35–38.
2. Walter Isaacson, "The Duel Over Gun Control," *Time* (March 23, 1981):33.
3. Don Kates, "Why Gun Control Won't Work," *Commonwealth* (March 13, 1981):136–38.
4. *Crime and Society.* New York: H. Wilson Co., 1979.

The following sample of persuasive speech illustrates the principles and techniques discussed in this chapter.

Sample Speech

Persuasive Speech
by Jan Moreland
Illinois State University

Commentary

This is a strong introduction. Jan tells a story that we can easily identify with, gives us some statistics, and shocks us with the fact that nothing is being done. The introduction ends with a straightforward statement of purpose. Given that most audience members were probably unfamiliar with this issue, this is a strong move. If the audience had a large contingent of chemical company representatives, this approach would be much less effective.

This main point contains an impressive array of evidence. Jan includes personal examples, statistics, and argument from authority. This section leads the uninformed audience member to the inevitable conclusion that chlordane should be banned. It seems so obvious that a listener might wonder if some counterarguments have been ignored.

Speech

Recently I saw a commercial on television for a major pest control company. The commercial depicted a young couple frantic that their home would be consumed by termites. So, like many Americans they called the Terminix man, who came to their house, killed the termites, and saved the day. As I watched the commercial, though, I thought about Beatrice Nelson. Beatrice Nelson, a middle-aged Colorado housewife, found herself lost and disoriented one evening two years ago. Her husband rushed her to a nearby emergency room where she was examined by toxicologist Dr. Daniel Tautlebaum.

Tautlebaum found that Beatrice was so confused that she could not remember days of the week or the names of any U.S. presidents. He was bewildered until he was told that a month earlier Beatrice had an exterminator at her house to spray for termites, as she puts it, just to be safe. Ironically, the result of that action made Beatrice anything but safe. The exterminator used a nerve-damaging pesticide called chlordane, which was not only effective in ridding the home of termites, but in robbing Beatrice of part of her mind. Even now, Bea cannot pass simple neurological tests, or remember simple details of her life.

Unfortunately, Bea is not alone. In fact, the Environmental Protection Agency hotline, which is an 800-number set up for reporting complaints, problems, and illnesses associated with pesticides, received over 7,500 phone calls concerning chlordane last year alone. And, according to the National Coalition Against the Misuse of Pesticides, or N-CAMP, there are currently eighty-four cases in litigation against the manufacturers of chlordane and the pest control companies who use it.

Obviously, the problem of chlordane poisoning is not a small one. But what is more frightening is that there is nothing being done to prevent exterminators from using the chemical around our homes. Now the impact of chlordane poisoning cannot be fully understood until we first look at the problem surrounding the chemical, then examine why it's still on the market, and finally, discuss some solutions that prevent any further harm.

Perhaps the director of the citizens group People Against Chlordane, Pat Manichino, said it best when he said, "The problem is not the use or application of the chemical. The problem is chlordane, and until we face that fact, the problem will never be solved. You see, chlordane is a termiticide that attacks the central nervous system in termites. Unfortunately, it can have the same effect on human beings as well."

The chemical is so dangerous, in fact, that in 1982 the National Academy of Science conducted a study for the United States Air Force to determine the level of chlordane contamination in their on–base homes. The study's finding: there is no level below which no adverse biological effects will occur. And, the study went on to say, that at a level of only five micrograms per cubic liter of air, a home should be evacuated. Now the frightening fact here is that according to a January 1987 report on National Public Radio, over three hundred thousand homes will be treated with chlordane this year alone. Three hundred thousand homes treated with a chemical that is unsafe at any level.

Now the EPA disputes this evidence, and believes that proper training of exterminators and proper application of the chemical would prevent contaminations. But, the EPA should have done their homework. Four years ago, health officials in New York and Massachusetts were so concerned about chlordane poisoning that they placed several restrictions on the chemical's use and application. But, according to Nancy Ridley of the Massachusetts Health Department, none of the restrictions were effective. She said, We had just as many cases reported and our restrictions were much tighter than the ones the EPA is proposing.

In addition, the Belsicoff Corporation, the manufacturers of chlordane, stated in a June 1984 issue of *Pest Control Technology* that quote: It is impossible to eliminate risks, spills, or accidents on any given job using chlordane. And, there's a catch. Even when the chemical is applied properly, contaminations occur.

According to a study conducted by Ross Lighty, chemist at North Carolina State University, air samples were taken in homes where the application of chlordane was strictly supervised and label instructions were followed to the letter. The air samples revealed levels approaching five micrograms per cubic meter, the same level at which the NAS recommends evacuation. Pat Manichino states that any regulation that allows for the use and application of the chemical cannot prevent spills or accidents and, therefore, they are all inadequate.

Manichino's point is well-taken. The continued use of chlordane has prompted thousands of phone calls yearly to organizations such as the EPA hotline and N-CAMP complaining of adverse symptoms from chlordane. For example, Kelly Purdell of Houston, Texas, began to feel so confused and, well, crazy as she puts it, that she was ready to admit herself to a psychiatric ward before officials found high levels of chlordane in her home and condemned it. The home of the Delaney family was so contaminated that Charleston officials condemned it as well. But perhaps the worst example is that of Charles Hanson. When his home became contaminated two years ago, he and his family were forced to evacuate, forced to live in rented houses and motels. They're still making mortgage payments on their contaminated home.

Well, now that we know that we are dealing with such a dangerous chemical you might be asking yourself, "Why is it still on the market?" Good question. And the EPA believes they have an answer. EPA official Doug Camp states that there is not enough evidence to suggest that enough people have been harmed. Good answer, Doug. But, in defense of the agency it is important to understand that evidence is not always readily available, because the public is generally uninformed. For example, when was the last time you asked your Orkin representative what he uses to kill termites? Or better yet, when was the last time you suffered a headache, sore throat, sinus problems, or any number of other minor ailments and attributed them to your exterminator? It never comes to mind, does it? And, according to Diane Baxter of N-CAMP, that's part of the problem. She states that some of the symptoms can begin so subtly, that we don't even consider the idea that we may have been poisoned.

Because this point is much weaker than the first point, placing it in the middle of the speech was probably a good idea. By asking a series of questions, Jan is able to point out why the EPA hasn't found enough hard evidence. This is an effective tactic because it involves the audience in understanding why the EPA has not acted.

This conclusion presents us with a very workable solution. We don't have to rely on the EPA or the exterminator. There is another chemical that works and we can take the initiative and insist it be used. This solution provides a very satisfactory way of dealing with what seemed to be an impossible situation.

Overall, the entire speech is impressive. The speech grabs and maintains attention, is clearly organized, is backed by convincing evidence, and offers a workable solution to an important problem. The only real weakness in the speech is the nagging suspicion that there must be contradictory evidence, a concern that could have been dealt with by using a two-sided presentational approach.

Now, at this point, it is important for me to tell you that no deaths have been linked to chlordane so far. And, according to Leah Wise of the Massachusetts Health Department, that's another reason the chemical hasn't been removed from the market. She says, "In this country we tend to be more concerned with mortality than morbidity, so if people are just getting sick we don't pay too much attention."

The scope of the chlordane problem has become too broad for any of us to ignore any longer. Especially when we consider that homes have been contaminated to the point of condemnation and people have suffered permanent neurological damage while the EPA sits by and watches. Well, they say there is not enough evidence to suggest that enough people have been harmed. Until, and if that evidence is found, the EPA will not ban chlordane. Not enough evidence? How many people have to suffer permanent neurological damage before we have enough evidence?

Also, we need to make agencies such as the EPA aware when we do experience problems with a chemical. They want evidence, let's give it to them. We can do this by notifying the Environmental Protection Agency hotline. Now, if you would like that phone number I will be available after this speech to give you that number and the numbers of N-CAMP and People Against Chlordane. These can get you in touch with someone who can help you if you feel that you or someone you know has been poisoned. Also, if you have any questions about the chemical. The final step that we as individuals can take is to ask our local health departments to check any home that we are considering to buy or rent for high levels of chlordane.

The use of chlordane must be stopped. And the responsibility lies with us. A combination of the individual steps that we can take and the national level steps the EPA should take, can prevent our families, our friends and ourselves from ever suffering the painful consequences from chlordane poisoning. Yes, as that commercial depicted we may be frantic over the fear of termites, but perhaps we should be afraid of the exterminator as well.[7]

Summary

In order to persuade audiences, you must present your ideas in a coherent fashion. Criterial, comparative advantage, residual reasoning, proposition-to-proof, motivated sequence, and problem-solution structures can be used to organize your ideas. The choice of which of these organizational formats to use is determined by the type of audience you are addressing. Audiences can be classified into three categories: friendly, neutral, and hostile. Refutation tactics are important in the persuasive process. Some general principles to consider when outlining the persuasive speech include (1) Using more constructive than destructive arguments; (2) limiting the number of arguments, and developing the strongest arguments most fully; (3) placing your most convincing arguments at the beginning and the end of your speech, with your opponents' arguments most often placed in the middle of your speech; and (4) presenting both sides of the subject, so the audience will perceive you as well-informed and objective, and less likely to be swayed by counterarguments they may hear later.

Exercises

1. Examine the reasoning in Jan Moreland's speech (the sample speech included in this chapter). Is the evidence reasonable? Is there any reasoning from sign? From example? How would you counter her claims?
2. Select a current persuasive speech (a good source for these is *Vital Speeches*) and identify the organizational pattern being used. Also, determine how the speaker accounts for opposing views.
3. Pick any topic that interests you. Write two versions of a persuasive message on that topic. The first version should present a one-sided argument and the second a two-sided argument. Have some friends respond to the two messages. Be prepared to discuss your friends' responses in class.

Assignments

1. Develop a ten-minute persuasive speech.
2. Prepare a critique of a persuasive speech delivered in your class. You should consider the effectiveness of (1) the logical, emotional, and ethical appeals; (2) proofs; (3) the overall organizational format; (4) the person's delivery. You should also identify any fallacies in reasoning. The critique should be organized into a three-minute presentation. This presentation should be done—impromptu fashion—immediately after the persuasive speech has been given.

Suggested Reading

Clark, Ruth Ann. *Persuasive Messages*. New York: Harper & Row, 1984.

Freeley, Austin J. *Argumentation and Debate: Critical Thinking for Reasoned Decision-Making*. 6th ed. Belmont Calif.: Wadsworth, 1986.

Simons, Herbert W. *Persuasion: Understanding, Practice, Analysis*. 2d ed. New York: Random House, 1986.

Notes

1. Gary Cronkhite, *Persuasion Speech and Behavioral Changes* (New York: Bobbs-Merrill, 1969): 195.
2. Cronkhite, *Persuasion Speech and Behavioral Changes:* 196.
3. Ruth Ann Clark, *Persuasive Messages* (New York: Harper & Row, 1984): 42–45; M. Allen, J. Hale, P. Mongeau, S. Berkowitz-Stafford, W. Shanahan, P. Agee, K. Dillon, R. Jackson, and C. Ray, "Testing a model of message-sidedness: Three replications." *Communication Monographs* 57 (1990): 275–291; Jerold L. Hale, Paul A.Mongeau, and Randi M. Thomas, "Cognitive Processing of One- and Two-Sided Persuasive Messages," *Western Journal of Speech Communication* 55 (No. 4) (1991): 380–389.

4. Kathleen Kelly Reardon, *Persuasion: Theory and Context* (Beverly Hills, Calif.: Sage, 1981): 142.

5. Mary John Smith, *Persuasion and Human Action* (Belmont, Calif.: Wadsworth, 1982): 229–30.

6. Arthur A. Lumsdaine and Irving L. Janis, "Resistance to Counter-Propaganda Produced by a One-Sided Versus a Two-Sided Propaganda Presentation," *Public Opinion Quarterly* 17 (1953): 311–18; M. Allen "Meta-Analysis Comparing the Effectiveness of One-Sided and Two-Sided Messages," *Western Journal of Speech Communication* 55 (No. 4) (1991): 390–404.

7. This speech was reprinted with permission from *1987 Championship Debates and Speeches*. Edited by John K. Boaz and James R. Brey (Normal, Ill.: American Forensic Association, 1987): 150–52.

15 The Speech to Entertain

All work and no play makes Jack a dull boy.

We have to inform and to persuade if we are to get the world's work done. But sometimes a speaker's purpose is to entertain. As we pointed out earlier, whatever the main goal of a speech is, it will also contain elements of other purposes as well. For example, before you can persuade you will most often need to give information. The speech whose major purpose is to entertain the audience is often informative or persuasive in nature also, an example being a popular lecture, such as a travelogue or talk on some phase of art.

The speaker's purpose in a speech to entertain is to give the audience momentary pleasure and enjoyment by arousing pleasurable emotions and avoiding disturbing responses. As a rule, ideas should be simple, easy to grasp, and should not make heavy demands on the intellect. The key qualities of such a speech are lightness, originality, and appropriateness—to speaker, audience, and occasion. This chapter describes four types of entertaining speeches: humorous speech, after-dinner speech, popular lecture, and book review.

The Humorous Speech

Humor is the major component of the humorous speech, and the intent of both speaker and listener is to enjoy a laugh together. To assure that both speaker and listeners know what to expect in the situation, the speaker should set the mood in the introduction and then begin meeting those expectations. The humorous speaker takes neither the theme nor himself or herself too seriously, but sets out to tell some amusing incidents about the theme, without too much stress on facts or logic and certainly without any malicious intent toward anyone. The speaker uses imaginative illustrations, figures of speech and twists of meaning, amusing character sketches, all with the willing participation of the audience in the spirit of the occasion.

Sources of Humor

The nature of humor is ephemeral. It depends so much on timing and the mood of the moment that it threatens to disappear as you analyze it. There are, however, some principles that can be agreed upon. Certain kinds of utterances cause people to laugh. We will list several types of these and give you examples of each.

Overstatement, or Exaggerated Description

A description of two rivers, "The Powder River—a mile wide and an inch deep!" and "The Platte River is too thick to drink and too thin to plow!"

An 80-year-old widow went on a blind date to a drive-in movie with an 80-year-old widower. When she came home, her daughter asked how it went.
"Terrible," said the mother. "I had to slap his face three times."
"You mean he got fresh?" said the daughter.
"No," said the mother. "I thought he was dead."

A Soviet dissident was condemned by the Soviet judge to a Siberian work camp.

"The sentence is too light," the dissident protested.

"What do you mean?" asked the judge.

The dissident replied, "Well, if America is so bad, why don't you send me there?"

Understatement

President Calvin Coolidge was known as "Silent Cal." He returned from church one Sunday morning and was asked by Mrs. Coolidge what the minister had talked about.

"Sin."

"Well, what did he have to say?"

"He's against it."[1]

Puns, or Plays on Words

A diamond is a chunk of coal that made good under pressure.

Some ants were minding their own business when they were startled by a golf ball landing in their midst. The unfortunate golfer arrived and started flailing away at the ball. With each errant stroke, he killed ants by the thousands. Finally, when only two ants remained, one turned to the other and said, "I suppose it's about time we got on the ball!"

Irony

To gain the most attention, it's hard to beat a great big mistake.

"If God had really intended men to fly, He'd make it easier to get to the airport." George Winters.

That activity is about as meaningful as rearranging the deck chairs on the Titanic.

Unexpected Twists

"Superstition is foolish, childish, primitive and irrational—but how much does it cost you to knock on wood?" Judith Viorst.

Two women met on the street.

"Oh, my goodness, you're pregnant. Congratulations!" said the first woman. "Are you expecting a boy or a girl?"

"Certainly," said the second.[2]

A cynic is a person who knows the price of everything and the value of nothing.

If at first you don't succeed, you are running about average.

"In the long run the pessimist may be proved right, but the optimist has a better time on the trip." Daniel L. Reardon.

The Incongruous or Absurd

A young man joined the Army and found himself assigned to the Airborne Infantry. Much against his will, he went through training to be a parachutist. The day came to make his first jump, and he was still resisting every foot of the way. As the first soldier approached the open door of the plane, the sergeant bawled, "Yell 'Geronimo' and pull your ripcord!" And the same for each one, "Yell 'Geronimo' and pull your ripcord!", till he came to our reluctant warrior, who was last in line. Terrified, the recruit braced his feet against the bulkhead and refused to jump. So the sergeant placed a foot in the middle of his back and booted him out of the plane, shouting, "Yell 'Geronimo' and pull your ripcord!" The sergeant closed the door and started to the front of the plane, when to his amazement he heard a knocking from outside the plane. He opened the door and there hovered the recruit, vigorously flapping his arms and saying, "What did you say that word was?"

So-called "sick" jokes often fall into this category:

"Other than that, Mrs. Lincoln, how did you enjoy the play?"

Considerations When Developing a Humorous Speech

The examples of humor we gave earlier may be used by the speaker to develop a humorous speech, but even good material will not create the desired effect unless the speaker has or can develop the sense of timing and the light touch that such a speech requires. The following are some pointers to help you present a successful humorous speech.

Subject Selection and Organization

When you give a humorous speech you should choose a subject that is particularly appropriate to this audience. This subject can be used to organize the speech by becoming the theme or central thread that runs through the speech and provides a coherent framework for your humorous anecdotes and remarks. Commonplace experiences seen from a new perspective can be an excellent source of humor. For example, a conference of debate coaches might enjoy accounts of outlandish incidents that occurred at debate tournaments. Similarly, an incident with an office for its setting could strike close to home at a business luncheon. This somewhat informative theme helps keep you from sounding like an amateur stand-up comedian reciting a series of one-liners.

Tact

Always exercise good taste. Do not make your listeners feel embarrassed or uncomfortable by holding them up to ridicule or pain. Your listeners should feel comfortably pleased with themselves and with you. If you choose to select anyone to be the target of a joke, select yourself.

A good sense of humor is universally admired. Apt witticisms that disparage the speaker but do not at the same time poke fun at the audience's values can raise an audience's estimation of the speaker's sense of humor.[3] Comedians like Rodney Dangerfield often use this tactic.

Delivery

Delivery should be casual and impromptu. As with all speeches, achieving the style of delivery you want requires a great deal of practice. If you don't get laughs where you think you should and do get laughs at unexpected places, don't let it upset you. Be careful not to create expectations that are hard to fulfill. For example, if you tell an audience that the joke you are about to tell is hilarious and your listeners don't think so, you are going to have to work harder to get them to laugh at the next line. It is better to leave out such previews and let the material speak for itself.

Avoid getting carried away by success. It's better to leave your listeners wanting more than to have them wish you would sit down.

After-Dinner Speech

Once upon a time, in the days of the Roman Empire, a mob was gathered in the Coliseum to watch as a Christian was thrown to a hungry lion. The spectators cheered as the wild beast went after its prey. But the Christian quickly whispered something in the lion's ear and the beast backed away with obvious terror on his face. No amount of calling and foot stomping by the audience could get the lion to approach the Christian again. Fearlessly, the Christian walked from the arena.

The emperor was so amazed at what had happened that he sent for the Christian and offered him his freedom if he would say what he had done to make the ferocious beast cower in fear. The Christian bowed before the emperor and said, "I merely whispered in the lion's ear: 'After dinner, you'll be required to say a few words.' "[4]

Among the many occasions on which a humorous speech to entertain may be appropriate is at a dinner or banquet. Not all "after-dinner speeches" are humorous, but most are entertaining (or at least are meant to be). The after-dinner speech can be a challenge because it must be interesting, but not too taxing on the audience, and it demands humor, but not just a string of jokes. The occasion of the speech is typically a lighthearted one, whose major purpose is to follow a social dinner with relaxing entertainment.

Organizing the After-Dinner Speech

The following outline will help you organize your after-dinner speech.

I. Select a topic suitable to the audience and to the occasion, one that looks on the lighter side of a topic.
II. The introduction of the after-dinner speech should arouse interest and be in harmony with the mood of the occasion.
    A. Tell a story or an anecdote, or give an illustration.
    B. Present a quotation or a verse.

III. The body of the speech should have a single essential idea that you state vividly; then you should proceed to illustrate and develop it with supporting ideas. Even though there are digressions, the speech must progress.
   A. Humor is important, but it must fit your subject and seem to develop spontaneously.
   B. Develop the subject in a way that establishes good fellowship; especially examine humor to see if it will amuse and not offend this audience.
   C. Be brief. Use no more than one or two main points and no complicated forms of support.
   D. Be original. It is permissible to borrow, but you should compose most of what you say yourself. Personal experience is good, but more important than *what* happened is the fresh or amusing way you look at things.
IV. Conclude with a striking or novel restatement of your central idea. As you did in the introduction, you may use a quotation, a short piece of poetry, or a brief anecdote to bring your speech to a rousing finish.

Popular Lecture

The speech to entertain is not exclusively restricted to humor. The speaker may use mystery, suspense, or adventure, as well as humor, to divert and entertain. The speaker presents ideas and incidents that entertain because they are novel or unusual, active and involving, and are described in vivid terms. If your purpose is to entertain your audience, your manner should be lively and vigorous, and should show enjoyment and enthusiasm for the subject. Some often-used forms of development for such a speech include striking comparison or contrast, a humorous exaggeration, an apt quotation, bits of dialogue, a witty or surprising comment, concrete examples, or a dramatic anecdote, perhaps based on human interest stories or human peculiarities.

Many of these require that the speaker use storytelling techniques. The basic elements of any narration are theme, action, character, setting, and mood. In your speech you may also use suspense, dialogue, dialect, and the introduction of topical elements, like familiar street names or local events. It's especially important to decide which and how many details to include, then throw out any (1) that are not directly necessary to the listeners' understanding and enjoying the story and (2) that seem inappropriate for this audience or occasion. Don't be longwinded or include unnecessary details that hold up the flow of the action. Similarly, in the development of character, present the necessary details of description, but pare them down to absolute essentials so you do not impede the flow of the narrative. It may be possible to suggest a picture of the character by word choice in the dialogue, or perhaps by a touch of dialect.

A book review may be primarily serious or primarily humorous, depending on the literature on which it is based.

The popular lecture should be organized, but it tends to be rather loosely knit and not necessarily balanced in the length of time spent on each segment. You probably won't need anything so formal as a summary conclusion; more likely you will use a humorous ending that continues the mood of easy enjoyment, or perhaps you will choose an inspirational closing. Throughout the speech (introduction, body, and conclusion) you should rely heavily on the use of "factors of attention" (see pages 64–69); those factors in the speech that can cause the audience to sit up and take notice and to maintain attention throughout.

Your manner in the popular lecture should not be formal or assertive. It should instead be good-natured, casual, and spontaneous, one that promotes an atmosphere of shared enjoyment. The audience comes with no expectation of receiving concrete information on which to take notes or to try to remember; listeners are encouraged to relax, have a good time, and leave feeling good and having learned something of interest about the topic. Sir James Jeans' speech in chapter 12 is an example of a popular lecture.

Book Review

The book review is a presentation whose purpose is to entertain. Its lecture-demonstration format combines elements of the informative speech and oral reading of literature. It may be primarily serious or primarily humorous, depending on the literature on which it is based.

Such reviews are often presented to clubs or other organizations, to acquaint the audience with a current fiction or nonfiction book, to provide the listeners with insights regarding the work, and to stimulate listeners to read it. When you give a book review, you may focus on the literary worth of the book itself, or you may use the work as a springboard from which to discuss some social custom or problem.

The book review typically will include the following:

1. Information about the author's background, point of view, personal eccentricities, typical themes, and previous works, which will arouse interest in hearing about the book.
2. A brief synopsis of the plot, characters, and setting.
3. Reading of short, selected passages from the text to illustrate the points you make in the review.
4. An analysis of the theme or problem presented.
5. A final significant quotation from the book.
6. A statement regarding the significance of the work, generally as well as to you, the reader, and to the audience, and a recommendation that your listeners read the book themselves.

The following is an abbreviated version of a book review.

> My report concerns *Texas* by James A. Michener.[5] As you are probably aware, Michener uses "historical novels" to shed light on a variety of contemporary issues ranging from apartheid in South Africa to religious differences in Israel. His concern in Texas, or Tejas, as it probably should be called given the extensive yet unacknowledged Spanish influence, is to get the reader to appreciate why Texas is unique among the states.
>
> As with most of his work, Michener employs a chronological development. Although *Texas* does employ a somewhat different organizational tactic than those he normally uses, he begins this book with the governor of Texas establishing a blue-ribbon commission to explore and preserve Texas history. The composition of the panel represents a cross section of Texan culture. The panel includes scholars, oilmen, prominent women, Hispanics, athletes, and so forth. The commission travels to various parts of the state as the story unfolds in that region.

[At this point in the book review, we would develop major themes of the book and illustrate them with quotations from the book. The conclusion would urge people to read this book because it deepens one's appreciation for the unique nature of Texas and, in turn, the United States. In particular, it helps one understand the extensive differences between Hispanic and Anglo influences in Texas.]

Key to a successful book review is the ability to pick a well-written book that has redeeming value; then all you have to do is pick out an appealing message and read selected passages to encourage the audience to read the book.

Summary

The speech to entertain embraces one of the three broad purposes of any speaker: to inform, to persuade, and to entertain. Four types of entertaining presentations are humorous, after-dinner, popular lecture, and book review. Overstatement, understatement, puns, irony, unexpected twists, and incongruity may be used in a humorous speech. Subject selection, organization, tact, and delivery are important factors in the humorous speech. The after-dinner speech should be interesting and relaxing to the audience. A popular lecture and a book review are two ways of communicating with an audience in an informative and entertaining way. Still another way is through the oral interpretation of literature, which we cover in an appendix to this text.

Exercises

1. Bring examples of humor to class. Analyze those materials in light of the sources of humor discussed in this chapter.
2. Watch a popular talk show. Examine how the host creates humorous interludes and how she or he does so.

Assignment

Develop a five-minute speech to entertain. You can use any of the four methods discussed in this chapter, or the method discussed in the appendix.

Notes

1. Charles S. Mudd and Malcolm O. Sillars, *Speech: Content and Communication,* 3d ed. (New York: Thomas Y. Crowell Company, 1975): 410, reprinted by permission of publisher.
2. Leo Rosten, *The Joys of Yiddish* (New York: McGraw-Hill, 1968).
3. Mei-Jung Chang and Charles R. Gruner, "Audience Reaction to Self-Disparaging Humor," *The Southern Speech Communication Journal* 46 (Summer 1981): 419–26.
4. Reprinted by permission of the publisher, from *How to Be the Life of the Podium* by S. H. Simmons: 13–14, © 1982 by AMACOM, a division of American Management Associations, New York. All rights reserved.
5. Excerpt written for illustrative purposes.

16 Speaking for Special Occasions

Chapter Outline

Forms for Special Occasions

In certain circumstances, a speaker is called upon to deliver a ceremonial address the purpose of which is to extend or to receive a courtesy. The introduction of a speaker, the speech of tribute, presenting or accepting an award or gift, the speech of welcome, and a commencement address are five such speech forms that are discussed in this chapter. Social rituals such as these usually are characterized by a prescribed order and content, and by a high degree of formality and attention to ceremony. Perhaps the key factor in all of these speech situations is "appropriateness." To determine what is appropriate in each circumstance, the speaker should analyze closely the audience and the occasion. What are the ritualistic customs inherent in a Fourth of July celebration, in a high school commencement, or in a sports or scholastic award banquet? What expectations do the audience members bring to the occasion about what would be appropriate for the speaker to say? Because the audience typically knows the established formula already, the speaker's task becomes one of performing his or her function with some originality but without violating the accepted rules.

In these ceremonial speeches, the speaker seeks to provide a modest amount of information and to reaffirm shared beliefs, values, and attitudes, which is what the audience expects to have done. The speaker chooses a topic and the forms of development that will accomplish this goal, paying especial attention to choice of language. The speech should be brief, so every word and phrase should be the right one, carefully chosen to bring about the desired emotional response. For this reason the speaker might choose to memorize the speech, or almost memorize it and deliver it from a manuscript or a detailed outline.

Included here are some general principles you should follow when you give a special occasion speech:

1. Question the person who asked you to speak about (a) the order of the program; (b) how long you are to speak; (c) how your speech pertains to the other parts of the ceremony; and (d) where you will be and what you should be doing during the other segments.
2. Make good use of specific examples, illustrations of real people in real situations, and other forms of development that have strong emotional appeal.
3. Choose vivid, colorful language to express your ideas. The words you select should arouse sensory images and reflect the correct level of seriousness and formality for the occasion.
4. Try to be original. Avoid the trite generalizations that occur all too often in this kind of presentation.
5. Rehearse the speech very thoroughly, giving attention to the techniques for effective delivery in whichever style you choose to use—extemporaneous, memorized, or manuscript.

A fool uttereth all his mind.

Proverbs 29:11

Introduction of a Speaker

At no time is the blunt advice given by Toastmasters International—"Stand up. Speak up. Shut up."—more useful than when you are asked to introduce a speaker. Your speech of introduction should accomplish three goals:

1. It should arouse the attention and interest of the audience and establish a connection between speaker, speech, audience, and occasion.
2. It should establish the main speaker's credibility.
3. It should create a receptive atmosphere that will help the speaker to achieve the speech purpose.

Nothing should be said that does not advance one of these three main purposes.

Arouse Attention and Establish a Connection

The introduction of a speaker should capture the attention of the audience by arousing its curiosity about the speaker and the subject. To help the speaker to accomplish the purpose of the speech, the introduction must be consistent in style and manner with the major speech to follow. The subtleties of the role of introducer can be compared with that of a piano accompanist who is always subordinate to the soloist but whose skillful support is absolutely essential to the success of the total program.

Establish the Main Speaker's Credibility

When you make an introduction you should motivate the audience to like and respect the speaker so it will respond favorably to his or her information or appeal. To establish the credibility of the main speaker, you can present information that the speaker could not modestly present—such as professional attainments, education, publications, governmental appointments, organizations to which she or he belongs, offices held and awards won—and thereby establish the speaker's fitness to discuss the topic.

You can further enhance the person's credibility by presenting the speaker as a genuine human being who shares the values and aspirations of the audience. Behind-the-scenes details about the speaker's family or hobbies, quotations from the speaker's writings or anecdotes about the speaker can often be used to reveal something about his or her character or sense of humor.

Speak with sincerity and enthusiasm. Be complimentary, but don't embarrass the speaker with too much praise. In particular, do not praise his or her speaking abilities; these the speaker's listeners will have an opportunity to assess for themselves. Focus instead on the speaker's attitudes or ideas.

PEANUTS reprinted by permission of UFS, Inc.

***Help to Achieve
the Speech Purpose***

The introduction should build anticipation and create enthusiasm for what is to follow. You should stimulate interest in the speech by establishing the importance, relevance, and timeliness of this subject to this audience. Focus your attention on the speaker, and let the speaker present the details of the topic. The audience did not come to hear your views on the subject, but rather those of the speaker.

Your purpose is basically informative, but it is persuasive as well; by your enthusiasm convince the audience that it should give favorable attention to what the speaker has to say.

***Problems to Avoid in
Introducing a Speaker***

When you are introducing a speaker, there are certain rules that you should follow:

1. Don't try to glorify yourself by showing off how well you know the speaker or how much you know about the topic.
2. Don't tell the audience how it will react to the topic or to the speaker's abilities as a public speaker. Don't say, "You will now hear an interesting and inspiring speech," or "This speech will really be funny."
3. Don't embarrass the speaker by overpraising him or her in lavish, exaggerated terms.
4. Be professional. If you're not adept at humor, don't try to be funny, especially not at the speaker's expense. Be mindful of whether the use of humor suits the occasion.
5. Avoid trite phrases such as, "It is an honor and a privilege," and, "someone who needs no introduction."
6. Be brief. Your speech should be about one to three minutes long, never longer than five minutes. Say enough to make the speaker look good, but don't get carried away. You're a necessary part of the preliminaries, but you're not the feature attraction.

Chief Justice and President William Howard Taft recounted this anecdote: "I remember once when I was in politics, we had a meeting at which there was to be one of these preliminary addresses.

One guest captured and held the platform and when he finally finished, I remarked, 'I will now present Mr. So-and-So, who will give you his address.' Mr. So-and-So arose and stated, with some heat, 'My address is 789A-22nd Street, New York City, where my train goes in fifteen minutes. Good night!' "[1]

Another graphic example of the appropriateness of brevity is the introduction of President Wilson given by Shailer Mathews. This introduction is the ultimate tribute to the speaker being introduced, one that indicates without saying it that the speaker's name and credibility need not be stated: "Ladies and gentlemen, the president of the United States!" Since that occasion, this masterpiece of understatement has been the accepted form when introducing the president. A lesser-known speaker may need to be given a psychological boost with the audience, but it is better to say too little than too much.

Preparing the Speech of Introduction
Consult the Speaker

Interview the speaker well in advance to learn about the speaker and the topic. Obtain copies of publicity materials or a biographical sketch. These may contain excellent quotations, colorful facts, or descriptive language that you can use in your introduction. Ask the speaker directly what items you can highlight to set the stage for the speech.

Don't trust the accuracy of information you get from any source other than the speaker. Check the accuracy of your information (titles and so forth) and be sure you know how to pronounce the speaker's name correctly! If necessary, write it phonetically, then practice it until you are sure of it.

Content of the Introduction

To decide what should be included in the introduction, ask yourself the following questions:

1. How much does the audience already know about the speaker? You don't have to repeat those things the audience already knows.
2. What is the audience's attitude toward the speaker? Are the audience members so skeptical or hostile that I need to emphasize the speaker's credentials to foster a more receptive climate?
3. Does the occasion call for a serious or a light tone?
4. Does the audience need specific information to be able to understand the speaker's message?
5. Do I want to stir up controversy, deflect it, or plant questions in the hearer's mind?

The following outline will help you when organizing a speech of introduction.

I. Use an opening that arouses audience attention.
   A. Perhaps you can share an anecdote that relates to the occasion.
   B. Give the name and identity of the speaker.
   C. Announce the subject and the title of the speech, even if it is printed in the program.
      1. Stress the importance and appropriateness of the subject briefly, with only a reference or two.
      2. Relate it to the audience.
II. Establish the speaker's credibility.
   A. Tell why the speaker is qualified to speak on the subject and give the speaker's experience, position, special abilities. Check your information carefully to avoid factual mistakes about the speaker's education, titles, and experience.
   B. A chronological list of accomplishments can be boring, so include only the most important. Adding a story about the speaker or a quotation by or about the speaker makes these credentials more interesting and personal.
   C. Except for the speaker's name and the subject of the talk, don't include information that will be printed on the program.
III. Conclusion
   A. Essential points such as the speaker's name and the title of the speech should be restated.
   B. Climactic order is good, but don't try for an artificially strong climax.

Since the bulk of the speech can be prepared in advance, have the facts firmly in mind. You shouldn't have to look at your notes to get the name of the person you are introducing. And above all, don't mispronounce or stumble over the speaker's name! To achieve the appearance of speaking impromptu requires exact preparation and thorough rehearsal.

On the Occasion of the Speech

When the occasion of the speech is at hand, it will be helpful to follow this outline we suggest for you.

I. Arrive in plenty of time to be sure you are there to greet the speaker when she or he arrives.
   A. If the program chairperson has not attended to such details as placement of a table, chairs on the platform, a speaker's stand, and testing of the amplifying equipment, then you should take care of any necessary physical arrangements.

B. Acquaint the speaker with the sequence of events, including the "cue line," which should alert the speaker that she or he is on. If you plan to shake hands after you finish the introduction, make this clear so the speaker will not be caught with his or her hands full of note cards or visual aids.

II. When the moment arrives gain the audience's attention.
  A. Pause to allow the audience to settle down.
     1. To adapt to the situation, you may need to make impromptu remarks to allow the audience time to quiet down, to stall until the tables are cleared or until late-comers are seated, or perhaps to ask the audience to move toward the front.
     2. Avoid any negative references. If the crowd is small, don't comment on it or apologize for it.
  B. Turn and gesture toward the speaker, then look only at the audience.
  C. Speak slowly and distinctly, loud enough to be easily heard and understood by the guest speaker and the audience.

III. Deliver your prepared speech with vitality and in a manner that projects sincere enthusiasm.

IV. Signal your conclusion by the tone of your voice, your body language, and by the nature of your comments.
  A. Announce the speaker's name and topic, and initiate the applause.
  B. Take a step back from the lectern, face the speaker in a welcoming manner, clap for a second, then move quickly to your seat.
  C. If the occasion is formal, such as a banquet or a large audience, you should continue to applaud until the speaker reaches the lectern, shake hands in welcome, then quickly take your seat.

V. Be a model listener yourself, attentive to the speaker, but at the same time be alert to any problems such as malfunctioning sound equipment or external noise.

Sample Speech of Introduction

The following speech of introduction was delivered to 600 or so students enrolled in a basic public speaking class at Washington State University. The students were assembled to hear a guest lecture from two distinguished scholars about communication apprehension (the fear of communicating).

Commentary	Speech

Commentary

Speech

This speech establishes the speakers' credentials in terms these students can understand. It points out the speakers are "of quality," but it does not create unreasonable expectations about the speech. All in all, it seems to serve to pique interest and get the audience ready to listen to these speakers.

Hi, I'm Joe Ayres. It is my privilege to introduce tonight's guest lecturers—James C. McCroskey and Virginia P. Richmond, both from West Virginia University. It gives me great pleasure to introduce these scholars for both personal and professional reasons. On the personal side, I like these folks. They may be at West Virginia but they are really westerners at heart. They are honest, hard-working, and straight-talking. They also have a great sense of humor.

On the professional side, there are a couple of reasons I've admired the work these scholars have produced. First, there is the sheer quantity of it. They have authored or co-authored more than 200 articles and books. That figure rolls easily off the tongue but when you stop to think of the work that number represents—it's truly mind-boggling. You've all written term papers for classes. Well, writing an article for publication is a little like that. You find a topic, read about the topic, draft, and redraft the paper. You have to do all that when you write a research-based article, but you also have to read all relevant material, design the study, collect the data, write the article, submit it for publication, and rewrite it, which usually involves additional work before it is finally accepted (like rewriting, gathering more data, and so on). Conservatively, I'd estimate it takes 10 times as much effort to produce a good article as it does a good term paper. Now, multiply that by 200. Wow!

I suppose I've given you the impression that all Jim and Virginia do is lock themselves in their offices and write articles. Not at all. Jim serves as the chair of the department and Virginia as the graduate coordinator—full-time jobs in and of themselves. They have both served as president of the Eastern States Communication Association. They have both edited or are editing major journals. They serve on committees. They are outstanding teachers, as their awards will attest. They even find time to visit with us.

The most important reason I'm impressed with their work is because of its quality. There are any number of tests of quality research. Does it address significant questions? Does it provide solid answers to those questions? Does it influence others work? and so on. In Jim and Virginia's case, the answers to those questions is a resounding YES. In organizational communication, interpersonal communication, intercultural communication, and instructional communication, their work has profoundly affected our understanding of how communication works. You may not know it but their work has directly influenced you. You are all enrolled in a public speaking course, and the way we have designed that course was influenced by research these scholars did.

You will have the opportunity to judge for yourself the quality of their ideas as they develop the topic for tonight's presentation, "Whatever Happened to the Strong Silent Type?"

Let's give Jim and Virginia a great big Cougar welcome.[2]

Speech of Tribute

The speech of tribute is a ceremonial address and may be one of three types: (1) the speech of praise that lauds a living person, perhaps on the occasion of someone retiring or moving away; (2) the eulogy, which pays tribute to an illustrious dead person; or (3) the speech of dedication. We will consider these three categories together, because their similarities far outweigh their differences. Chief among their differences is the fact that the passage of time adds historical perspective and allows you to be more candid and objective. Thus, the speech of tribute, which is given after the passage of time, is more general and diffuse in its sentiment when compared with the sharpness and intensity of reaction to more immediate events and persons.

Organization

The organizational patterns most frequently used in a speech of tribute are topical and chronological, or a combination of the two. In the introduction to the speech of tribute, the speaker focuses on the occasion that inspires the speech, perhaps an achievement of an individual, the occasion or anniversary of his or her death, or the dedication of a building or a monument to a person, group, or institution.

A thematic approach is an effective organizational technique for these speeches. The speaker selects a central theme in the subject's life and carries that idea throughout the speech, illustrating it with specific events. Each incident should be told vividly and interestingly, avoiding complicated details. When you deliver a speech of tribute you should focus on the person's praiseworthy achievements and attributes, but it is important to do so sincerely. Magnify the subject's virtues, but don't carry this to extremes or it will no longer be credible. The style of language used in these speeches tends to be elevated and formal, to the degree that is in keeping with the mood of the occasion.

Here is one way you might proceed:

I. Introduction
   A. Establish a relationship between the occasion, the audience, and the person (or group) being honored.
   B. Recount a striking incident in the person's life that illustrates a basic trait of the person's character or exemplifies the person's work.
II. Point out the significance of this person's contribution to society.
   A. This person's achievement was beyond what is expected or what duty requires.
   B. This person's achievement was made in the face of overwhelming difficulties.
   C. Add accounts of other events and incidents that further develop the point.
III. Conclusion
   A. An account of an incident that sums up the person's best qualities is an effective means of concluding.
   B. An effective way to amplify these qualities is to use an inspirational statement that shows how adopting the person's attitudes could benefit the audience, urges deeper devotion to the cause she or he represents, and evokes a desire to be like the person being honored.

Adlai Stevenson, former governor of Illinois and the Democratic nominee for president in 1952, was a low-key but effective speaker.

A Eulogy

The following is a tribute given by Adlai Stevenson, then governor of Illinois, on the occasion of the funeral of his friend, Lloyd Lewis. Speaking after their mutual friend, Marc Connelly, Governor Stevenson's words are a spontaneous outpouring of his deep feelings of grief at the sudden death of his friend and neighbor.

Farewell to a Friend
Adlai E. Stevenson

Commentary

Adlai Stevenson's speech of tribute has a very uplifting tone. His words are simple and sincere, words chosen to bring comfort to the friends who are gathered there and to himself. The theme of friendship is very clear and effective. He refers to the place where the cemetary is located and reaffirms the close ties they all share with each other and with the deceased. Especially effective is the repetition of "April," first as the present date, then as a symbol for the renewal of life and friendship.

Speech

I have been asked to share in these farewells to a friend.

I think it is a good day for this meeting. It is April now and all life is being renewed on the bank of this river that he loved so well. I think we will all be happy that it happened on this day, here by the river with the spring sky so clear, and the west wind so warm and fresh. I think we will all be the better for this day and this meeting together.

He was my neighbor. He was the neighbor of many of you. He was a very good neighbor; quick in time of misfortune, always present in times of mirth and happiness—and need.

I think Mr. Connelly was right when he said he was the most successful man he ever knew. I don't know much about the riches of life, and I suspect few of you have found the last definition. But I do know that friendship is the greatest enrichment that I have found.

Chapter 16

Everyone loved this man. He enriched others and was enriched. Everyone was his friend—everyone who knew him or read him. Why was that? Why is he the most successful man that many of us will ever know? Our answers will differ. For me it was his humility, gentleness, wisdom, and wit, all in one. And most of all a great compassionate friendliness.

I think it will always be April in our memory of him. It will always be a bright, fresh day, full of the infinite variety and the promise of new life. Perhaps nothing has gone at all—perhaps only the embodiment of the thing—tender, precious to all of us—a friendship that is immortal and doesn't pass along. It will be renewed for me, much as I know it will for all of you, each spring.[3]

Commencement Address

Another very specialized form of public presentation is the commencement address. This speech and this occasion typify the kind of speech we are discussing in this chapter. You have all heard at least one of these addresses, chances are good that you knew exactly what you would hear and how it would be said. But that's the way it should be. There is not a lot of variety in the content of other important rituals, either, such as the marriage ceremony, or a baptism or initiation. The important thing about these social utterances is that they should be appropriate to the occasion and should meet the expectations of those who have gathered for the ceremony.

The occasion of graduation represents a coming of age for a group of people, a point at which they have completed a phase of their preparation and are ready to go on to the next step of schooling or into their life's occupation. The commencement address typically consists of three main parts: (1) congratulations for the graduates' achievements thus far; (2) advice on the obstacles the graduates will encounter next, and how their preparation will enable them to overcome those obstacles; and (3) an inspirational charge to the graduates that by meeting and conquering the challenges ahead, they may make a contribution to the progress and betterment of society.

Content and Delivery

The commencement address should be short, highly structured, relatively formal in its choice of language, and dignified in its delivery. We have spoken already of its highly predictable themes, and those themes are best developed by emotional proofs. A moving quotation from literature or a quotation from an authoritative source can be a very effective and inspirational form of development. Everything about the address should be consistent with the tone of the ceremony, of which it is a part, and appropriate to the larger occasion.

In all three kinds of ceremonial speeches, as in the introduction of a speaker, the purpose is to give information but also to convince the audience. The speaker seeks to deepen the listener's appreciation for the praiseworthy ideals or accomplishments of the person or group being honored or for the significant occasion.

Presenting a Gift or Award

When a gift or award is presented to an individual or group in recognition of some outstanding achievement, it will be accompanied by a speech of presentation. This speech has as its main purpose the expression of honor, recognition, and appreciation for the recipient's excellence in athletics, scholarship, political life, industry, or religious service. The speech should include reference to four major factors: (1) the occasion; (2) the award itself; (3) the recipient; and (4) those whom you represent, the donors.

The Occasion

People usually gather especially for the purpose of presenting this award; an awards assembly, a sports or scholarship banquet, or a media event such as the presentation of the Emmy or Grammy awards.

The Award

The award almost always consists of some tangible token of recognition such as a medal, trophy, certificate, ribbon, scholarship, or other gift. When you present an award you should describe the gift itself, noting any special qualities that make it particularly significant or valuable. These same admirable qualities can be attributed to its recipient. If the award is a useful item, it would be desirable to indicate its appropriateness as an award to this person, on this occasion.

Most often, the award is a token, not necessarily valuable in itself. Even if the gift does have some monetary value, you should not present it as if it were a payment. You should go beyond the material attributes of the gift to point out its symbolic importance as a token of appreciation for the recipient's achievement or contribution. Discuss the history and background of the award: when and why the tradition was founded, who donated it, its first or most notable recipients, and the conditions under which it is awarded.

The Recipient

In making the presentation of an award, you should formally and publicly acknowledge the worth of the recipient by pointing out, not exaggerating, his or her good qualities and accomplishments. Your sincerity should always be evident, so do not overpraise.

The criteria for selection should be described, as well as how this particular individual or group met those criteria. Be laudatory, but selective, recounting only facts that are particularly significant.

The Donor

The donor's contribution should be officially recognized in the presentation of an award. Credit should be given to the donors and the reasons for providing the gift, in part to heighten the donor's pleasure and satisfaction for having done so. If the gift is given as a memorial, you should note the qualities that made the person worthy of being commemorated.

As a speaker, you are the donor's representative and you will want to express the donor's sincere pleasure at playing a part in the occasion and approval of the choice of this person to receive the award.

"Don't go away...I'll go get my acceptance speech."

Copyright © 1992; Reprinted courtesy of Bunny Hoest and Parade Magazine.

Delivery

The speech of presentation should be carefully constructed, thoroughly rehearsed, and delivered extemporaneously. Your manner should project the genuine, sincere desire of the donor(s) to honor the recipient. In your presentation, you should take care to focus the audience's attention not on yourself, but on the award and on the recipient.

Eye contact throughout most of the speech will be directed toward the audience, but you should look at the gift when you are describing it and reading the inscription. If possible, hold the gift up for the audience to see. When you actually make the presentation, look at the person receiving it, still projecting your voice so the entire audience can hear. Hold the item in your left hand and pass it to the left hand of the recipient, while you both shake with your right hands. Congratulate him or her. Then give the recipient a chance to respond.

Accepting a Gift or Award

When you accept a gift or an award, sometimes a simple "Thank you very much" will be the appropriate response, but often it is desirable to say a bit more so that you can express your appreciation and the audience can share your pleasure in receiving the honor. This will depend on the kind of award, the expectations of those conveying the honor, and your own feelings in the situation.

William Faulkner was one of America's most influential novelists of the twentieth century.

If you think there is a chance you might receive an award of some kind, plan ahead what you will say. In such a speech you should include (1) your appreciation; (2) attention to the award itself; (3) thanks to those who provided the gift; (4) acknowledgement of the assistance of those who helped you earn the award; and (5) a brief indication of your plans for the future.

If you are surprised, say so. Express appreciation for the honor of receiving the award. Show admiration for the gift. Indicate your realization of its significance; extend your thanks to the donors of the gift and to the person who has presented it.

Whenever possible, share the honor with others. If it represents a team effort, include the others who participated in the effort, or if you were inspired by someone, acknowledge this debt. If it is appropriate, explain how receiving this award may affect you in the future. What effect could it have on your efforts to achieve, or your opportunity to go further?

A Speech of Acceptance

In most cases, your response will be brief, perhaps fifteen seconds to two minutes. The only exceptions are those few very special occasions, such as accepting a Nobel Prize for Literature, when the clear expectation is that the recipient will have prepared a major address as a response. William Faulkner's speech on that occasion is considered to be a classic example of the formal acceptance speech.

On Accepting the Nobel Prize for Literature
William Faulkner

Commentary

Speech

William Faulkner's speech accepting the Nobel Prize for Literature received great acclaim at the time, and it continues to stand out as a model of its kind. He begins by revealing his intent to use the prize money in a worthwhile project and his desire to share the benefits of the acclaim as well. He seizes this opportunity to communicate his strongly felt beliefs about the solemn responsibilities borne by him and his fellow writers. He expresses his optimistic view of the nature of humans and points to the important role to be played by writers in helping humans not only to endure but to prevail.

I feel that this award was not made to me as a man, but to my work—a life's work in the agony and sweat of the human spirit, not for glory and least of all for profit, but to create out of the materials of the human spirit something which did not exist before. So this award is only mine in trust. It will not be difficult to find a dedication for the money part of it commensurate with the purpose and significance of its origin. But I would like to do the same with the acclaim too, by using this moment as a pinnacle from which I might be listened to by the young men and women already dedicated to the same anguish and travail, among whom is already that one who will some day stand here where I am standing.

Our tragedy today is a general and universal physical fear so long sustained by now that we can even bear it. There are no longer problems of the spirit. There is only the question: When will I be blown up? Because of this, the young man or woman writing today has forgotten the problems of the human heart in conflict with itself which alone can make good writing because only that is worth writing about, worth the agony and the sweat.

He must learn them again. He must teach himself that the basest of all things is to be afraid; and, teaching himself that, forget it forever, leaving no room in his workshop for anything but the old verities and truths of the heart, the old universal truths lacking which any story is ephemeral and doomed—love and honor and pity and pride and compassion and sacrifice. Until he does so, he labors under a curse. He writes not of love but of lust, of defeats in which nobody loses anything of value, of victories without hope and, worst of all, without pity or compassion. His griefs grieve on no universal bones, leaving no scars. He writes not of the heart but of the glands.

Until he relearns these things, he will write as though he stood among and watched the end of man. I decline to accept the end of man. It is easy enough to say that man is immortal simply because he will endure: that when the last ding-dong of doom has clanged and faded from the last worthless rock hanging tideless in the last red and dying evening, that even then there will still be one more sound: that of his puny inexhaustible voice, still talking. I refuse to accept this. I believe that man will not merely endure: he will prevail. He is immortal, not because he alone among creatures has an inexhaustible voice, but because he has a soul, a spirit capable of compassion and sacrifice and endurance. The poet's, the writer's, duty is to write about these things. It is his privilege to help man endure by lifting his heart, by reminding him of the courage and honor and hope and pride and compassion and pity and sacrifice which have been the glory of his past. The poet's voice need not merely be the record of man, it can be one of the props, the pillars to help him endure and prevail.[4]

Speech of Welcome

A speech of welcome is given to acknowledge publicly the arrival of a new person or group of people into the community or into an organization. The visitors may be coming to attend a convention or seminar or to participate in a commemorative celebration.

As a speaker on this occasion, your purpose is to show friendliness and hospitality. Public courtesies such as this perform much the same function as they do in private life, that of creating a bond of goodwill among the participants and making both hosts and visitors feel that the appropriate sentiments have been expressed.

The speech of welcome should include the following elements: (1) identification of the welcoming agency; (2) pleasure in welcoming the newcomers; (3) complimentary facts about the guests; (4) the purpose of the visit; and (5) prediction of a pleasurable and worthwhile outcome from the visit.

Presenting the Speech of Welcome

In presenting a speech of welcome, first you should identify the group you represent. Associate the values of your group with those of the person or group being welcomed. Refer favorably to the honored individual or group by citing some of their specific attributes or accomplishments, again taking care not to overdo it.

Discuss the goal of the visit and the significance it holds for the audience. It may be useful to recount events that led to the visit or how it was arranged. You can then give the visitors some information about the place or organization to which they are being welcomed, and to enumerate the plans your group has made to entertain them.

Conclude with your good wishes for a pleasant stay and a prediction of the worthwhile outcomes to be expected from the interchange. This phase of the welcome might include the presentation of some token of welcome— the key to the city or a certificate of honorary membership.

The mood of this kind of occasion is dignified and formal, but it needs to show warmth and sincerity as well. This is no place for note cards, so when you are making a welcoming speech you must have carefully prepared your remarks and have them firmly in mind, with attention to such details as correct pronunciation of names and accuracy of titles. Again, this is a short ceremonial occasion in which your purpose is to affirm shared values and ideals.

Responding to a Welcome

All that has to be said about the speech that responds to a welcome is that it is exactly the reverse of the speech of welcome. You are the recipient of a formal courtesy, and your response is one of appreciation for that kindness.

Your response should be very brief and include these essential elements: (1) name the group for whom you are speaking; (2) compliment the group that has extended the welcome, and express thanks and appreciation for the hospitality; (3) note the significance of the occasion and the purpose for the group's visit; and (4) say that you expect the experience to be a pleasant one.

Public Relations Speech

The public relations speech is not a new phenomenon, but it is one that is becoming increasingly prominent. Both individuals and institutions recognize the need to promote a positive public image, and many business executives actively seek opportunities to influence public opinion by giving public relations speeches. The *Public Relations Journal* reported, "Many corporations retain experts to concentrate on researching and cataloguing material, writing manuscripts, screening and selecting invitations, and coaching executives on speech discipline and techniques."[5]

Public relations speeches are of two general types: (1) the speech that seeks to create goodwill for a person or organization; and (2) the speech of justification that attempts to rebuild the subject's credibility after it has come under attack. These are both sales speeches and are essentially persuasive in nature, although they appear on the surface to be speeches to inform. They do in fact present a great deal of information in their development, but the essential intent is to persuade the audience to buy not a specific product, but the positive image of the organization. If the public relations speaker is to be successful, the persuasive appeal must be unobtrusive. To accomplish this, the public relations speaker must skillfully blend facts with suggestion, presenting the facts in such a way as to indirectly build support for the organization.

Speech to Create Goodwill

Government agencies, business organizations, and university extension programs often have lectures or demonstrations that are suitable as programs for clubs and organizations. In this context, the aims of the organization furnishing the program can be presented to the audience in a positive light. When it is your purpose to present a speech to create goodwill, you can construct the speech in this way:

I. Arouse the audience's interest and advance a worthwhile motive for speaking.
   A. Present some interesting and novel fact to arouse curiosity.
   B. Say that you intend to increase the audience's understanding of the organization by presenting some facts about it.
II. Detail the positive aspects of the organization.
   A. Describe the operations of the company by selecting interesting aspects that are new to the listeners.
   B. Represent the leaders of the company as individuals of merit and high principles.
   C. Describe your organization's effort to solve some important social need.
      1. Support this point inductively by citing specific instances of its constructive efforts.
      2. Point out any worthwhile achievements made by your company.

D. Establish a direct tie between the company's values and activities and the social and economic well-being of the audience.
III. Conclude with a strong summary.
   A. Point out the ways in which your company contributes to the community and the world, now and in the future.
   B. Show the audience how it can specifically benefit from the services and products of your company.

Speech of Justification

In the case where the speech is a response to public criticism, the speaker presents a particular action or policy in such a way as to allay resentment and rebuild a positive image.

For example, a government official might seek to justify tax policies that seem to favor wealthy constituents at the expense of the poor, or an oil company executive might uphold the company's motives in drilling in locations that might damage the environment. Richard Nixon's "Checkers" speech, as well as his later speeches regarding Watergate, are examples of speeches of self-justification by an individual.

Summary

Ceremonial speeches include introduction of a speaker, the speech of tribute, the commencement address, presentation and acceptance of a gift or award, the speech of welcome and response to the welcome. For all of these, the ceremonial occasion dictates both subject and treatment. These are short speeches, highly structured, and relatively formal in tone. Vivid language, illustrations, and quotations are used to dramatize the ideas and events being celebrated. The speaker's purpose is often persuasive; he or she seeks to deepen the audience's appreciation for the traditions and ideals it already holds.

The purpose of the public relations speech is the "selling" of an image, by persuading the audience of the goodwill and helpfulness of the speaker's organization.

Exercises

1. Discuss how you would introduce a prominent member of your community.
2. Assume your class was going to dedicate the building you are meeting in to someone who has worked in or is currently working in the building. Decide to whom you would dedicate the building and what you would say.
3. Decide how you could develop a speech of tribute for a historically prominent person on the occasion of his or her birthday.
4. Prepare a short written critique of an introduction that is given for a speaker. This should be on a speech given outside of class and should comment on the items discussed in this chapter. Be prepared to discuss your critique in class.

Assignments

1. Prepare a one- to three-minute speech of introduction for a prominent person. Determine what the characteristics of the occasion will be and the title of that person's speech. Your speech of introduction should contain an appropriate attention getter, establish the main speaker's credentials, and should result in a receptive atmosphere for the speaker.
2. Prepare a two-minute speech of tribute, welcome, or presentation of an award that adheres to the criteria discussed in this chapter. You will need to construct the hypothetical occasion for the speech and explain it to the audience before you begin. For example, you might assume that Dan Rather is going to visit your campus to dedicate a new building for the School of Communication and that it is your job to welcome him on behalf of the university community.

Suggested Reading

Bryant, Donald C., and Wallace, Karl R. *Fundamentals of Public Speaking,* chap. 22. 4th ed. New York: Appleton-Century-Crofts, 1969.

DeVito, Joseph A. *The Elements of Public Speaking,* chap. 11. New York: Harper & Row Publishers, 1981.

Notes

1. Albert J. Vasile and Harold K. Mintz, *Speak With Confidence,* 2d ed. (Cambridge: Winthrop Publishers, Inc., 1980): 199–200.
2. Joe Ayres, *Speech of Introduction,* delivered in September of 1991 at Washington State University.
3. The text of Adlai Stevenson's "Farewell to a Friend" is taken from the printed record of the services conducted for Lloyd Lewis at Libertyville, Illinois, on April 23, 1949. It appears in the volume *American Short Speeches,* ed. Bower Aly and Lucile Folse Aly, (New York: The Macmillan Company, 1968).
4. William Faulkner, *The Faulkner Reader: Selections from the Works of William Faulkner* (New York: Random House, Inc., 1953): 3–4.
5. Carl R. Terzian, "Going to Communicate: Try Speaking!" *Public Relations Journal* (May 1976): 16–17.

Appendix

Performance of Literature*

By Gail Miller

Values of Performance of Literature to the Public Speaker

The oral interpretation of literature offers many concepts and techniques that are of special value to the public speaker. A speaker may present a piece of literature—prose (such as prose fiction, an essay, or a speech), poetry, or drama—either because the theme of the selection presents in vivid dramatic fashion a point the speaker wishes to make, or because sharing the literature will in itself be a pleasurable and entertaining experience for both reader and listener. There are numerous occasions on which you might read literature aloud: in a classroom setting, in a family gathering, or to a public audience. You might also include short pieces of literature as forms of development in an informative or persuasive speech.

Donald C. Bryant and Karl R. Wallace very early affirmed the value of oral reading of literature as a training experience for the public speaker: it can help to sharpen the speaker's perception of the effect language can have on listeners, and help the speaker learn how to use the voice and body more effectively. By interpreting good literature aloud, the speaker acquires a feel for the flow of language and can experience firsthand the impact that expert word choice and dramatic structure can have when effectively presented. An understanding of these techniques can be used to advantage by any public speaker.[1]

In the business setting, speakers frequently deliver speeches from a manuscript. For students interested in a career in management, training in oral reading is recommended "to enhance their future ability to practice management with more imagination, more vision, more skill, more art."[2] Mark L. Knapp's survey revealed that speech training provided by business organizations to their employees included public speaking and specifically manuscript reading as a critical concern.[3]

---

*This appendix is a revision and expansion of portions of *Effective Public Speaking,* 2d edition. Printed with the permission of Gail Miller.

Janet Palmer, an interpretation scholar who is now a communication consultant, has noted that business managers who do a great deal of public speaking perform many of the same functions as interpreters and can benefit from the humanistic approach of interpretation.[4]

Public speakers engage in audience analysis in order to construct more effective messages. Ronald Pelias has found that the experience of performing literature increases the ability of the performer to adopt and understand the perspectives of others.[5] The importance of intercultural communication in the corporate world is underscored in the results of a 1988 study by Herbert W. Hildebrandt, in which he compares Asian and U.S. corporate executives and concludes that for both "they must understand something of other persons and their culture in order to succeed."[6] The sensitivity to the needs and feelings of people who come from different backgrounds can be gained by oral performance of literature, which can help the public speaker and the corporate manager to communicate with and influence diverse audiences.

For the social scientist or public activist, an awareness of what kinds of arguments most effectively shape public opinion and behavior, and the skill to present those arguments well, can be an important factor in understanding and influencing social issues. An effectively presented piece of prose or poetry about child abuse or nuclear destruction, for instance, can sometimes create more conviction and involvement than any amount of facts, figures, and well-marshaled arguments. Emotional issues are effectively addressed in emotional terms.

Oral interpretation teaches performers how to balance their responses to the emotional and logical appeals in the work, something that public speakers strive for as well. Robert Ivie has said that interpretation is valuable in part because it helps us to "play" as an added dimension to language.[7]

The language skills gained by the oral interpreter can be grouped under analysis and writing, rehearsal, and performance, all of which are the stock in trade of the public speaker as well.

Speech writing demands sensitivity to the nuances of language and style. An interpreter examines the language and style of a variety of fine writers and thus has many models for his or her own writing, and practice in writing a series of analyses of the literature to be performed builds writing competence and confidence. Rehearsal is a vital part of the preparation process of both interpreters and public speakers. By paying attention to feedback, interpreters learn to monitor their performance behavior and gain self-critical skills. An additional benefit received by the interpreter of literature is a heightened awareness of the emotional, inner life that is shared by the speaker and the listeners.

Performance of literature gives the speaker practice in concentrating on several factors simultaneously, including switching between multiple characters, variety of focus, and changes in scene and viewpoint. Interpretation also develops timing skills, which are important for pointing up a line or for creating dramatic effect.

Definition of Oral Interpretation

The oral interpretation of literature is not the same as public speaking, nor is it the same as acting, but falls about halfway on the continuum between them. When the speaker performs a piece of literature aloud, he or she is not merely *reading* from a manuscript but is *entering into* all of its dimensions—logical, physical, and emotional. This is what a speaker always does to communicate conviction to an audience—a major difference is that here the speaker is interpreting the words of another writer. It is not at all unusual today that a speaker in public life should deliver an address written by another person, often without any acknowledgement that this is the case.

Choosing a Selection

To prepare for the experience of performing literature, you must first choose a selection you want to share with the audience. The first place you should look for material is within your own experience. From a class or from your own personal reading, what short story, novel, speech, poem, or play do you remember? If a selection struck you as interesting and caused you to remember it, the chances are very good that other people, especially people as similar to you as are most of your classmates, will enjoy the selection also.

Select literature of good quality. If it has been included in an anthology, this is a good indication that knowledgeable people consider it to be well-written. Good writing will be easier for you to read well and will merit the time you spend in preparing it for performance.

It is possible for a piece of material to have impact when read silently but not be effective when read aloud. Choose a selection that is rich in description, words that arouse sensory reactions: sight, sound, smell, taste, and touch. These "word pictures" cause the listeners to participate actively in the literature, by reminding them of similar feelings they have experienced or of people they have known. Good writing has a breadth and depth that allows different people to find different interpretations, and the same person to find something new in the writing at different stages in his or her own life.

In addition to (1) the suitability of the selection for the reader and the audience, and (2) the intrinsic quality of the literature, the speaker must be concerned with (3) the time limits of the occasion.

Cutting and Editing

You must be able to read your selection in the time available. Don't guess at how long it is—time the selection by reading it aloud, just as you intend to present it. *Never* plan to read a little faster to make it conform to the time limits. A poem should be performed in its entirety, but the performance of prose fiction or drama in the classroom most often requires that lines be deleted (editing) or even entire sections be removed (cutting) in order to stay within the time limits of the situation. When you shorten a piece of literature, be sure to maintain the style and tone of the original work.

One approach to cutting is to begin your reading before the climax or high point of the action and continue to the end. This way your performance will have both tension and release, which creates a satisfying resolution for the audience. The introduction for such a reading should include relevant background information about characters and events leading up to where you begin to read.

Some general guidelines for cutting a piece of prose include:

Expository passages that give information about characters and situations at the beginning of prose fiction selections and plays can be eliminated. This information can be included in your introduction.

Long descriptive passages and even a complete episode can be cut if the selection maintains unity without it. Minor characters may be eliminated if the scene is clear without them.

Tag lines, such as "he said," or "she remarked," can be cut if the audience does not need them to distinguish between characters when the selection is read orally. Lines such as, "She turned away weeping," can be performed (shown) rather than spoken (told).

To have impact and to provide a satisfying experience for your audience, your selection must appear complete: it must have a beginning, a middle, and an end. Not every piece of writing will lend itself to being cut. If you cannot abstract a section that has a cohesive feeling, then select something else to read.

Analyzing the Selection   The more you know about the material, the better prepared you are to interpret it for someone else. To prepare yourself to present a piece of literature you should first examine it from all sides:

1. Investigate the background of the selection. What can you find out about the time frame in which or about which it was written?
2. Who is the author? To understand what is being said, it helps to know who is saying it.
3. Who is speaking in the selection? Speakers in literary works can be analyzed on two levels, the physical and the psychological. The physical level includes the speaker's age, sex, physical characteristics, level of attractiveness, and general state of health

and strength. The psychological level focuses on the speaker's internal state and includes his or her education, occupation, attitudes, beliefs, emotions, thoughts, and experiences.

4. To whom is each speaker speaking? Who is the intended audience of the selection as a whole?
5. Where is the speaker speaking? Where did the action being described take place?
6. When is the speaker speaking? Is the action taking place in the present or being remembered from the past?
7. What is the speaker speaking about? What is actually being said, the logical content? What is the climax, the high point toward which the selection builds? Are there any unfamiliar words you need to check for meaning or pronunciation in order that you and your audience will understand what the author means?
8. How is the speaker speaking? Is the language simple or formal? What attitude does the speaker convey: sincere, or perhaps sarcastic? What is the overall mood being expressed, and does that mood change at given points?
9. Why is the speaker speaking? Is the purpose to amuse us, to shock or surprise us? What is the theme of the selection; is there perhaps a moral to be drawn?

To illustrate these principles, following is the script of a short story "The Open Window" by H. H. Munro (Saki), with a sample analysis that answers these nine questions.

The Open Window
Saki (H. H. Munro)

"My aunt will be down presently, Mr. Nuttel," said a very self-possessed young lady of fifteen; "in the meantime you must try and put up with me."

Framton Nuttel endeavoured to say the correct something which should duly flatter the niece of the moment without unduly discounting the aunt that was to come. Privately he doubted more than ever whether these formal visits on a succession of total strangers would do much towards helping the nerve cure which he was supposed to be undergoing.

"I know how it will be," his sister had said when he was preparing to migrate to this rural retreat; "you will bury yourself down there and not speak to a living soul, and your nerves will be worse than ever from moping. I shall give you letters of introduction to all the people I know there. Some of them, as far as I can remember, were quite nice."

Framton wondered whether Mrs. Sappleton, the lady to whom he was presenting one of the letters of introduction, came into the nice division.

"Do you know many of the people round here?" asked the niece, when she judged that they had had sufficient silent communion.

"Hardly a soul," said Framton. "My sister was staying here, at the rectory, you know, some four years ago, and she gave me letters of introduction to some of the people here."

He made the last statement in a tone of distinct regret.

"Then you know practically nothing about my aunt?" pursued the self-possessed young lady.

"Only her name and address," admitted the caller. He was wondering whether Mrs. Sappleton was in the married or widowed state. An undefinable something about the room seemed to suggest masculine habitation.

"Her great tragedy happened just three years ago," said the child; "that would be since your sister's time."

"Her tragedy?" asked Framton; somehow in this restful country spot tragedies seemed out of place.

"You may wonder why we keep that window wide open on an October afternoon," said the niece, indicating a large French window that opened on to a lawn.

"It is quite warm for the time of the year," said Framton; "but has that window anything to do with the tragedy?"

"Out through that window, three years ago to a day, her husband and her two young brothers went off for their day's shooting. They never came back. In crossing the moor to their favorite snipe-shooting ground they were all three engulfed in a treacherous piece of bog. It had been that dreadful wet summer, you know, and places that were safe in other years gave way suddenly without warning. Their bodies were never recovered. That was the dreadful part of it." Here the child's voice lost its self-possessed note and became falteringly human. "Poor aunt always thinks that they will come back some day, they and the little brown spaniel that was lost with them, and walk in at that window just as they used to do. That is why the window is kept open every evening till it is quite dusk. Poor dear aunt, she has often told me how they went out, her husband with his white waterproof coat over his arm, and Ronnie, her youngest brother, singing 'Bertie, why do you bound?' as he always did to tease her, because she said it got on her nerves. Do you know, sometimes on still, quiet evenings like this, I almost get a creepy feeling that they will all walk through that window—"

She broke off with a little shudder. It was a relief to Framton when the aunt bustled into the room with a whirl of apologies for being late in making her appearance.

"I hope Vera has been amusing you?" she said.

"She has been very interesting," said Framton.

"I hope you don't mind the open window," said Mrs. Sappleton briskly; "my husband and brothers will be home directly from shooting, and they always come in this way. They've been out for snipe in the marshes today, so they'll make a fine mess over my poor carpets. So like you men-folk, isn't it?"

She rattled on cheerfully about the shooting and the scarcity of birds, and the prospects for duck in the winter. To Framton it was all purely horrible. He made a desperate but only partially successful effort to turn the talk on to a less ghastly topic; he was conscious that his hostess was giving him only a fragment of her attention, and her eyes were constantly straying past him to the open window and the lawn beyond. It was certainly an unfortunate coincidence that he should have paid his visit on this tragic anniversary.

"The doctors agree in ordering me complete rest, an absence of mental excitement, and avoidance of anything in the nature of violent physical exercise," announced Framton, who laboured under the tolerably wide-spread delusion that total strangers and chance acquaintances are hungry for the least detail of one's ailments and infirmities, their cause and cure. "On the matter of diet they are not so much in agreement," he continued.

"No?" said Mrs. Sappleton, in a voice which only replaced a yawn at the last moment. Then she suddenly brightened into alert attention—but not to what Framton was saying.

"Here they are at last!" she cried. "Just in time for tea, and don't they look as if they were muddy up to the eyes!"

Framton shivered slightly and turned towards the niece with a look intended to convey sympathetic comprehension. The child was staring out through the open window with dazed horror in her eyes. In a chill shock of nameless fear Framton swung round in his seat and looked in the same direction.

In the deepening twilight three figures were walking across the lawn towards the window; they all carried guns under their arms, and one of them was additionally burdened with a white coat hung over his shoulders. A tired brown spaniel kept close at their heels. Noiselessly they neared the house, and then a hoarse young voice chanted out of the dusk: "I said, Bertie, why do you bound?"

Framton grabbed wildly at his stick and hat; the hall-door, the gravel-drive, and the front gate were dimly noted stages in his headlong retreat. A cyclist coming along the road had to run into the hedge to avoid imminent collision.

"Here we are, my dear," said the bearer of the white mackintosh, coming in through the window; "fairly muddy, but most of it's dry. Who was that who bolted out as we came up?"

"A most extraordinary man, a Mr. Nuttel," said Mrs. Sappleton; "could only talk about his illness, and dashed off without a word of good-bye or apology when you arrived. One would think he had seen a ghost."

"I expect it was the spaniel," said the niece calmly; "he told me he had a horror of dogs. He was once hunted into a cemetery somewhere on the banks of the Ganges by a pack of pariah dogs, and had to spend the night in a newly dug grave with the creatures snarling and grinning and foaming just above him. Enough to make any one lose their nerve."

Romance at short notice was her speciality.

Sample Analysis

1. Investigate the background of the selection.

   The period of 1900–1914, when Saki was writing, could be characterized as a time of change for Great Britain. Things were falling apart in the Empire, with wars in India and South Africa, and the establishment of the welfare state at home. Germany was mobilizing, which led France and England and Holland to form mutual defense alliances and to prepare for the war to come. All of these factors led to high taxes and growing tension.

2. Who is the author?

   Hector Hugh Munro (1870–1916), who wrote under the pen name Saki, early distinguished himself as a political satirist and sketch writer. His unique vein of fantasy and wit found its best expression in his short stories, which were published between 1900 and 1914. He enlisted for service in World War I at the age of forty-four and was killed in action.

3. Who is speaking in the selection?

   The primary storyteller is the narrator, who speaks in the third person, using "he" and "she." He can know the thoughts and feelings of some but not all of the characters. The narrator in this story is considered to be a male, since the author and the major character are male. A member of the educated British upper class, his language is somewhat formal: "An indescribable something about the room suggested masculine habitation."

   Framton Nuttel is a fastidious upper-class British man. He is shy and retiring and suffers from a nervous disorder.

   Mrs. Sappleton is a middle-aged, polite upper-class English matron.

   Vera, a young lady of fifteen, is self-confident and imaginative.

4. To whom is each speaker speaking?

   The narrator is most likely speaking to an audience of fellow upper-class Englishmen, or to a general audience.

   The characters speak to each other.

5. Where is the speaker speaking?

   The setting is the sitting room of Mrs. Sappleton, in a well-to-do English country home.

6. When is the speaker speaking?

   The time is an October afternoon about 4:00 P.M., which is tea time in England. Framton's hat and walking stick are elements that suggest the turn-of-the-century era.

7. What is the speaker speaking about?

   The narrator describes the visit of Framton Nuttel to his hostess, Mrs. Sappleton. Framton is taken in by the niece Vera's imaginative, impromptu ghost story and flees in terror when the ghosts seemingly appear. Vera has a ready answer for that, also.

8. How is the speaker speaking?

   The speakers use the elevated language of the upper class of that time. The narrator is very descriptive; his tone is one of amused tolerance toward Framton ". . . who labored under the tolerably wide-spread delusion that total strangers and chance acquaintances are hungry for the least detail of one's ailments and infirmities, their cause and cure."

9. Why is the speaker speaking?

   The storyteller's purpose is to tell an amusing tale with a message that people are not always what they seem. One should beware of seemingly demure young ladies of the upper class.

Getting Ready to Perform

The process of getting ready to perform a piece of literature is exactly the same as the process followed by the speaker who writes a speech and then delivers it from a manuscript. In both cases the gathering, arranging, and wording of ideas has been done before, and now the speaker's efforts are concentrated on *presenting* those words to achieve the desired effect—whether to inform, to persuade, or to entertain.

Physical Preparation of the Script

The script should be typed double-spaced, with each sheet numbered and placed on a solid backing, such as construction paper, or in a rigid notebook.

Prepare the Introduction

The first step is to prepare the audience. An introduction to a piece of literature performs the same functions as does the introduction to any other type of presentation: (1) it establishes a bond of goodwill between speaker and audience; (2) it sets the mood; and (3) it gives any necessary information to prepare the audience for the material to follow. As a reader, you create interest in the material by pointing out its relevance to you and to your listeners, and by conveying your own enthusiasm for the selection.

Rehearse

Using the script you have prepared, practice reading the selection many times, and over a period of time; it is much better to read it twice a day for ten days than to read it twenty times on the day before performance.

Reading from a manuscript is *different* from extemporaneous speaking, but is not *easier*. For almost every reader, the natural tendency is to underplay the feelings and actions described in the selection. Work to enlarge these scenes and make them not postcard, but billboard size. It will help you to make use of your muscle memory if during this rehearsal phase you actually move through the actions being described, planning to eliminate most of this large movement during the performance. If you make them larger than life at this stage, you may maintain the images strongly enough in performance. Time your total performance again and make further cuts in your script if they are needed to conform to your time limitations.

No matter how many times you rehearse or present a selection, you should strive to make it fresh and new each time. This requires your intense and immediate concentration, to experience and to stimulate the audience to experience the ideas and images *firsthand,* not just as if they were being read *about*.

Performance
Becoming

The interpretive reader does not stand outside the literature and talk *about* it, but makes every effort to enter into the literature and to portray it from the inside out. The act of "becoming" the speakers and expressing the moods and feelings of the scenes described is very much a participation sport, consisting of (1) vocal responsiveness, (2) physical responsiveness, and (3) emotional responsiveness to the literature.

Vocal Responsiveness

To create characters or express moods, the speaker has the following vocal variables to work with: (1) voice quality; (2) volume and intensity; (3) vocal pitch; (4) rate of speed and pauses; and (5) use of dialect. The speaker must also pay close attention to accuracy of pronunciation and enunciation.

Vocal Quality

Vocal quality is created by the overtones of the voice. Each vocal mechanism is different, and the size and shape of the mouth, nose, and sinuses create a quality that is distinctive to each individual. This is how you can recognize friends on the phone, even before they identify themselves.

Volume and Intensity

Certainly your audience needs to be able to hear your selection to appreciate it. Assess the room in which you will be speaking and the size of the audience to be sure your volume and projection will allow your audience to hear comfortably. Intensity is a function of the amount of energy being expended in speaking; a whisper can communicate as much urgency as a shout. Variations in the use of volume and of intensity can be used to establish and differentiate between characters, and to stress and give emphasis to important words and ideas. The climax and, most often, the concluding lines of the selection should be stressed.

Pitch

Pitch refers to the position of the voice, whether high or low, on the musical scale. Your own natural pitch range will be the most desirable one to use, aiming for maximum variety within that range to create interest and to promote understanding by your audience. Strive to keep a relaxed throat; tension will drive the pitch up into an unpleasant range. Different characters portrayed within a selection can be suggested by assigning each a different pitch level, as well as by other factors. For example, a woman typically has a higher pitch than a man, and a child could be read with an even higher pitch (all within the reader's normal pitch range, without going into falsetto or unnaturally low).

Rate of Speed and Pauses

A common error for beginners, or anyone who tends to be nervous in the public speaking situation, is to speak or read too fast, causing credibility to suffer because the speaker is perceived as being ill at ease and lacking in confidence. A comfortable overall rate is important, and so is the need for variety in rate. Reading speed should be keyed to what is being said in the selection: a description of a calm, lazy canoe ride should be presented at a slower pace than a description of a wild ride through white-water rapids.

Pauses are important in establishing mood. Pauses also play a large role in indicating structure, taking the place of the periods, commas, and other punctuation that clarify written material. A pause before and/or after an idea will make it stand out as important. It is especially effective to pause between the introduction and the beginning of the selection, and also to *hold* your audience after the last line to allow that last important idea to take full effect.

Dialect	The use of dialect can be a valuable aid to establishing character and distinguishing one speaker from another. The setting of the story can be suggested also; the South, the frontier West, New York City, or a particular section of England, for example.
Pronunciation and Enunciation	Correct pronunciation requires attention to the sounds that make up the words and the order in which they occur. Enunciation, or articulation, is the correct formation of the sounds that make up the word. The principal articulators are the lips, teeth, and tongue, lower jaw, and the hard and soft palates. Incorrect or careless enunciation results in speech that may be difficult to understand and that conveys a negative image of the speaker. Such errors draw attention away from the ideas and feelings in the literature you are reading.
Physical Responsiveness	It will do no good to *say* how exciting a game is if your bodily stance and lack of muscle involvement indicate that you are bored and uninterested. "Less is more" when it comes to large movements, such as walking and sweeping hand gestures; practice economy of movement. Make good use of muscle tone and facial expressions, and of head and shoulder gestures. You will usually stand, or perhaps sit on a high stool, and you may either hold the script or place it on a lectern. The script should be placed or held about chest high to maximize your ability to maintain eye contact. Your listeners need to be able to see your bodily responses and to feel that speaker and audience together are sharing the enjoyment of the literature being read.
Performance Focus	Focus refers to where the performer looks at a given moment in the literature. Shifts between who is speaking and who is being spoken to must be made clear to the audience in performance. There are three kinds of performance focus:

1. Open focus. Eye contact includes the entire audience, for example, when a narrator is "telling the story" to the audience.
2. Closed focus. For example, when two characters talk to each other, lines spoken by one may be addressed toward one side of the audience and lines spoken by the other toward the other side of the audience. This (plus vocal and physical changes) helps the listeners to keep the characters separate.
3. Inner-closed focus. The focus is slightly above and removed from the audience, as if thinking aloud.

Emotional Responsiveness Imagery and Sensory Showing	A writer uses descriptive language to recreate objects or experiences. Our actual or vicarious experience with what is being described enables us to recreate the images and our feelings about them in our minds. The word "cat" in a piece causes you to visualize a particular cat you have known.

The author may provide more details that cause you to picture "an old cat" or "a Siamese cat." Sensory images appeal to our senses: sight or visual; hearing or auditory; taste or gustatory; smell or olfactory; touch or tactile; temperature or thermal; overt action or kinetic; and our sense of muscular tension or body position, kinesthetic.

Other kinds of images are called literary or figurative images. They serve to communicate the author's ideas and feelings more vividly and clearly, in a kind of shorthand form. The Scottish poet Robert Burns used a simile to describe his love: "My luv is like a red, red rose." We can't know exactly what Burns felt for this woman, but we know the kind of response we have to a beautiful red rose and can experience vicariously the feeling he had for his loved one. Both sensory and literary images make our language seem newer and more alive.

Sensory Showing

It is not enough for a performer to understand and to respond personally to the sensory imagery in a selection, but these images must be projected into the audience as well. This process is called sensory showing, and it involves the use of "muscle memory." Remember what it felt like to throw a ball, to clench your fists in anger, or to cuddle a baby. Then "act out" the muscle tension and the psychological set as you read the words that describe such an action or feeling. Listeners will mirror your nonverbal cues with their own bodies, thus drawing them into the image.

Responding to Feedback

Feedback is equally important to the performer of literature as to the public speaker. No matter how much preparation a performer has done in rehearsal, there are always adjustments that must be made when you finally face an audience. You may need to adjust your timing in response to audience reaction or feedback, perhaps pausing for laughs or to share strong feelings. If you do not allow this time, listeners may withhold their reaction for fear of missing something. You may need to adapt your volume level or body position, and perhaps enlarge your gestures and facial expressions if you get nonverbal feedback, which indicates the audience cannot see or hear you.

Remember, you're onstage from the moment you leave your seat to perform, so don't behave in a way that creates a feeling of uncertainty. Smile and look confident, and your audience will believe you! Deliver your introduction as yourself—do *not* read it. After you complete the introduction, pause, look down, look up in character as the speaker in the selection, and begin. As your performance draws to a close, slow down and give importance to the final lines to signal the end and give the audience a sense of finality. Then pause afterward to give yourself and your audience time to share that climactic last line before you break the connection and return to your seat.

Items to Consider When Reading Literature Aloud

1. Look first within your own experience to choose literature to read aloud, then go to anthologies or collections of writings by well-known authors.
2. Determine if the piece (or an edited version of the piece) can be read in the time available.
3. Analyze the background of the literature and of the author, and the literature itself.
4. Prepare the script.
5. Plan your introduction.
6. Rehearse aloud many times.
7. When you perform, deliver your introduction extemporaneously.
8. Respond to the emotional content of the selection. Utilize vocal and physical techniques of interpretation and sensory showing to create scenes in the audience's imagination.
9. Emphasize important words and phrases, and show the build toward the point of climax. Pay especial attention to the ending; emphasize its importance by using intensity, pitch inflection, and slowing of rate.
10. Use pauses effectively between the introduction and the selection, during the selection, and after you have delivered the last line.

Notes

1. Donald C. Bryant and Karl R. Wallace, *Fundamentals of Public Speaking,* 5th ed. (New York: Appleton-Century-Crofts, 1976).
2. Denise R. Mier, "Learning the Art of Management Through the Art of Oral Reading," *Communication Education* 32 (July 1983).
3. Mark L. Knapp, "Public Speaking Training Programs in American Business and Industrial Organizations," *Speech Teacher* 18 (1969): 129–134.
4. Janet Palmer, "The Manager as Performer: Axioms of Performance Theory in Executive Communication Consulting," *Communication Excellence Institute* (San Dimas, Calif., 1988).
5. Ronald Pelias, "Oral Interpretation as a Training Method for Increasing Perspective-Taking Abilities," *Communication Education* 33 (April 1984): 143–151.
6. Herbert W. Hildebrandt, "International/Intercultural Communication: A Comparative Study of Asian and U.S. Managers," *World Communication* 17, No. 1 (1988): 49
7. Conversation with Robert Ivie, August 25, 1988.

Gail Miller has a PhD in Performance of Literature from the Speech Communication Department of the University of Texas. She is currently teaching at the University of Idaho.

Credits

341

Index